STO

**DO NOT REMOVE
CARDS FROM POCKET**

TRAGEDY AND PHILOSOPHY

Also by N. Georgopoulos

ART AND EMOTION: The Aesthetics of E. Papanoutsos
(*editor and translator*)
BEING HUMAN IN THE ULTIMATE (*co-editor*)
CONTINUITY AND CHANGE IN MARXISM (*co-editor*)

Tragedy and Philosophy

Edited by

N. Georgopoulos
Kent State University, Ohio

St. Martin's Press　　New York

First published in the United States of America in 1993

Printed in Great Britain

ISBN 0–312–08938–4

Library of Congress Cataloging-in-Publication Data
Tragedy and philosophy / edited by N. Georgopoulos.
p. cm.
Includes index.
ISBN 0–312–08938–4
1. Tragic, The.   I. Georgopoulos, N.
BH301.T7T72   1993
111'.85—dc20   92–37143
                                                              CIP

Contents

Acknowledgments   vii

Notes on the Contributors   ix

Editor's Introduction   1
N. Georgopoulos

1   Nietzsche's Critique of Aristotle's   19
Theory of Tragic Emotions
John P. Anton

2   The Disjunction of the Tragic: Hegel and Nietzsche   39
Roland Galle

3   Tragic Thoughts and the Entertainments of   57
Possibility
Leon Rosenstein

4   Tragedy: Its Contribution to a Theory of Objects   70
and the Emotions
Richard F. Kuhns

5   The Role of Philosophy in the Development   86
of Tragic Drama
E. F. Kaelin

6   Tragic Action   104
N. Georgopoulos

7   Philosophy and Tragedy in the Platonic Dialogues   123
Drew A. Hyland

8   Philosophy and Tragedy: The Flaw of Eros and the
Triumph of Agape   139
Carl R. Hausman

9   Being at a Loss: Reflections on Philosophy
      and the Tragic   154
      William Desmond

10   Myth, Tragedy and Dialogue: The Language of
      Philosophy   187
      John M. Anderson

Index   217

Acknowledgments

The essays included in this volume are published here for the first time. They were written specifically for it. I wish to thank the authors individually for their patience and for their confidence in this project – for making it possible. Also, I wish to thank Dr Henry Tapp, Chairman Emeritus of the Department of German, Kent State University, for his translation of Roland Galle's essay *Die Disjunktion des Tragischen: Hegel und Nietzsche*. In addition, I am grateful to Kent State University's Research Council for granting me a semester's leave from academic duties to work on this project. I must likewise acknowledge Dr Eugene Wenninger, Dean, Research and Sponsored Programs, and the Research Council for material assistance in the preparation of the manuscript.

Notes on the Contributors

John M. Anderson has been Chairman of the Philosophy Department and Director of the Humanities Program at Pennsylvania State University. He is Evan Pugh Distinguished Research Professor of Philosophy Emeritus of the same institution. He is the co-editor of *Man and World*. His publications include *The Individual and the New World; Calhoun; Natural Deduction; the Realm of Art,* and *The Truth of Freedom.*

John P. Anton has been Associate Dean of the Graduate School at S. U. N. Y., at Buffalo, and Fuller E. Callaway Professor of Philosophy at Emory University. He presently teaches philosophy at the University of South Florida. He has written or edited a number of books, including *Aristotle's Theory of Contrarieties; Critical Humanism as a Philosophy of Culture: The Case of E. Papanoutsos; Naturalism and Historical Understanding; Science and the Sciences in Plato; Philosophical Essays,* and *Essays in Ancient Greek Philosophy.*

William Desmond is Chairman and Professor of Philosophy at Loyola College. He is author of *Art and the Absolute: A Study of Hegel's Aesthetics; Desire, Dialectic and Otherness: An Essay on Origins; Philosophy and Its Others: Ways of Being and Mind.* He is also the editor of *Hegel and His Critics,* as well as the author of many articles and essays in metaphysics and the philosophy of art.

Roland Galle is Professor of Literature at the University of Essen, Germany. He is the author of numerous articles and of *Tragödie und Aufklärung: Zum Funktionswandel des Tragischen zwischen Racine und Büchner* and *Gestandis und Subjektivitat: Untersuchungen zum Französischen Roman zwischen Klassik und Romantik.*

N. Georgopoulos teaches philosophy at Kent State University. He is the co-editor of *Continuity and Change in Marxism* and *Being Human in the Ultimate,* and the editor and translator of *Art and Emotion: the Aesthetics of E. Papanoutsos.* His essays on tragedy and art have appeared in several books and journals.

Carl R. Hausman is the author of *Novelty and Creativity* and *Art and Metaphor*, and co-editor of *The Question of Creativity*. His articles in the philosophy of art and metaphysics have been published in several journals and books. His book on Pierce is scheduled to appear this year. He is also co-editor of the *Journal of Speculative Studies*. He is a member of the Philosophy Department at Pennsylvania State University.

Drew A. Hyland served as chairman of the Philosophy Department at Trinity College. He is presently Charles A. Dana Professor of Philosophy at the same institution. He is the author of *The Origins of Philosophy: Its Rise in Myth and the Pre-Socratics; The Virtue of Philosophy: An Interpretation of Plato's Charmides,* and *The Question of Play.*

E. F. Kaelin teaches philosophy at Florida State University. He has written extensively on contemporary interpretations of art and literature. His books include *An Existentialist Aesthetic; Art and Existence: A Phenomenological Aesthetics; The Philosophy of Aesthetics: A Phenomenological Approach; The Unhappy Consciousness: The Poetic Plight of Samuel Beckett – An Inquiry at the Intersection of Phenomenology and Literature,* and *Heidegger's Being and Time: A Reading for Readers.*

Richard F. Kuhns is Professor of Philosophy at Columbia University. He is the co-editor of *Philosophies of Art and Beauty* and author of the following works: *The House, the City and the Judge: The Growth of Moral Awareness in the Oresteia; Perception, Understanding and Style; Structures of Experience: Essays on the Affinity between Philosophy and Literature; Psychoanalytic Theory of Art,* and *Tragedy – Contradiction and Repression.*

Leon Rosenstein is Professor of Philosophy at San Diego State University. He wrote his Dissertation on tragedy at Columbia. His articles on Plato, Aristotle, Hegel, Nietzsche, Cassirer and Heidegger, and on art and tragedy, have appeared in many philosophy journals.

Editor's Introduction

Some twenty-five years ago Walter Kaufmann opened his *Tragedy and Philosophy* by questioning what he called the presumption of Socrates, Plato and Aristotle that they were superior in wisdom to the tragic poets. In a sense his book was an effort to set the record straight, to show not so much who are the wisest, the philosophers or the tragic poets, but that the latter too were wise. 'Let us disown', he wrote,

> two equally extreme generalizations: one sees the poet as a singularly wise philosopher, the other, as a man whose business is with words and sounds, with language, possibly with plot and characters, but not with anything remotely philosophical. Both views approximate the truth about *some* poets. Regarding the great tragic poets, the first though wrong, is much more nearly right: Aeschylus and Euripides, Goethe and Ibsen were, beyond question, intellectuals, full of ideas; and while Sophocles and Shakespeare were not quite *that* intellectual, they, too, projected their own vision of the world and man's condition. (pp. 93–4)

While Aristotle's poetics, according to Kaufmann, dealt with the technique of tragedy or what he called the artistic dimension, and the poetics of Romanticism explored the historical dimension, his own poetics focuses on 'the philosophical dimension' of tragedy. He explains this dimension by referring to it as the content of a given poem that is inseparable from the plot and diction, or the meaning *in* the poem as a whole, or the poet's thoughts independent of the statements and arguments of the characters, thoughts that cannot be systematically put forth prior to or apart from the particular tragic poem. What the tragedian does is to communicate his views, his philosophy, but not as a philosopher would. His mode of communication is not discursive or theoretical but dramatic and therefore indirect. The bulk of Kaufmann's book is taken up by analysis of a number of tragic dramas showing what the views of the respective dramatists were, how these views compare to the views of philosophers (while Plato believed in the compatibility of the virtues, Sophocles realized that some of the virtues are

1

profoundly problematic), and to what extent these views were understood or misunderstood by those philosophers who wrote on these tragedies or on tragedy in general (Euripides is not the rationalist Nietzsche took him to be).

The present volume shares little with Kaufmann's book of the same title. It would be surprising if a volume with a title such as this did not in some fashion or other deal with at least some of the great philosophers who wrote on tragedy, did not make allusions to those issues first brought up by Aristotle, or did not refer to individual tragedies. The present volume does all these and to that extent it has something in common with Kaufmann's *Tragedy and Philosophy*. Thus Anderson examines *Oedipus* and *Antigone*; Kuhns *The Seven Against Thebes* and *Othello*; Kaelin *The Oresteia*, Sophocles' and Euripides' *Electra*, and Sartre's *The Flies*; Desmond spends a great deal of time on *King Lear*, and Georgopoulos on *Moby-Dick*. Anton discusses Aristotle's and Nietzsche's theories; Galle and Desmond focus on Hegel and Nietzsche; Georgopoulos speaks of Hegel and Langer; and Kaelin alludes to Schiller's views. The traditional Aristotelian themes are also considered: the tragic flaw, catharsis, the tragic emotions, the action of tragedy.

If, however, the writers in this volume turn to individual tragedies, their aim is not to discover the respective tragedian's philosophical views and to what extent these views are compatible with the views of philosophers on the subject, for instance, of justice. With the exception of Kaelin, whose phenomenological reading of the tragedies he examines tries to show how the underlying philosophical ideas of the playwrights structure the events of their narratives, the writers in this volume are not concerned with the 'philosophical import' of individual tragedies or of tragedy in general, at least not in the sense meant by Kaufmann. Tragedy *and* Philosophy here does not refer to philosophy contained in tragedy; it does not mean Philosophy *in* Tragedy. In fact Georgopoulos explicitly questions the soundness of Kaufmann's approach. More generally, Rosenstein rejects the idea that tragedy as art contains philosophy, or a particular philosophy. Anderson, less directly, holds the same. And some writers reverse Kaufmann's approach and speak of philosophy as tragic, of Tragedy *in* Philosophy. This does not mean, however, that there is, among the writers in this volume, a consensus regarding their approach, still less an agreement as to the nature of tragedy and the meaning of the tragic. Anton, for example, doubts the legitimacy of the concept 'tragic' and the notion of a 'philosophy of the tragic'. There is not even agreement as to what philosophy or the philosophical is, although the majority of the writers share a more or less common view as to the notion of traditional philosophy or to philosophy as traditionally understood. For Rosenstein, for example, philosophy is the giving of a rational account of its subject which ultimately is the One reality, an account which on the rational plane is consistent and complete. For Hausman, it is the systematic pursuit and the exhaustive account of the Whole of things. For Anderson, philosophy, particularly since Descartes, has been the pursuit and attainment of objective knowledge, or the truth as absolute clarity. Kuhns sees the model of philosophy as being that of science. And in Desmond's words, philosophy has considered Being as completely intelligible. But not all writers, themselves philosophers, espouse as their own such a view of philosophy. Not only do they come up with new ways of considering tragedy and the tragic; a number of them offer new ways of philosophizing. These new conceptions of philosophy emerge out of a context that all essays (including those that do not go beyond philosophy traditionally understood) share: the relation between tragedy and philosophy. All the essays address themselves to this relation. This is what overrides their diversity, unifies them into one volume and justifies its title.

Sometimes the relation is presented in terms of contrast, even clash, reminiscent, if vaguely, of the old quarrel Socrates refueled in the *Republic*. But no one here speaks negatively of tragedy, or considers it inferior to philosophy. In fact for Rosenstein and Kuhns, tragedy is richer than philosophy. There is much, according to the latter, that the philosopher can learn from tragedy. Desmond goes further. With its traditional stress on the determinate knowledge of the determinate, philosophy is incapable of attaining the extremity and radicality of tragedy. Only when philosophy gets rid of its official image, can it measure to tragedy's ontological depth. For Anderson, both tragedy and philosophy are ontologically deep. Both share a common origin and both move in the same direction. But in offering dialogue at the point where tragedy ends, philosophy moves beyond tragedy, epitomizing it.

At other times the relation between tragedy and philosophy is seen in terms of their affinities. By drawing parallels between the tragic agent and the nature and goal of the philosophical activity, Hausman supports his thesis that philosophy is tragic. Desmond, too, argues that to the extent philosophy becomes mindful of the meaning of being at a loss, it approximates tragedy. More specifically, Hyland's entire essay is to show that Plato's conception of philosophy is tragic. In a curious way, one that gives an interesting twist to the tradition, all these latter essays turn not to Aristotle but to Plato either to support tragedy or to exhibit its closeness to philosophy. The essays in this volume could be seen as falling into two more or less separate groups. One group is Aristotle oriented; the other Plato oriented. This division, however, is not made along traditional lines. It is not that the latter group is critical of tragedy in a way that is often attributed to Plato, while the former group justifies tragedy, finding a place for it in the *polis*. Rather, the division is drawn along non-traditional lines and is, I believe, of a deeper philosophical significance. The first group explicitly or implicitly aligns itself with Aristotle or the Aristotelian tradition, returns to the *Poetics* either to give the correct interpretation or to retrieve insights and reinterpret, enlarge and modernize themes first brought up by Aristotle. The second group returns to Plato, not to what his characters said about tragedy, but to his own philosophical practice, finding that practice akin to tragedy. The name of Aristotle hardly appears in these essays. Desmond mentions Aristotle only once and only to question the honored place Aristotle occupies in the ancient world. He suggests that this honor should be given to Plato. He finds Plato's and Aristotle's philosophical activity antithetical – the former's alone is tragic.

It is not so much out of respect for the tradition but for Aristotle's insights that this volume opens with an essay that clarifies and defends his most famous insight: his notion of catharsis.

At least up to Nietzsche's time there were two main interpretations of what Aristotle meant by catharsis. According to the one which was held by Lessing and which may be called moral, tragedy familiarizes us with the dangerous emotions of pity and fear so that we exercise them with moderation. According to the other, which was put forth by Jacob Bernays and which may be referred to as psychopathological, tragedy arouses the two harmful emotions in order that we discharge them and thus restore psychic equilibrium. It was the latter interpretation that was prevalent in Nietzsche's time and it was this he sided with. He took catharsis to mean the purgation of these deleterious emotions. It was on the basis of this interpretation that he criticized Aristotle. It is Anton's thesis that Nietzsche's criticism is based on a misinterpretation of what Aristotle took to be the nature and function of the tragic emotions and the end of tragedy. Anton himself sees the *Poetics* as presenting a theory of the process of producing a particular kind of art, and argues that catharsis is a formal element in this art; not an emotional end-effect on the spectator, but a structural feature of the plot, the soul of tragedy. He supports his interpretation by drawing a distinction between *pathe* (emotions) and *pathemata* (incidents or events charged with emotions), a distinction Nietzsche overlooked. Thus, according to Anton, when in his famous definition Aristotle speaks of *pathematon katharsin*, catharsis refers not, as Nietzsche took it, to *pathe* but to *pathemata*, and denotes not purgation but clarification – the clarification or illumination of the incidents that make up the plot. It is not that in tragedy, for Aristotle, emotions are not aroused; they are not purged. Aroused, they become integrated to the tragic incidents and are thus aesthetically transformed into tragic emotions. As such, they come to illuminate these incidents and sustain our compassionate understanding. As clarification then, catharsis, along with other elements, contributes in completing the plot. As Anton sees it, the completion of the plot (*mythos*) is, for Aristotle, the purpose of a tragic performance. By showing the intimacy between tragic emotion and rational insight, Aristotle's account of tragedy reveals the *logos* of the tragic *mythos*. Finally, it is this completion, the formal integration of the components of the *mythos*, that the pleasure proper to tragedy derives from – a pleasure which obviously enough is not at odds and therefore need not be reconciled with the witnessing of incidents in themselves horrific. Thus, according to Anton, Aristotle did not recognize the existence of the so-called 'paradox of tragedy' which Nietzsche read into Aristotle's theory and then accused him of not solving.

In turning next to the concept of the tragic, Anton, here too, finds Nietzsche in the wrong in accusing Aristotle for having missed the essence of the tragic and in claiming to have gone beyond him and the Greeks. Nietzsche accused Aristotle of missing what Aristotle was not even looking for. For Aristotle, and for all the Greeks, the tragic was a literary device and a dramaturgical concept. For Nietzsche, it was turned into an ontological and a value concept – it became de-hellenized. The Greeks never made reference to the tragic in connection with the philosophical concerns about nature and human nature. For Nietzsche, the tragic became the center of all philosophical concerns. From a dramatic art Nietzsche turned tragedy into an art of existence – the joyful acceptance of the absurd, and as such, into a means of salvation. In doing so, Anton argues, Nietzsche moved away from the Greeks and close to the Christian tradition. His model for the tragic art of life had already been worked out by Augustine and the church fathers – the will of God became the will to life, eternal salvation was taken over by eternal creativity; salvation in creativity. In the final analysis, Nietzsche's misinterpretation of Aristotle's account of the tragic emotions and the function of tragedy, is not, in Anton's judgement, the error of a scholar. It has its source in his invention of the tragic sense of life – an un-Aristotelian, un-Greek, neo-Christian notion.

Galle's essay provides an explanation of how the concept of the tragic came to be, in Anton's words, de-hellenized. It can be seen as an elaboration and even a justification of Anton's critique of Nietzsche's concept of the tragic. Galle does not speak of Nietzsche's misunderstanding of Aristotle, but of the appropriation of the tragic by post-Enlightenment philosophers, paradigmatically Hegel and Nietzsche, and shows how in this appropriation the tragic was disjoined. According to Galle, the Enlightenment, represented by Voltaire, brought about a structural change of tragedy. By adapting his plays to the rational demands and taste of his times, Voltaire in effect eliminated the tragic constellation – he presented the tragic as a threat to be overcome. Galle sees Hegel's and Nietzsche's theories of tragedy as different attempts to rescue the tragic from this crisis. Both attempts failed. Hegel tried to reintegrate the tragic into an Enlightenment view of the world without having to abandon its classic dimension. However, by seeing the tragic conflict as that between the split parts of the Rational/Divine and by relativizing the catastrophe in the final reconciliation which, unlike the Aristotelian tradition, he considers integral to tragedy, Hegel, for Galle, remained within the Enlightenment. Voltaire paralyzed the dimension of the tragic by means of the Enlightenment-based idea of *perfectabilité* for his characters. Hegel attempted to regain this dimension lost in Voltaire, by preserving the conflict and the catastrophe. But by retaining the idea of *perfectabilité* at the level of historical progress, he brought about the disjunction of the tragic.

If Hegel's view of the tragic is his attempt to reconcile tragedy to the Enlightenment, Galle sees Nietzsche's as his attempt to negate the Enlightenment. For Nietzsche, tragedy realizes in aesthetic form the anthropological basis by which humans acknowledge the bestial without turning against themselves in guilt. Guiltless, tragedy celebrates the martial and the cruel; it affirms suffering. It is Galle's view that Nietzsche's conjuring away of history under the sign of cruelty and his conception of the hero as the hypostatization of the primal human condition does as little justice to the traditional practice of tragedy as does Hegel's assimilation of the tragic to the idea of progress. Both end up by disjoining the tragic, the former with the relativization of the tragic conflict, the latter with the apotheosis of the conflict. Galle sees this disjunction as the consequence of the two philosophers' relation to the Enlightenment. More generally, he sees it as a consequence of the way each considered reality. Both use the tragic principle they extrapolate from tragedy to profile their philosophy, while at the same time they come up with a view of tragedy that is conditioned by that philosophy. Their concept of the tragic reflects their philosophy and their philosophy determines the concept of the tragic. If Anton, centering on Nietzsche, questions the very notion of a philosophy of the tragic, Galle concludes that the philosophy of the tragic since the eighteen-hundreds, best represented by Hegel and Nietzsche, is not really an interpretation of tragedy. It is a reflection on a particular formulation of human destruction conditioned by a philosophical construct of reality. Such a construct is disjoined. It owes its philosophic form to just this disjunction.

For Rosenstein, philosophical constructs of reality are extraneous to tragedy. On this basis alone he would reject both Hegel's and Nietzsche's theories. He would agree that Nietzsche's tragic sense of life is foreign, not only to Aristotle's account of tragedy, as Anton has argued, but to any account that takes tragedy, as Rosenstein's does, on its own terms and for what it is: art. Tragedy, for Rosenstein, neither reproduces nor refers to life or reality. Its world is a virtual, invented, worked-world with its own laws, conditions and criteria of rightness, inapplicable to the extra-artistic world. As such, tragedy cannot be the expression of a particular philosophy, e.g. the tragic philosophy or the tragic view of life, nor, more generally, can it contain philosophy as an isolable sub-category. The thoughts that may be contained in a tragedy are not interpretations of reality or expressions of moral or metaphysical theses, but suggested explanations of the events of the play-world which in each instant is unique. Rosenstein wants to explain the nature and function of this unique playworld. He does this by first turning to Aristotle. His purpose, however, is not, as it was with

Anton, to interpret correctly and therefore to defend Aristotle. Although rooted in Aristotle, his essay carries us in a different direction and beyond the context of Greek culture within which Anton moves. Rosenstein uses the *Poetics* as a heuristic device: he adopts, reinterprets, reconstructs aspects of Aristotle's argument initially to support and clarify his own position regarding the events and the thoughts in tragedy, and on the basis of this to establish a distinction between tragedy and philosophy beyond the obvious distinctions often granted by critics and philosophers.

For Rosenstein, the unique worked-world of tragedy, Aristotle's poetic invention, is a unified whole constituted by the coordination of content and means. It is to this whole in 'play', and not simply to the plot line, the themes and thoughts, as it is often with philosophers, that we become attuned when we respond to tragedy as art-work. In this attunement our various faculties are brought into play – our imagination is set free and we are entertained with possibilities. The purpose of the destructive events depicted in tragedy and of the thoughts expressed in it is not, respectively, to provoke our pity and fear and to refer to reality and the lives we must live in it. Rather, the purpose of both, and this is Rosenstein's thesis, is to stimulate our attention and thereby entertain us with possibilities. The attuned stimulation that is our response is accomplished by the sensuous media as they become integrated with the so-called content, bringing about its transformation. The possibilities tragedy entertains us with are different from those provided by philosophy. Philosophy is tied to perception and its reasons; tragedy transforms perception by and for the imagination. Philosophy delimits the relations in the actual world; tragedy proposes new relations of possibility by creating new worlds. Philosophy considers possibilities insofar as they conform to and confirm perceived actualities; tragedy expands the actualities of perception into a plentitude of possibilities by the imagination to occasion much thought. Tragedy exemplifies what Kant found at work in all poetry. For Rosenstein, however, tragedy creates not only as Kant thought in connection with poetry, a plentitude of ideas and images, but also of interrelated feelings and sensations, and therefore its pleasure is not, as with Kant and the philosophers, merely an intellectual pleasure, but sensuous and emotional as well. The distinctness and complexity of the pleasure of tragedy is due to and commensurate with the distinctness and complexity of the possibilities Rosenstein associates with tragedy. It is the complexity of these possibilities, stimulated in part as they are by the 'thoughts' in tragedy, that account for the richness of tragedy and its difference from philosophy.

Kuhns, too, finds tragedy richer than philosophy. His reasons, although related to Rosenstein's, are different. For Kuhns, too, the world of tragedy is a virtual world. But it is not a world unto itself. In responding to it that world crosses over to the real world of culture and contributes to it by helping assess, direct and shape the emotions of the audience. To this extent Kuhns' account of tragedy is closer to Aristotle's than to Rosenstein's. It is, we could say, an updating and an enlargement of Aristotle's discussion of the emotions and of catharsis by means of a new interpretation of the psychoanalytic theory of art. While for Rosenstein the worked world of tragedy entertains us with possibilities, for Kuhns this same world helps us mature as sentient beings living in a cultural tradition. Whatever else tragedy does, this, in Kuhns' view, is one of its central functions. In this, he argues, philosophy has much to learn from tragedy. Kuhns finds a discrepancy between philosophy's claims to direct and order the emotions on behalf of living well, and the actual living of those who do philosophy. The behavior of the latter contradicts their claim to having insights into character and human nature. When philosophy talks of the emotions, it remains at the level of argument. Having read a philosophical text, we do not feel deeply or differently. The possible increase in knowledge is not accompanied by a growth of the affective side of our life. Philosophy has little power in molding character or bringing about cultural integration. By contrast, in witnessing a tragic performance we go through an emotional growth. It is Kuhns' thesis that this comes about in great part by the way tragedy presents objects – objects such as Philoctetes' wound, Clytemnestra's body, the shields in *Seven Against Thebes*, Othello's handkerchief. Philosophy, too, considers objects, but it treats them as fixed, static and neutral. In tragedy objects are dynamic and multireferential, metaphorically powerful and emotionally loaded, and as such they relate to the audience as participants in a cultural tradition in a changing way. In the experience of a tragic drama we undergo a developmentally complex affective maturation, a cultural growth and integration.

In interpreting objects in terms of their function in psycho-sexual-political conflicts, tragedy, according to Kuhns, affords us a more complete epistemology and politics than philosophy does. It

generates a theory of action and show how objects work in the
individual's development of growing up in the family and in the
society. It is by turning to tragedy, with its ability to reach what
Freud called the primary process of thought, which formulates the
instinctual drives, that philosophy, limited as it is to what Freud
called the secondary process of thought, can come to understand
its own conflicts. Philosophy, to be sure, has its own way of
interpreting tragedy. Kuhns does not see the need for a quarrel.
Instead he calls for the alliance of philosophy and tragedy or poetry
for the sake of their mutual enrichment – an alliance that even Plato
affirmed, not through his characters but in his own practice of
writing dialogues.

If Anton argued that Nietzsche misunderstood Aristotle's
account of the effect of tragedy, Kaelin wants to show that both
Aristotle and Nietzsche, in fact the entire aesthetic theory from
Aristotle through Schiller to Nietzsche, has mislocated the investigation of tragedy from the artistic facts of the matter into the
demands of the various theories themselves. Thus he deviates what
he takes to be Aristotle's, Schiller's and Nietzsche's question (how
it is that the act of contemplating suffering and pain determines a
positive response in the audience) from the theoretical problem to
its source: the tragic phenomenon. The effect of tragedy is to be
found in the tragic art-work itself, not in the theoretical explanations of our response to it. Thus he turns to four dramas: the
Oresteia, Sophocles' and Euripides' *Electra* and Sartre's *The Flies*,
and traces the transformation of significance of the myth of the
house of Atreus through the four successive re-interpretations. By
means of a phenomenological analysis of these plays he shows how
it is the relation between the surface description of the individual
characters, acts and circumstances, these first order events, that
reveals the underlying philosophy (the different philosophical
ideas of the respective writers) as the principle that orders these
events and structures the dramatic narrative, pointing in this way
to the inseparability of form and philosophical 'content'. With their
respective moral, metaphysical and psychological treatment,
Aeschylus, Sophocles and Euripides aimed at a tragic effect of the
original myth. Thus in opposition to Aristotle, Kaelin sees several
manifestations of the tragic 'essence', as many as there are ways of
modifying the dramatic interpretations of the original myth. In the
hands of the three Attic tragedians the myth has already been
successively transformed, but these transformations have been

within the framework of what Kaelin calls their naturalistic philosophy. *In The Flies* the same myth is altered in such a basic way that it transevaluates the naturalistic values of the Greek tragedians into the existential values of Sartre's philosophy. Because of its drastically different dramatic techniques, *The Flies* places into greater relief what was also true of the Greek tragedies. The reversal of the significance of the original myth in *The Flies* is seen by Kaelin as being itself an instance of the transevaluation of values which he, in agreement with Nietzsche, considers one of the determinants of the tragic experience. For Kaelin it is this transevaluation of values and the joy of participating in the creation of a new value that constitutes the effect of tragedy; its positive value created out of the negative values of pain and suffering, the 'tragic lift'.

Kaelin's thesis is that one need not appeal to another medium to account for this phenomenon; it can be found only within an experience of the tragic dramas themselves – not in anyone's aesthetic theory. If tragic dramas are indirect expressions of the dramatist's philosophical ideas, what those ideas are and how they effect the development of tragic drama can be found only through a phenomenological analysis of the narrative structure of dramas. Like the dramas he considers, Kaelin's essay has a plot and a subplot. The plot or text is the question of the relationship of philosophy and tragic drama. The subplot or subtext is that only in a phenomenological description of literary techniques can one find an answer to the question. The phenomenological deep reading of the dramatic texts will show what the case actually is, if only we drop the theorizing, whether of Aristotle, Schiller or Nietzsche.

Like Kaelin, Georgopoulos drops the theoretical approaches to tragedy and like Rosenstein considers tragedy in its own terms. He is not doing so, however, in order to give a correct account of what Kaelin calls 'the tragic lift', or to explain, as Rosenstein does, the distinct pleasure of tragedy. His concern is not, as with Aristotle, the effect of tragedy. He is in agreement with Aristotle that it is the action that defines tragedy. But his interpretation of what makes the action tragic and what its significance is, is quite different not only from Aristotle's views but also from views as diverse as those of Hegel and Langer. Unlike them, he considers as central the circumstances in the midst of which the protagonist is placed, sees these circumstances as non-human and views the action as a response to the claims made on the human protagonist by the non-human circumstances. In this response the protagonist reaches his/her human limits and at the moment of the catastrophe cracks these limits, opening to what destroys him/her.

Georgopoulos locates the significance of the protagonist's action in its correlativeness to the tragedian's action. As it is the protagonist's response to the non-human circumstances that defines his actions and qualifies him/her as tragic, so it is the tragedian's response to his uncanny themes and his openness to the other to which they point as their origin that define his activity as artistic and qualify him as creative. In and through the tragic action, the tragedian and possibly and subsequently we, in activities that open to the other, come to be engaged in a happening of emergence that originates in what is other. Such a happening does not occur, in Georgopoulos' view, only in tragedy. It is not only through tragedy that we come to be involved in activities that open to the other. All involvement in art is, in his view, constituted by such activities. From the perspective of the activities that constitute them, all artworks are tragic. What distinguishes a tragedy from other works, plastic or not, is that in the former such activities become more evident. Tragedy provides an awareness of a process that comes to be in human being's participation in that in which what is other than human also participates, a process that has its source there – the creative process. Georgopoulos concludes by suggesting that when philosophy expresses the need for human being to be related to the mystery by opening to its wonder, its activity, like the activity of art, is analogous to the activity that involves the tragedian and us in tragedy. Philosophic action, like art action, is tragic action.

The themes of limit and of the other that Georgopoulos brings up in connection with his discussion of the tragic action are addressed again, separately or together, in a variety of ways, by all the writers that follow, beginning with Hyland. It will be recalled that Kuhns closed his essay by calling for an alliance of philosophy and tragedy, and alluded to Plato's practice as affirming this alliance. Hyland takes up where Kuhns left off; he returns to Plato's practice. His thesis is not so much that by writing dialogues Plato proved in practice what Socrates denied within the dialogues, but rather that Plato's dialogues exhibit a tragic dimension. Using *Oedipus the King* as an operative example, he finds five dimensions of the human situation that he associates with tragedy. A situation is tragic to the extent one is subject to fate; a striving to overcome that fate; this attempt condemns the hero to it; this is understood only at the end; the attempt to overcome his fate enables the tragic hero. In Hyland's interpretation, Aristophanes' speech about eros in the *Symposium* conforms to the first four of these dimensions. According to Aristophanes, we cannot achieve our original wholeness; we are condemned not only to incompleteness, but to a striving to overcome that incompleteness which itself is bound to fail. What is missing from Aristophanes' narrative is the dimension of nobility of the erotic striving. That is why his speech remains a comic portrayal of the human condition. It is Socrates' speech, in Hyland's view, that provides that dimension and so fulfills the tragic portrayal of *eros*. Socrates preserves the tragic elements of Aristophanes' speech, but completes them by going beyond Aristophanes' account of the erotic nature of human beings. For Socrates eros is not limited to love between individuals. In addition he finds other and higher manifestations of experienced incompleteness and the striving to overcome it. It is in its higher manifestations that Socrates shows that eros can be a source of nobility. Eros is not only the source of consolation for human beings; it is also the source of the noblest human aspiration, of philosophy itself. The paradoxical character of eros' parentage (poverty and plenty) makes the human situation not less but more tragic. Not only are humans fated to aspire toward a goal to which they are doomed to fail, but this aspiration ennobles them. Thus, for Hyland, the account of eros, i. e. the account of the human situation, in the *Symposium* is tragic. The project of completeness or wholeness as the love of wisdom is not attainable. This becomes particularly evident when we view Socrates' speech not in isolation and not as an alternative to the other speeches. Plato invites us to hold together Aristophanes' (and Alcibiades') account of eros as the pursuit of individuals and the bodily, *and* Socrates-Diotima's account of eros as the pursuit of the higher object of knowledge – an impossible enterprise. This impossibility is precisely Plato's point. The philosophic enterprise, erotic as it is, tries to hold the whole together, as one. As such, it is destined to failure. But by trying to bring about the impossible this pursuit is noble. Philosophy, like the human erotic condition of which it is its highest expression, is tragic.

For Hausman, too, Plato's thinking is tragic. Hausman, however, does not limit himself to Plato. He uses Plato to shed light on the larger picture of philosophy as such. Understood as the love of

wisdom, philosophy, he argues, is inherently tragic. Whether
committed to pre-twentieth century metaphysical and epistemological ideals or committed to contemporary limitations of
philosophical aims conceived according to the linguistic turn,
philosophy loves wisdom (a state of knowledge that concerns the
whole of things) in the sense that it is unrelenting in its critical
efforts and is intent on asserting its claims categorically and
exhaustively. This character of philosophy is tragic in Hausman's
sense in that what is tragic is something or someone noble in
intention but headed toward an inevitable failure because of the
nature of the tragic agent. Thus, philosophy has a flaw that is at
bottom like the tragic flaw of literary tragic heroes. Hausman
admits that insofar as his own essay is intended to be philosophical
and about philosophy, it too falls prey to its own claims and
therefore it too is flawed. Like philosophy in general, his essay
cannot escape failure. However, he locates this failure not in his
claim that philosophy is tragic, but in his larger philosophical
outlook presupposed by and at the basis of this claim: philosophy's
inevitable failure. Hausman accepts the failure of his own position,
and on the basis of this acceptance proposes a possible course for
future philosophy. Thus he adopts a form of fallibilism akin to
Peirce's, and argues that if philosophical love is widened to include
what Peirce understood by agape, the inevitable failure of
philosophy can be seen as implying a flaw that is a virtue. This does
not diminish the failure, but suggests that failure is admirable
insofar as it is the expression of a condition of the inevitability and
limitation of the agency that engages in philosophizing. As free-
giving, agape is the openness to something other than the agency
and the agapistic effect. It leaves open to what it loves the
possibility of departure from its own determination. So if philosophy is agapistic as well as erotic it can accept its flaw and thus it
can be free in a sense more radical than that which characterizes
the tragic hero and the traditional philosophical drive, for it can
support that freedom as integral to the necessity of that drive. It is
in this acceptance and in this freedom that lies the future of
philosophy for Hausman. As agapistic, philosophy must drive
toward wisdom, but at the same time it must be open, ready to
accept its inevitable failure. Philosophy should not try to overcome
its tragic nature, but foster it by insisting on its own growth which
is possible by virture of its own failure. It must be open to new and
even conflicting claims – claims that may imply its own failure. As

Oedipus' flaw turns out to be (in *Oedipus at Collonus*) his own redemption, so philosophy's inevitable failure can be its own superiority over itself.

Failure is at the heart of Desmond's essay too. But Desmond speaks of failure in an active, existential way – failure as breakdown or loss. Because of this his essay has a different texture and dimension from Hausman's essay to which it is otherwise intrinsically related. Desmond centers his essay on Lear's Howl: 'Thou't come no more, Never, never, never, never'. He locates the tragic in this Howl, in Lear's being at a loss in the face of this Never. Tragedy, for Desmond, reveals one of the ultimate forms of being at a loss. In a tragic situation we are confronted with absolute limits; pushed to the dead end of being. As such and in contrast to Hausman, he sees tragedy as being at odds with philosophy understood in the traditional sense as systematic science. Philosophy strives to overcome loss, to place reason where tragedy faces rupture, to construct meaning where tragedy undergoes suffering. Philosophy is not and in principle could never be at a loss. As systematic science it excludes the tragic or, in its 'love for truth', it hides a hatred for the tragic. It is Desmond's conviction, however, that being at a loss is a constitutive dimension of being human. When philosophy is a mindfulness that thoughtfully tries to be at home with being in being at a loss, it is no longer philosophy as systematic science. As such, philosophy considers as essential losing, breakdown, the irruption of the indeterminate. Desmond's conception of philosophy includes but is not exhausted by the will to systematic science; it has a plurivocal identity. What is more than science in philosophical mindfulness is related to the metaphysical meaning of being at a loss and hence to the tragic. He sees Plato's philosophy as paradigmatic of this mindfulness. Plato's dialogues make us realize that philosophy is always already at a loss. In fact philosophy, as Desmond understands it, comes to know itself at its own breakdown. The philosopher's self-identity can be forged in the awareness of being at a loss. And as the *Phaedo* shows, it is in death, the death of a non-universalizable particular, that the philosopher's extreme being at a loss is manifest. This does not mean for Desmond that philosophical *logos* must give up before the ultimate experience at a loss. Talking must continue, but as plurivocal. As plurivocal, philosophy can break through in thought beyond breakdown. That there is more to philosophy as plurivocal Desmond illustrates in terms of Lear's Never. When Lear says

Never, he is addressing a particular thou – the ultimate being of Cordelia as his beloved child. Particulars, intimates of being, have an ontological richness, an inward otherness, invisible to conceptual discursivity. Such public discursivity cannot capture the intimacy of being expressed in Lear's Howl. To see what is revealed in this tragedy is co-extensive to our own complete transformation, to the death of the ordinary self. Desmond likens the tragic insight to an asphyxiation by a knowing we cannot possess, and finds the value of this insight, which he offers as a possible metaphysical consolation to the tragic, in what he calls the posthumous mind: a thinking of being as if from beyond death. Having been brought to a complete loss of being, to the edge, we come to see, in wonder, the marvel and mystery of being.

Like Desmond, Anderson brings himself and us to the limit, the edge, the *aporon* at which the tragic scenario leaves the hero, the tragedian and us. And like him Anderson, too, speaks from this edge. For Anderson, however, this edge is a threshold, one opening to indeterminate possibility. As such the aporon is seen as the scene of freedom. If in Desmond's view the tragic makes us aware of the marvel of being, in Anderson's view tragedy as art offers to the audience as well as to the tragedian the recognition of freedom as hope. Anderson's speaking at the edge is the articulation of this freedom. If Desmond's language is, at the edge, the language of philosophy as plurivocal, Anderson's language, at the edge, is the language of philosophy as dialogue. The aporon and the wonder evoked is at the center of their respective essays. For Anderson, both tragedy and philosophy are responses to wonder. His essay traces the development of philosophy from wonder. He finds the first human response to wonder in the generation of myth. In the course of time this response has been developed with the aid of art. Wonder interwoven in myth and brought to presence by art bespeaks, according to Anderson, the call exciting our yearning in that which is beyond us.

Anderson sees the early development of tragedy by art in Greece as a major achievement in the development of myth to formulate and comprehend human being. He presents the contribution of tragedy to this task in terms of *Oedipus* and *Antigone*. A fundamental part of our lives is that we are aware of limitation as a horizon. It is this horizon, according to Anderson, that these tragedies plumb, as have done all tragedies since tragedy's origin and growth from the myths of prehistory. We say we are finite but something more, something we cannot say yet. Becoming the more-we-can-be is for Anderson our tasks as humans. That we strive to become what we are not, and so ourselves, is to be aware of the root of meaning as wonder. Not to accept freedom is to be blind to what we are not, blind to possibility, to the radiance of absence. To seek and accept this absence is to live truly, to be free. By representing the objective world as illusion and by bringing the protagonists to the threshold of possibility beyond that, Sophocles' tragedies are seen by Anderson as symbolizing human being's openness to that absence, to indeterminate, unqualified possibility.

In addition to tragedy, the early Greeks also developed philosophy as a mode for pursuit of wisdom, which is for Anderson the understanding of human nature. This development, however, included the recognition and sharpening of objectivity as a basic concept which, developed as science, diverges from the views of myth and art. The issue of the societal focus on finite circumstance rather than myth was sharpened. Anderson sees this ambiguity in philosophical views presented in the thought of the Pre-Socratics. After the development of tragedy laid a foundation, and the Pre-Socratics extended it with this ambiguity, religion continued the development on this line by replacing Wonder with Revelation. This objectification of myth and art eliminated, at least in principle, for Anderson, the horizontal character of wonder. The importance of non-objectifying, horizonal, comprehension is a theme running through Anderson's essay. Philosophy, for him, can be understood as the Greeks for the most part did understand it, as a variation in the development of myth similar to that of art and religion. But Anderson brings to our attention that the Greeks also understood philosophy as being more concerned with society problems, politics, argumentation and dealing with nature. To some extent they anticipated the scientific view of the Renaissance. Thus they introduced the problem which is a significant contemporary issue in philosophy: Wisdom or Practical Scientific truth? Anderson's essay emphasizes that Wisdom is necessary even in the pursuit of scientific knowledge. It also suggests how philosophy can and does serve both goals.

Philosophy is presented by Anderson as a non-objectifying discipline which, while questioning any objectification, even that of art, also presents transcendence as a moment beyond.... developed best in human dialogue, that is, the recognition of and respect for the otherness of the others. Tragedy brings human beings (protagonist, artist, audience) to stand upon the threshold of the infinite, the aporon – wonder. It places humans at the edge of possibility. As dialogue, philosophy begins where the tragic scenario leaves off – at the edge, at the curtain-fall. It is the free response to origins by one on the threshold to another standing there. Dialogue offers presence to each of the persons it frees to stand on the threshold of possibility. These persons, as the mutual recognition of the mystery each other is, are the presence in their dialogue. Their mutual response accepts the wonder of each as the emergence of mystery. Philosophizing, for Anderson, offers dialogue as a movement beyond science and religion, but also beyond tragedy (and comedy) as a further insight into human being, its nature and its meaning.

1
Nietzsche's Critique of Aristotle's Theory of Tragic Emotions[1]

JOHN P. ANTON

I

When Nietzsche criticized Aristotle's views on tragedy in *The Birth of Tragedy*, he based his attack on two central issues. The first concerned the relationship between the tragic emotions, pity (*eleos*) and fear (*phobos*), both being painful experiences, and the aesthetic result of the art of tragedy, 'the proper pleasure of tragedy' (*he oikeia hedone tes tragodias*). Nietzsche claimed that Aristotle made two errors in his formulation of the tragic experience and especially of the concept of catharsis because he misidentified both. Following Bernays, Nietzsche took the latter to mean 'purgation of emotions'.[2]

The second issue concerned the relationship between the effects of tragedy and the basic needs of human nature. Again, Nietzsche concluded, Aristotle mistook the connection between the two. As a result Aristotle was unable to establish the continuity between the meaning of catharsis in the *Politics*, Book 8, and in the *Poetics*. In effect, Nietzsche chastized 'the moralist' Aristotle for casting asunder the continuity between these two treatises. Virtually, this means that Aristotle did not keep together his aesthetics and his ethical doctrines.

As I hope to show, Nietzsche's criticism of Aristotle's theory of tragic emotions, i.e. pity, fear and tragic pleasure, was based on a peculiar misunderstanding of the *Poetics*. He had developed a philosophical view about the nature of the tragic that began with Hegel and reached him through Schopenhauer, which he then used to study Greek dramaturgy as well as to project a theory of his own. As we know, Nietzsche's radical and novel ideas in *The*

Birth of Tragedy have influenced deeply the literary and philosophical circles of Europe, and continue to do so to this day. However, the undervaluing of the Aristotelian theory of tragic emotions to which his thesis is committed is by no means a minor issue, and therefore should not be left unanswered.

Nietzsche counterposes his own theory to Aristotle's conception of tragedy. Whether Nietzsche's position constitutes an advancement is still open to debate. There are two issues here: (a) the premises on which he based his attack, and (b) whether Nietzsche interprets Aristotle judiciously. Both take us back to his own conception of the tragic.

Nietzsche was a romantic theorist who thought about tragedy as reflecting concealed primitive powers that produce in human beings terrifying and insoluble conflicts. Hence for Nietzsche poetry deserves to be the leading spiritual activity, for its task is metaphysical disclosure. This means that art as tragic poetry reveals the deepest layers of human nature. We find here certain common features with the ancient Greeks, but with a difference. True, the ancients defended the high mission of the poet, but not on the same grounds as the moderns do. The Greeks saw with a critical eye the interdependence of opposites, whether moral, aesthetic or ontological, but refused to admit that there can be conflicts, however extreme, to which no resolutions may be found. This is a basic difference that separates Nietzsche's from Aristotle's model of human nature.

Nietzsche's method of viewing Aristotle allows him to advance two important criticisms. The first points to 'the paradox of tragedy', i.e. how is it possible to derive aesthetic pleasure from viewing horrible and destructive actions, which he claims that Aristotle formulated in such a way as to enable him to dissolve rather than solve it. He arrived at this conclusion first by linking the paradox with Aristotle's *Poetics* and then by introducing considerations that upon close inspection invariably tend to distort Aristotle's position. Nietzsche's view is that there is no real paradox in tragedy. Hence Aristotle *addressed* a contrived issue. But in dismissing the paradox Nietzsche came in fact closer to Aristotle, who also did not recognize its existence although for different reasons, chief among them being that the pleasure derived from the formal integration of the components of the *mythos* and not from the purgation of emotions due to the perception of horrific incidents. Nietzsche missed this similarity on this particular point.

However, having read the paradox into Aristotle's theory, Nietzsche thought it incumbent upon himself to criticize Aristotle. In carrying out the criticism, he attributed to Aristotle a distorted view of catharsis. This he did first by attacking the theory of tragic emotions, which is the main topic of this paper.

The second criticism, namely that Aristotle failed to connect the meaning of catharsis as found in the *Poetics* to that in the *Politics*, was far more serious. It implies that Aristotle's social philosophy is incoherent. The accusation is that Aristotle is guilty of divorcing politics and aesthetics, and therefore is guilty of compromising the Greek view about the unity of human values and institutions. The charge is of the gravest nature. For this reason alone it should not go unanswered.

The issue is by no means a dead one. Richard McKeon has defended the view that Aristotle's theory of tragedy is cast in aesthetic as well as extra-aesthetic terms, and although *Politics* VIII and *Poetics* deal with art, we have in the former a 'political utterance' while in the latter we are given an 'aesthetic utterance'.[3] If so, it would follow that Aristotle could not insist that tragedy is best understood in its own right and terms, as a reading of the *Poetics* alone would lead one to conclude. Arguing against McKeon's revival of Nietzsche's charge, N. Georgopoulos published a paper that comes close to my own position. He makes a point of recognizing McKeon's distinction between the two contexts but objects that 'tragedy may be used as a political instrumentality in the state or it may reflect doctrines or motivations in its speeches', which permits one to say that 'in either case it does not function as a work of art'. In contrast, Georgopoulos states that Aristotle is refusing to acknowledge that "a tragedy presents a world which is self sufficient and unto itself", and adds that tragic drama 'being an imitation does not fundamentally differ from the rest of the imitative activities that characterize the practical, i.e. the moral life of men. Like them, the artistic activity has its final cause in that life and contributes to its enhancement'. It points in the right direction.[4]

II

The Greeks have been paid high tribute for their contributions to humanity, especially for creating the theater and inventing tragic drama. It is also commonly recognized that Aristotle was the first and foremost theorist of the art of tragedy and the first to write a systematic treatise on the art of poetry. Some twenty-three centuries later, a young professor of classical philology, Friedrich Nietzsche, turned into an aspiring radical philosopher, published in 1872 his book *The Birth of Tragedy* and offered a brilliant new interpretation of the rise of tragic art in ancient Greece. By 'new' he literally meant an original thesis on the subject. He spared no labour in his effort to justify his claim that he was saying things no one before him, not even Aristotle, had suspected. His was going to be the decisive victory in the war of the moderns against the tyranny of the ancients.

Nietzsche praised the Greeks in what turned out to be an underhanded compliment. Given the extraordinary achievements of their culture, the Greeks still failed to understand what they had in fact discovered. In Section 17 of *The Birth of Tragedy*, after declaring his to be the first complete theory of the tragic myth and the best explanation of the chorus of Greek tragedy, he states that the real meaning of tragic myth was never articulated by any poet before his own arrival on the scene. Nietzsche announces that he is the first tragic philosopher, which also means, the first philosopher. The claim is that he was the first to understand what the Greeks did as tragic artists and why. As for uniting artistic self-consciousness and reflective insight, Nietzsche and not Aristotle is the real philosopher of the Greek achievement. The tragic experience, as the articulate emergence of the tragic view of life, was only dimly seen until Nietzsche came upon the battlefield.

Nietzsche held these theses to the end. He re-stated them with the same boldness in his last work. *The Will to Power.*[5]

What is tragic? – On repeated occasions I have laid my finger on Aristotle's great misunderstanding in believing the tragic affects to be two depressive affects, terror and pity. If he were right tragedy would be an art dangerous to life: one would have to warn against it as notorious and a public danger. (#851, 449)

Again:

I have been the first to discover the tragic. The Greeks, thanks to their moralistic superficiality, misunderstood it! Yearning for nothingness is a denial of tragic wisdom, its opposite. (#1029, 531)

The warning is also meant to instruct the reader. In effect it suggest that tragedy, if it has the affects Aristotle had diagnosed, renders innocuous the warning Plato issued so passionately against that art in his *Republic*. Confident in his judgment and satisfied with his critique of Aristotle, he did not see that his premises implied a strange conclusion: if Plato's warnings were wrong-headed and Aristotle's restoration of the importance of tragedy was half-hearted, then all warnings, including Nietzsche's own about taking Aristotle seriously, become superfluous. Shielding against 'depressive affects' becomes unnecessary. There is nothing that can make the art of tragedy dangerous to life. The fact is that Nietzsche concluded that both Plato and Aristotle were wrong: the one on moral grounds, the other on intellectual. Together they make an unreliable guide to life and art. The same basic view was also stated in *Twilight of the Idols*:

> Saying Yes to life even in its strangest and hardest problems, the will to life rejoicing over its own inexhaustibility even in the very sacrifice of its highest types – *that* is what I called Dionysian, *that* is what I guessed to be the bridge to the psychology of the *tragic* poet, *not* in order to be liberated from terror and pity, not in order to purge *oneself* of a dangerous affect by its vehement discharge – Aristotle understood it what way – but in order to be *oneself* the eternal joy of becoming, beyond all terror and pity – that joy which included even joy in destroying.

> And herewith I again touch that point from which I once went forth: *The Birth of Tragedy* was my first revaluation of all values. Herewith I again stand on the soil out of which my intentions, my *ability* grows – I, the last disciple of the philosopher Dionysus – I, the teacher of the eternal recurrence.[6]

In *Ecce Homo*, also written in 1888, he repeats the same thesis.[7] And in *The Antichrist*, First Book, Section 7, he declares:

> Aristotle as is well known, considered pity a pathological and dangerous condition, which one would be well advised to attack now and then with a purge: he understood tragedy as a purge. From the standpoint of the instinct of life, a remedy certainly seems necessary for such a pathological and dangerous accumulation of pity as is represented by the case of Schopenhauer

(and unfortunately by our entire literary and artistic decadence from St. Petersburg to Paris, from Tolstoi to Wagner) – to puncture it and make it *burst*.[8]

Schopenhauer had complained he could not find in the ancients the feeling of resignation to which everything tragic in life ought to lead. He concluded that the ancients had a lop-sided and misleading view of the tragic. Nietzsche, in his early work, repeats the reservations but gives different reasons. For both thinkers the ancients discovered the art of tragedy but missed the concept of the tragic, because they did not see that the tragic demands resignation.

The later Nietzsche protests from the other end of the spectrum. Schopenhauer failed to get close to the tragic but so did the ancients. The former on account of his misguided pessimism. The Greeks, because of their trust in reason, fell victims to their anti-life optimism. Hence tragic wisdom lies in the transcendence of both extremes. Nietzsche thus claims victory and the privilege to declare: 'I have the right to regard myself the first tragic philosopher'. What is presupposed in the thesis is the conviction that Aristotle held in fact the view that the function of tragedy is to effect purgation of deleterious feelings. It is the ghost behind the 'paradox of tragedy'. Presumably, Aristotle evidently never understood that he was haunted by this ghost. He simply meant well, but paid a high price for his innocence: he missed the tragic.

Nietzsche's mistake was in accusing Aristotle of identifying the end of tragedy to be *katharsis pathon*. Even if he had read correctly the text where Aristotle writes *pathematon katharsin*, still he would not have been free of error. I should state parenthetically at this point that if we take the Aristotelian formulation at its face value, we must read the expression *perainousa* in a way that keeps us close to the text, for here the verb *perainein* refers back to something that was already under way and is now brought to an end. In other words, the process of catharsis had started at an early stage of the unfolding of the tragic *mythos* but it takes the tragic emotions of pity and fear for tragedy as *praxis mimetike*, etc. etc., to complete the catharsis of the 'such and such' incidents-events.

Nietzsche's quest for 'tragic wisdom' is one that seeks to find the meaning of the 'tragic view of life'. Nietzsche attained it. Aristotle did not even suspect its existence. He missed the tragic. So declares Nietzsche, and so do many of his neo-Romantic followers. The charge of failure can be predicated only on the interpretation that the intent of tragedy of Aristotle's view of catharsis is to effect the purging of the emotions of pity and fear. This approach to catharsis as the end of tragedy acquired more momentum during and after Nietzsche's time. It still lurks behind positions that argue in favor of a 'tragic view of life'.

Our basic question remains: did Aristotle actually fail to understand or identify the nature and function of tragic emotions and the end of tragedy? If not, then a diagnosis of Nietzsche's errors is in order. For to say that he made an honest mistake is not enough. The charge that the Greeks failed to grasp the full significance of their achievement is too serious to ignore. It is equally important to decide whether arguments can be given to support Nietzsche's claim that he actually went beyond the Greeks. It may well be that what we have here are not rival doctrines but a confusion due to the modern appropriation of certain key terms to which novel meanings were assigned to serve different philosophical and axiological ends. The overlapping of concerns cannot and should not be denied. But the use of common terms has confused the issues 'tragedy' and 'the tragic'; once extended metaphorically they perform tasks not to be found in the literature and philosophies of the ancients. In other words, being the brilliant philologist that he was, Nietzsche should have known better. However, this does not lessen the impact of his judgment or of his conviction that the answers he found were far more adequate to the issues he addressed than the ones the Greeks had provided in their most exalted and creative moments.

III

Nietzsche turned out to be a classicist with a vengeance. His writings reveal an ardent lover of Greece hugging his beloved object to submission. Whether his understanding of what Aristotle meant by tragic emotions is supported by the texts is a question to which I must now turn. The key to remove the difficulty lies in the correlation of the relevant texts: the *Poetics* and the *Rhetoric* with reference to (a) the difference between (emotions) *pathe* and events or incidents charged with emotions (*pathemata*), on the one hand, and (b) the species of pity (*eleos*) and fear (*phobos*) that are proper to the unfolding of the *mythos* in dramaturgy, on the other. First I must quote the celebrated definition of tragedy.

Tragedy, then, is an imitation [*mimesis*] of an action, important and complete, and of a certain magnitude, by means of language embellished, and with ornaments used separately for each part, about human beings in action, not in narrative; carrying to completion, through a course of events involving pity (*eleos*) and fear (*phobos*), the purification of those painful or fatal acts which have that quality.[9]

The disputed part that figures heavily in the diverse interpretations of the passage reads: *di' eleou kai phobou perainousa ten ton toiouton pathematon katharsin*). Now for certain clarifications.

1.　The term *pathemata* although interchangeable with *pathe*, may cover the same range of denotation. Thus, it is correct to say that: (a) *pathemata* means events, doings, incidents. In the context of the definition of tragedy the word refers to the quality and type of events proper to tragic poetry: pitiful (*eleeina*) and terrible (*phobera*). The emotions we experience vicariously when viewing such events are called either *pathe* or *pathemata*. (b) Such vicariously experienced emotions, *pathe*, in tragedy are, strictly speaking, two: a species of fear and a species of pity. The are the only, properly speaking, *tragic* emotions.[10]

2.　The emotionally charged incidents, *pathemata*, as constituent elements of a tragic plot or *mythos*, may vary, but in order to qualify as tragic elements they must have the power to generate corresponding emotions but only of the type that pertain to tragedy. But why only certain species of pity and fear? For an answer we must go to Aristotle's *Rhetoric*, Book II, the part *peri pathon*, where he discusses the diverse emotions:

Emotions are all those things which so change human beings as to cause differences in their judgments and are accompanied by pain and pleasure, such as anger, pity, fear and the other ones like them and their contraries.

The list of such contrary pairs includes the following:

(a)　anger and calmness: *orge, praotes*.
(b)　friendship and hatred/enmity: *philia, misos/echthra*.
(c)　fear and confidence: *phobos, tharsos*.
(d)　shame and shamelessness: *aischyne, anaischyntia*.
(e)　kindness and unkindness: *charis, acharistein*.

(f)   pity and indignation: *eleos, to nemesan.*
(g)   envy: *phthonos.*
(h)   emulation: *zelos.*

Only two emotions on this list are named in the definition of tragedy: pity and fear. Yet not all types or pity will do. Their specific quality depends on the circumstances or events that cause them. In *Rhetoric*, these two emotions are defined as follows:

(i)   Pity:
Pity may be defined as a feeling of pain caused by the sight of some evil, destructive or painful, which befalls one who does not deserve it, and which we might expect to befall ourselves or some friend of ours and moreover to befall soon.

(*Rhetoric* II. 8, 1385b 12–15)

(ii)   Fear:
Fear may be defined as a pain or disturbance due to a mental picture of some destructive or painful evil in the future. Of destructive or painful evils only; for there are some evils, e.g. wickedness or stupidity, the prospect of which does not frighten us: I mean only such as amount to great pains or losses. And even these only if they appear not remote but so near as to be imminent: we do not fear things that are a very long way off: for instance, we all know we shall die, but we are not troubled thereby, because death is not close at hand.

(*Rhetoric* II. 5, 1382a 19–27)

It is not necessary to append here yet another elaborate discussion on the history of the literature regarding catharsis and how the term came to mean 'about emotions'.[11] Rather, my concern is to stress Nietzsche's misconception of the concept and why he found it so handy when he attacked Aristotle. He never suspected that Aristotle never said such silly things. Such was the prevailing interpretation of the day, and Nietzsche took it over from his teacher without reservations. Part of the cause for the misinterpretation may be due to the fact that the Greek words *pathe* and *pathemata* sound alike and have a common root. But technically speaking they do not cover the same ground. Now to return to our definition of tragedy, what Nietzsche did not see was that what is being brought to an end in tragedy is not the catharsis of emotions (*pathe*) but the clarification of the incidents that comprise the plot, the *mythos*. Emotions are evoked all along, but they are not purged; they become integrated in the resolution. Nietzsche did not suspect this thesis, nor did it seem likely that he could have entertained it as a hypothesis. His mind was set on saddling Aristotle with the theory of purgation, the 'vehement discharge of emotions'. My own reading of the *Poetics* has led me to conclude that the completion of *mythos* and not the purgation of emotions is the purpose of a tragedy. As for the benefits of tragedy, the *oikeia hedone* and the *didaskalia* it offers, they call for a separate study.[12]

Briefly stated, my thesis is as follows: With the resolution of the dramatic play comes the clarification that brings the end into full view; at the same time the emotions converge to sustain our understanding and compassion. Contrary to what Nietzsche contends, Aristotle was on target. He brought to the foreground the intimacy between tragic emotions and rational insight needed to reveal the *logos* of a tragic *mythos*. And once the pieces are drawn together something else happens: the pleasure proper to tragedy (*oikeia hedone*), which is felt despite the witnessing of incidents in themselves pitiful and terrible. This way of rendering Aristotle's meaning was totally foreign to Nietzsche. He was looking for incurable flaws in the ancients. His mind was moving in another direction.

IV

At the time he was writing *The Birth of Tragedy* he believed that the persistent deficiency in modern aesthetics reflected the deep crisis of the European mind in the nineteenth century. The absence of an adequate aesthetic, he contended, had generated an incurable pessimism and thrown the consciousness of Europe into deep self-distrust. As a result, the intellectuals could not unravel the meaning of life. It was a criticism directed against the rationalism of the Enlightenment. The intellectuals had failed; having put their faith in scientific knowledge, they could not admit that 'art represents the highest task and the truly metaphysical activity in life'. That in 1872. Twelve years later, when he wrote his 'Self-Criticism' for the second edition of *The Birth of Tragedy*, he became more precise. He stated there that his task was 'to look at science in the perspective of the artist, but art in that of life'. With this aphorism and announcement, Nietzsche elevated the artist to the position of the supreme spokesman for the human condition. In his 1888 work, *Twilight of the Idols*, 'Reason in Philosophy', Aphor. 6, the artist became the tragic artist. In the Forth Proposition he states: 'The tragic artist is no pessimist: he is precisely the one who says Yes to everything questionable, even to the terrible – he is *Dionysian'*.[13] Thus Nietzsche after arriving at his 'improved thesis' was in a stronger position to repeat that Aristotle by recommending the purgation of the tragic emotions was not the thinker who could provide the framework for so exalted an aesthetic, cultural and philosophical mission as the one Nietzsche assigned to, and reserved for, the artist.

Put in plainer terms, Nietzsche was convinced that the Greek experience had run its course. In *The Gay Science* he wrote: 'I honor Aristotle and honor him most highly – but he certainly did not hit the nail, not to speak of hitting it on the head, when he spoke of the ultimate aim of Greek tragedy (80)'. Nietzsche was therefore free to explore the 'real' question, the great and ultimate question: *What is tragic?* He formulated his first answer in 1872, in *The Birth of Tragedy*. However, it contained one flaw: the influence of Schopenhauer. The removal of pessimism in subsequent reformulations, his 'improved thesis', as I called it before, led to a stronger rejection of Aristotle's views. The reason for the attack remained the same. In 1888 nothing had changed. The conclusion remained the same. He reiterated the same criticism: 'On repeated occasions I have laid my finger on Aristotle's great misunderstanding in believing the tragic effects to be two *depressing affects, terror and pity'*. Aristotle's aesthetics and the Greek mind had prejudiced the understanding of the idea of the tragic.

His *Der Wille zur Macht* contains a summation of many central doctrines, including the one related to Nietzsche's critique of Aristotle and the Greeks. He insists that the character of existence, reality, is terrifying, and that the actual, the 'real world' is 'false, cruel, contradictory, seductive, without meaning' (#853). To be able to live in this real world and endure its cruelties, human beings become creative and work out systems of beliefs, i.e. systems of 'lies' which they then take to be true: metaphysics, religion, morality and science. In fact, Nietzsche's criticism of scientific beliefs and of the other systems of 'lies' stems from the conviction that our constructions and abstractions are inadequate representations of existence and of the real world, especially of ourselves. We throw back to nature our beliefs, confident that they are nature's own truths. Such confidence is nothing but self-deception. Human beings believe the lies they create because they need to forget and overcome the cruelty of the world. Each accepts his own lies and calls them truths. All truths, including the truths of logic, are lies. The peace they give is false because we have lied to ourselves. In sum, we turn life into what life is not.

We create in order to escape from reality; we make metaphysics, religion, morality and science in our capacity as artists. There is only one way to stop this on-going self-deception, this life of lies. Our only choice is to recover our will as artists, and by means of art to will to transcend our lies. Only by being an artist can one know what the arts are and are not. The next step is to create more by removing all obstacles to creativity. Only creating in art gives the power to lie without falling into the error of accepting the lies we create. Only the artist can be supremely honest and not deceive himself. This means that art is the only lie that enables the artist to refuse the fruits of creativity as truths. Above and beyond the will to truth is *the will to transfigure*. Nietzsche declares art to be 'the real task of life, art as life's metaphysical activity'. Art now comes to take the place which for thousands of years philosophy had assigned to reason. Art practices a creativity that gives 'the highest state of affirmation of existence' which includes even the highest degree of pain: 'It yields the tragic-Dionysian state and joy'. (#853)

Having thus stated his case, the critique of traditions, institutions, cultural ideals, theories and methods, follows relentlessly. Of course, the Greeks wrote tragedies and theorized about them, but by being superficially moralistic "they misunderstood their great discovery". Aristotle misled the modern aestheticians into accepting "the triumph of the moral world order, or the purgation of the emotions through tragedy, as the essence of the tragic".[14] With Aristotle out of the way, Nietzsche felt entitled to announce what had never been heard before: 'I have been the first to discover the tragic'.

V

Philosophers as well as other theorists have proposed views on the nature of tragedy, yet it is not always clear what a 'philosophy' of tragedy is. One suspects that whereas Aristotle had a theory of tragedy, Nietzsche had a 'philosophy' of same. If indeed one has ideas about this literary genre, how should they be classified and to what sort of discourse do they belong? If 'philosophical', why should they be considered so, and what are their credentials? One way of solving the problem is to place them within another set of ideas, e.g. ethical, political, aesthetic, ontological, etc. But then, we still have to face the problem of method in classification and how to justify its results.

One of the problems concerning tragedy in recent times has been the question 'Is tragedy dead?' Is this in fact a philosophical question, and if so why? Should it rather come within the orbit of the historian of literature? If the 'philosopher' also wishes to answer the question, how is he to do it? Is it a question to be treated as part of a philosophy of culture, or is it one for a philosophy of history, a philosophy of art, and the like? But to answer questions of the sort one may have to view the literary genre 'tragedy' as a report on man's place in nature and in society and do so within a broader set of theoretical concepts. But then why is this a 'philosophical' task, if indeed it is? At this point the boundaries between enterprises begin to look fuzzy. There is need therefore to justify the claim that one can treat the results of the art of dramaturgy as disclosures of truth, even more concretely, as expressions of a 'philosophy of life', itself to be defended as carrier of truth. But even this, in turn, would call for explicit argument and evidence, not only as *'praxis'* but also as *'theoria'*.

To be philosophical nowadays is to produce work that abounds in argument, work that employs methods explicating arguments. If a 'philosophy of tragedy' is found lacking in argument, as is the case with much of Nietzsche's writings on the subject, his discussions, no matter how persuasive, can be viewed as either unphilosophical or non-philosophical. But Nietzsche's thesis aside, one must still face the problem of what it is to have a 'philosophy of tragedy', if the theory behind it is to command respect.

When we turn to Plato and Aristotle, with or without their ontological theses, we can still understand their positions as statements on poetry within a political theory. They would start in this case with the didactic force of the literary work and proceed to examine its effect on the common good without necessarily limiting its role to the moral concern. At least this much can be said about these ancient thinkers: they were prepared to relate poetry to the broader context of the political life. In this case, it should be of no surprise that a theory of poetry would be in part subordinate to a social theory. Thus, a theory or 'philosophy' of tragedy, if one prefers the latter term, as part of the broader concept of a philosophy of art, is included in the discourse of political philosophy that calls for the examination of the art of the good life and the evaluations of the institutions that sustain it. But to do so without having a firm grasp of the *natural* forces and conditions that constitute the physical environment within which human beings act, think and create, would be sheer folly, or at best, living in a world of fantasy. To proceed and call this set of natural forces, including the forces that drive the human being, 'tragic' is a peculiar extension of the term covering surprisingly more grounds that the Greeks would be willing to concede.

Be that as it may, Nietzsche raised the issue about the 'tragic' texture of life, and in so doing he, together with his immediate intellectual ancestors, was convinced that he had posed the ultimate 'philosophical' question. What was initially a literary device and a dramaturgical concept became an ontological and axiological term with fundamental claims to disclosing the nature of life and the world. So broadened, the term was no longer restricted to being one for posing issues within the theory of a literary genre, but one that asked for ultimate answers to the most urgent problems in culture and politics as art and creativity. The Greeks excluded the 'tragic' from their philosophies of nature and human nature, but not the moderns, at least not the ones who took science seriously and restricted the quest for truth within the efficacy of its methods. But those who sided with Nietzsche not only found it necessary to disparage science and the reliability of logic; they also took the final step in the direction of reassigning new meanings to old technical terms to convey the radical visions of the will of the modern. They did so with the explicit intent of putting in the place left vacant with the demise of what had become a bloodless *mythos*, without which, as Nietzsche insisted, tragedy was impossible, a different technique for the redramatization of a world in which the disoriented pathos of mankind could be transformed into liveable vision. And while this trend was getting under way, a great number of questions about the recasting of the functions of what tradition had defined as the tasks of philosophy were allowed to idle in the penumbra of rationality. One of the consequences was to throw into disarray the once venerated relationship between *mythos* and *sophia*, and to point that it has become almost impossible for technical 'philosophers' nowadays to attach any significance to Aristotle's dictum in *Metaphysics* A. 2.

982b 17–19: 'Even the lover of *mythos* is in a way a lover of *sophia*, for *mythos* is composed of wonders; therefore since they [the *philosophos* and the *philomythos*] philosophized to escape from ignorance, evidently they were pursuing science in order to know, and not for any utilitarian end'.

Just the same, we are not absolved from the responsibility of recasting the relationship of philosophy and tragedy, with or without a 'philosophy of tragedy'. Whether the splintering of our cultural substance will allow for the proper therapy to heal the wounds of the divorce of science and art, is another question. Nietzsche himself was convinced he had envisioned the only solution.

VI

In *Ecce Homo* Nietzsche wrote:

> I predict a new age of tragedy: the highest art of life-affirmation, tragedy, will be reborn when mankind is conscious, but *without any feeling of suffering* that it has behind it the hardest but most necessary of wars...[15]

What he meant by 'tragedy' was not the perfected form of dramaturgy but the supreme style of life or art of affirming the tragic. The upshot is that Nietzsche took tragedy off the stage and outside the classical theater to make it the art of life. Yet, he was inadvertently repeating a Greek idea, i.e. he was still staying within the boundaries of *techne*. He changed the label and added a modern element: the grim image of the primordial cruelty of life, the absurd character of existence. Here Nietzsche is not Greek, if he ever was. He is a disaffected Christian, one who could not trust the art of politics to secure the collective happiness of the citizens. His model for the tragic art of life, ironically enough, had already been worked out by the Church Fathers in the apologetic period, when the relevance of the Greek culture to the Christian world-view had to be decided.

Nietzsche worked in the shadow of the Augustinian tradition. And like the Eastern Fathers, Basil and the two Gregories, he assigned a limited place to the Greek mind in the new order to make it function as part of the wave of the future. And like

Augustine, he recast the signification of the tragic beyond anything the Greek word intimated. He turned it into the essential element in the soteriological drama of the universe. The Greek conception was pushed aside to make room for the emerging life of eternal creativity, the modern substitute for eternal salvation.

For Augustine and all the Church Fathers there can be but one tragedy: divine liturgy and the symbolic enactment of salvation. Like his spiritual ancestors, Nietzsche's first act of revaluation concluded another confrontation with Greek thought and art; the rest was a matter of salvaging what was worthy of assimilation. And like the churchmen, he modelled creativity after the radiating primordial divinity with its promise of rebirth. He discovers the real humanity in a vision of unending reforms, a revelation of the higher attainment in a series of rebirths. The key to his philosophy of reforms is the vision of the tragic, resurrected from the death to which the shallowness of Greek morality had condemned it.

As I stated earlier in this paper, Nietzsche took the tragic off the stage. But he did more than that. He took it out of the perimeter of the political life. The move would have been enough to leave Aristotle speechless; and he would have been equally shocked to learn about the new tragic emotions. Nothing makes the contrast sharper than the difference in their views on the nature of tragic pleasure. Again, Nietzsche missed what Aristotle said in the *Politics*. Where Aristotle saw pleasure coming at the conclusion of a dramatic play, Nietzsche read 'catharsis' or vehement discharge of dangerous emotions. Where Aristotle assigned to tragic pleasure a place in the education of the citizens, Nietzsche tied it to the transvaluation of values, to the triumph of becoming over being.

For Aristotle, the political man, the statesman, is not a tragic artist, nor is life itself tragic. The 'tragic sense' of life is a modern, indeed a neo-Christian invention, with Nietzsche being its chief prophet and preacher. What it conveys is a style of life, a sense of urgency for commitment to creativity, one that rests its case in the power to transcend all lies, including those of one's own making. Even the boldest of the Greeks, Heraclitus, not to mention Protagoras, could have ever gone that far. Probably Nietzsche never quite realized how high was the wall he had erected between his vision of life and that of the classical Greeks. It all started with the determination to reveal to himself and to others the will to life, something the theologians had known for at least two thousand years and had insisted on reserving exclusively for the will of God.

Nietzsche reached out to claim it. And ever since his declaration the world has not been the same. Creativity has become not God's act but man's obsession.

Notes

1. I wish to express my gratitude to the Academy of Athens, Greece, for inviting me to present an early version of this essay in May 1987. Initially, it was given as the Theodore Tracy Lecture at the Department of Classics, University of Illinois, Chicago, and later presented at the invitation of the Departments of Philosophy of Union College and the University of New Mexico. Portions of this essay appeared in my 'Mythos, Katharsis and the Paradox of Tragedy', *Proceedings of the Boston Area Colloquium in Ancient Philosophy*, edited by John Cleary. University Presses of America, vol. I, 1986, pp. 299–330, and are reproduced here with kind permission of the editor.
2. Henri Weil's 1847 thesis on the medical catharsis anticipated Jacob Bernays's 1857 view that catharsis stands for the purgation of emotions. As Bywater and others have shown, the interpretation had its antecedents in the Renaissance. Gilles Deleuze remarks on Nietzsche's way of reading Aristotle as follows: 'As early as *The Birth of Tragedy* Nietzsche attacks the Aristotelian conception of tragedy-catharsis. He points out the two possible interpretations of *catharsis*: moral sublimation and medical purging (BT 22). But whichever way it is interpreted, catharsis sees the tragic as the exercise of depressive passions and reactive "feelings" '. *Nietzsche and Philosophy*, p. 200, n. 12. For an extensive discussion and critical review of the chief interpretations of catharsis other than Nietzsche's, see E. P. Papanoutsos, 1953 and 1964.
3. R. McKeon 1936, (repr. 1952, reference to this edition): 'Literary Criticism and the Concept of Imitation in Antiquity',: in *Critics and Criticism*, ed. R. C. Crane (Chicago, 1952), p. 165.
4. Georgopoulos 1980, 207. Despite its merits, the rebuttal stops short of completely absolving Aristotle from the charge that tragedy is viewed from the perspective of 'moral character'. The problem I see in Georgopoulos' article is that his insight recognizes, but still does not encompass *in toto*, the political nature of man. The argument does not exhibit in detail the grounds for the continuity between *ethos* and *polis*. He admits that the political function 'underlies the entire analysis of the *Poetics* ...for catharsis is at the center of Aristotle's discussion, and however we interpret it, its significance will ultimately turn out to be a moral one, i.e. political, and so, of course the significance of tragedy itself will be moral...in its ability to enhance the moral and rational character of the members of the polis' (207–8). The allusion to the political, however, is not without

a certain vagueness, for it permits shifting the emphasis to moral character rather than to what the *Politics* declares to be the dominant value in community life: the common good of all normal forms of government. I think it is misleading to introduce terms that tend to suggest a separation of the aesthetic from the political or to say that the political is included in the 'moral'. Aristotle's contextual analyses do not support conclusions open to the objections many moderns have raised when they claim that his views on tragedy imply a moral reductionism or a separation of the aesthetic from the political, or even a special though defensible balance between the aesthetic and the moral. My point is that the *ousia* of tragedy and that of man are ultimately the same for Aristotle. Admittedly, Nietzsche and Georgopoulos do not mean the same thing by the term 'moral'; For Nietzsche, Aristotle is a 'moralist', a meaning that would be unacceptable and rightly so, to Georgopoulos.

5. For a recent and informative discussion on the problems surrounding the manuscript tradition and the interpretive issues of this work, see B. Magnus 1986.

6. In Section 5, 'What I owe to the Ancients', *The Portable Nietzsche*, pp. 562–3.

7. The passage occurs in Section 3 of the preface he had prepared for a new edition of the *Birth of Tragedy*, titled 'The Birth of Tragedy': 'In *The Twilight of the Idols* (Aph. 5 part 10) I finally discussed how far these doctrines enabled me to discover the idea of "tragedy", the conclusive recognition of the psychology of tragedy...This is what I called Dionysian, this is what I meant as the bridge to the psychology of the tragic poet. "Not to relieve one's self of terror and pity, not to purge one's self of dangerous emotion by a vehement discharge (this was Aristotle's misunderstanding of it) but rather, far beyond pity and terror, to be the eternal joy of Becoming itself – that joy which also involves the joy of destruction." ...In this sense I have the right to regard myself as the first *tragic philosopher*, that is to say, the extreme antithesis and antipodes of a pessimistic philosopher. Before me there was no translation of the Dionysian phenomenon into philosophic pathos: tragic wisdom was lacking; I have sought vainly for signs of it even among the great Greek philosophers – those belonging to the two centuries before Socrates. I still retained a doubt about Heraclitus, in whose presence, in general, I felt warmer and more at ease than anywhere else'. In the Modern Library edition, tr. Clifton P. Fadiman, p. 868.

8. *The Portable Nietzsche*, p. 574.

9. *Poetics* 6. 1449b 24–31; G. Else's translation with minor changes.

10. For instance in *Poetics* 11, 1452b 8: *pathos d' esti praxis phthartike e odynera*. Here pathos means suffering. The reverse, whereby the word *'pathos'* is also used to cover particular *pathemata*, may also be the case. Frequently *pathemata*, the plural form of *pathema*, is used to refer to incidents, rather than emotions.

11. References to the bibliography on the literature about the controversy in G. Else 1967, 225 n14.

12. I have discussed aspects of these benefits in my older paper, 'Tragic Vision and Philosophic Theoria', in *Philosophy and the Civilizing Arts: Essays Presented to Herbert Schneider on His Eightieth Birthday*. Edited and with Introduction by C. Walton and John P. Anton. Ohio University Press, 1975, pp. 1–23.
13. *The Portable Nietzsche*, p. 484.
14. *The Birth of Tragedy*, section 27.
15. Modern Library, p. 869.

Bibliography

Anton, John P. 1985. 'Mythos, Katharsis and the Paradox of Tragedy', in *Proceedings of the Boston Area Colloquium in Ancient Philosophy*, vol. I, John J. Cleary, ed. (University Press of America), pp. 299–325.

Anton, John P. 1973. 'Tragic Vision and Philosophic Theoria', *Diotima*, I, 11–31; 1975 reprinted with revisions in *Philosophy and the Civilizing Arts: Essays Presented to Herbert Schneider on His Eightieth Birthday*. Edited and with Introduction by C. Walton and John P. Anton. (Ohio University Press), pp. 1–23.

Arnott, W. Geoffrey. 1984. 'Nietzsche's View of Greek Tragedy', Arethusa 17/2, 135–49.

Arrowsmith, William. 1963. 'Nietzsche on Classics and Classicists', Arion, 2/1, 5–18, and 2/2, 5–27.

Benn, A. W. 1914. 'Aristotle's Theory of Tragic Emotions', Mind 23, 84–90.

Bernays, Jacob. 1857. *Grundzuge der verlorenen Abhandlung des Aristoteles über Wirkung der Tragödie*. (Breslau).

Delauze, Gilles. 1983. *Nietzsche and Philosophy*. Tr. Hugh Tomlinson from the 1962 edition, Presses Universitaires de France. (New York).

Else, Gerald. 1967. *Aristotle's Poetics: The Argument*. (Cambridge, Mass.: Harvard University Press).

Georgopoulos, N. 1980. 'Plato and Aristotle: Mimesis, Tragedy and Art', in *Essays in Honor of E. P. Papanoutsos*. (Athens, Greece), pp. 199–212.

Magnus, Bernd 1986. 'Nietzsche's Philosophy in 1888: *The Will to Power* and the *Übermensch*', *Journal of the History of Philosophy*, XXIV/1, 79–98.

McKeon, Richard. 1952. 'Literary Criticism and the Concept of Imitation in Antiquity', in *Critics and Criticism*. R. C. Crane, ed., (Chicago), pp. 147–75; reprinted from *Modern Philology*, XXIV (1963), 1–35.

Nietzsche, F. 1967. *The Birth of Tragedy and The Case of Wagner*. Translated with Commentary by Walter Kaufmann. (New York: Random House, Vintage Books).

Nietzsche, F. 1968. *The Will to Power*. Translated by Walter Kaufmann and R. J. Hollingdale, edited, with commentary by W. Kaufmann. (New York: Random House, Vintage Books).

Nietzsche, F. 1968. *The Portable Nietzsche*. Selected and translated, with an introduction, prefaces, and notes by Walter Kaufmann. (New York: Viking Press).

Nietzsche, F. [n.d]. *The Philosophy of Nietzsche*. Introduction by W. H. Wright. (New York: Random House, The Modern Library. [Note. The

abbreviation ML follows references to pages in Nietzsche's works
included in this edition].

Papanoutsos, E. P. 1948. 'La catharsis aristotelicienne', *Eranos* 34, 77–93.

Papanoutsos, E. P. 1955. *La catharsis des passion d' après Aristote*, Collection
de l'Institut Français d'Athènes. (Athens).

Papanoutsos, E. P. 1964. *Philosophika Problemata*. (Athens, Greece). Part IV,
'*Pathematon Katharsis*', pp. 219–98.

Weil, H. 1847. 'Über die Wirkung der Tragödie nach Aristoteles',
Verhandlugen der 10. *Uversammlung deutcher Philologen und Schulmanner
in Basel 1847*. (Basel), pp. 131–40.

Whitman, James. 1986. 'Nietzsche in the Magisterial Tradition of German
Classical Philology', *Journal of the History of Ideas*, XLVII/3, 453–68.

2

The Disjunction of the Tragic: Hegel and Nietzsche

ROLAND GALLE

Philosophic speculation on tragedy and the tragic did not develop until the period of German idealism, thus at a time in which tragedy itself had gotten into a far-reaching structural crisis. This crisis has served many critics as an indicator of the frequently diagnosed 'Death of Tragedy' in modern times. Thus we have to proceed from the remarkable phenomenon that large scale philosophic speculation on the tragic begins at a time in which the secular tradition of tragedy itself seems to have reached its end. Hegel's figure of speech of Minerva's owl, which doesn't begin its flight until nightfall, has been cited to comment on this striking relationship between the crisis of poetic practice and the onset of philosophic speculation relating to this practice. Hegel's image implies that a figure of life, of reality, in our case tragedy, has gotten old, has passed its peak and that in a countermove the idea of this figure now preserved in philosophic thought is, so to speak, saved.

With respect to the appropriation of the tragic, a continuity is postulated between those periods which have produced tragedies and have been able to give them a place in life, and those periods which philosophized about tragedy. French classicism was the last to do the former, and German idealism was the first to do the latter. Thus it would seem that what has changed between the seventeenth and nineteenth centuries is only the way in which the tragic is presented while its idea, even in its most varied forms, has remained the same.

In opposition to this, we will develop the thesis that the Enlightenment marks a turning point in the history of the tragic. This turning point is such that, in the wake of the Enlightenment, not only is the basis of the production of tragedies and their anchor in public life increasingly weakened, but also the philosophic appropriation of the tragic is disjoined. This disjunction is to be understood as the reason that from the early nineteenth century on, a dispute with the Enlightenment is immanent for the philosophic appropriation of the tragic. This appropriation has been decisively formed and made one-sided by the nature of this dispute. That this disjuncture eventually leads to an antinomy of aspects of the tragic, can be demonstrated by the paradigmatic positions of Hegel and Nietzsche. Hegel's outline of the tragic can be read as an attempt to reconcile tragedy with the Enlightenment. Nietzsche's theory can be interpreted as an extreme attempt to bypass the consequences of the Enlightenment by granting tragedy the status of a first-rate counter-Enlightenment cultural phenomenon. No doubt it would be hermeneutically profitable to interpret pre-Enlightenment tragedy itself as the point of interference of the aspects of the tragic revealed by Hegel and Nietzsche. However, we can not do this here.[1]

Here we shall first show how the influence of the Enlightenment has brought about a structural change in the form and *telos* of tragedy. Voltaire, as perhaps no other dramatist, is best suited for this purpose. Against the background of the crisis of tragedy as represented by Voltaire's theater, Hegel's theory is to be read as a response to this crisis, as an attempt to secure an original dimension of the tragic under the constraints of the Enlightenment. To what extent this attempt to save the tragic is itself shaped by the Enlightenment and thereby made one-sided, is clearly demonstrated by Nietzsche in his equation of the tragic with a prehistoric original condition. However, even Nietzsche's extreme reaction continues to be subject to the force of the Enlightenment, evidencing the impossibility of avoiding the fact that after the Enlightenment the view of the tragic is disjointed: the disjunction of the tragic.

I

According to both his own understanding and that of his contemporaries, Voltaire brought classic tragedy to its culmination. Today, however, we see how the inclusion of Enlightenment elements runs counter to his tragic designs, and that it has neutralized them aesthetically and made them historically ineffective.

Voltaire's first play *Œdipe* retains the dilemma, which

inescapably results from the confrontation of preserved tragic *mythos* and the demands of the Enlightenment. The strength of the play and its interest for us lie in bringing to light the impossibility of uniting the irreconcilable strengths of the Enlightenment on the one hand with those of tragedy on the other. In the forward to his second drama *Mariamne*, Voltaire already chooses a way out of the dilemma which amounts to an adaptation of the tragic schema to the rational demands and intuitive requirements of a changed public. This is summed up in the demand: 'il faut adoucir les caractères désagréables'.[2] Herewith Voltaire gives a first cue for the progressive recasting of the traditional constellation of tragedy under the influence of the Enlightenment. Not only the delineation of the characters is affected: in similar fashion the Enlightenment works on the linking points of the tragic development – on *hamartia*, *anagnorisis* and *peripatia* – above all it brings about a completely new way of ending the tragedy.

Enlightenment anthropology has a tendency to weaken or morally denounce character traits which demand an inexorable and destructive confrontation. As a result Voltaire's theater is characterized by the fact that the inflexibility and artistic isolation which function as the distinctive marks of the tragic hero from Sophocles' Oedipus through Shakespeare's and Racine's heroes up to Anouilh's Antigone, have either been reduced or remodeled or, insofar as they have been kept, have been morally stigmatized. Only priests and other fanatics still possess this inflexibility, thus excluding themselves from the circle of those worthy of iden-tification as heroes. Heroes suitable to the taste of the Enlightenment are characterized by so much self-relativization that the mechanism of a tragic outcome is thereby negated and made tendentious and as such avoidable. In *Alzire* there is a striking example of this when Guzman, who is introduced as an unscrupulous and cruel power-politician, finally pardons his chief opponent at the request of his father and in the following words: 'A father's will must be obeyed; / I will suspend my wrath, but urge me, sir, / No further'.[3] The completely new function which close familial ties attain in Voltaire's tragedy ought to be pointed out here merely as an aside. If the family in Racine's works – in accordance with a famous directive of Aristotle's – still has the task of sharpening the tragic constellation, in Voltaire a counterweight to the tragic threat is developed. In the cited passage the intimate father–son relations are activated in order to avoid the threatening catastrophic ending. Just as this change of the function of the family, which is in accord with the Enlightenment, weakens and relativizes the possible tragic, so the suspension of emotion ('suspendre ma colère') voiced in the following verse evidences the possibility of destroying the inevitability of the tragic. Guzman is granted a scope of action which estranges him from the main purpose of his own character, unconditional securing of power, and basically opens up alternative forms of conduct for him. The traditional model of tragedy knows only apparent alternatives to a tragic ending. Under the influence of the Enlightenment in Voltaire's theater the self-relativization of the main character is such that a tragic finale, wherever it may occur, can scarcely be based on the characters.

Besides the conception and disposition of the characters, the hamartia, the start of the tragic course, is also adapted to the requirements of the Enlightenment and neutralized in its effect. The discrepancy between the hamartia and the tragic consequences originally had the purpose of revealing the frailty of the socially normal world and of illuminating the overwhelming power of the subsequent tragic events that follow. On the other hand, the 'flaw' in Voltaire's tragedies testifies to the possible endangering of a world which is capable of moral order in the sense of the Enlightenment. The basic possibility of avoiding catastrophe is inherent in the quasi-tragic situation of the Voltairean theater. Thus Voltaire provides a keyword for his theater when he has a protagonist in *Les Guebres* cite hamartia as a 'detestable error'.[4] In *Zaire* Orosman kills the heroine because of jealousy, which the situation makes understandable but which is not justified and can finally be seen as an error and repudiated. This does not happen, as in *Othello* or *Phèdre*, due to the excess of an uncontrollable passion but due to an error which in the final analysis leaves the ordered world of the Enlightenment untouched.

Another especially significant example for the adaptation of the hamartia to the requirements of the Enlightenment is to be seen in the recasting of myth, as Voltaire does in *Oreste*. He expands his sources by a divine command to Orestes not to reveal his identity until his revenge is complete. Breaking this command can be seen as a fault; this fault is obviously needed to enable the tragic course of events foreseen in the myth to be made tolerable. At the same time its culmination, the matricide, is neutralized, in that Orestes kills Clytemnestra only unintentionally and inadvertently; the real target of his revenge is Aegisthus. This moralizing of the hamartia cushions the shock, which the Enlightenment world demands of every tragic revelation. While the Enlightenment aims at securing or attaining rationally provable positions of order, the traditional tragic end always implies the collapse of order, however established. Against this background, Voltaire's attempted moralizing of the hamartia and weakening of the tragic result shows the attempt to fit a tragic event into a concept of the world which conforms to the Enlightenment. The extent to which the prevalence of basic concepts of the Enlightenment neutralizes tragedy is seen in the finale of Voltaire's plays, in the transformation he wrought in the traditional tragic end. It is certain thât traditional tragedy closed with the prospect of a continuation of the community in which the tragedy occurred; the effect of the catastrophe was paramount and necessary for the catharsis. The concurrent destruction was frequently designed to show the order which was restored in a somewhat ironic light. However, the constellation at the end of Voltaire's tragedies is completely different. Reconciliation and compromise are so dominant that the catastrophe appears quite accidental. In the previously cited play *Alzire* there is a surprising final turn; Guzman, fatally wounded by Zamor, pardons his opponent, even gives his rival his wife and advises his father to adopt him as a son in his place:

> thou shalt admire and love me:
> Guzman too long hath made Alzire wretched,
> I'll make her happy; with my dying hand
> I give her to thee, live and hate me not,
> Restore your country's ruined walls, and bless
> My memory
> > (to Alvarez)
> > Alvarez, be once more
> A father to them, let the light of heaven
> Shine forth upon them; Zamor is thy son,
> Let him repair my loss.[5]

In view of this end it seems appropriate to speak of a quickly concluded reconciliation which demonstrates in an effective way the neutralization of the tragic. Guzman's possible reversal and the resulting interchangeability of the quasi-tragic rivals makes clear the previously mentioned self-relativization of the characters and the structure of errors of what has occurred as a presumably tragic misfortune. The end of the play retracts the staged conflict and discloses it as avoidable from the perspective of the rivals and even more from that of the audience. The outcome of tragedy in Voltaire's plays becomes increasingly a demonstration of such avoidability and appeal for the abolition of the tragic constellation. This conception of the tragic is carried to a logical conclusion in the considerably later play *L'Orphelin de la Chine*. Just as Guzman in *Alzire*, so now Genghis Khan, who has been introduced as a cruel conqueror, finally renounces all his original goals and brings about a conciliatory ending that signifies the triumph of virtue. At the beginning of the play, the virtuous Zamti, Genghis Khan's opponent, voices the strongest tragic situation conceivable for the Enlightenment when he says: 'A prey to robbers: what hath it availed us / That we have trod in the fair paths of virtue?'[6] The play becomes a harmonizing answer to this problem. For a long time it looks as though the opponents of Genghis Khan will not be able to attain their goal of saving the youngest heir to the throne of the vanquished and otherwise already murdered ruling family, and thus they are resigned to committing suicide. At the very moment, however, when a collapse of hope called for by the Enlightenment seems inevitable and when a tragic end seems unavoidable, Zamti and his wife Idame are reprieved from death by Genghis Khan himself and proclaimed the true victors:

> I admire you both,
> You have subdued me, and I blush to sit
> On Cathay's throne, whilst there are souls like yours
> So much above me; vainly have I tried
> By glorious deeds to build myself a name
> Among the nations; you have humbled me
> And I would equal you.[7]

This reconciliation is rounded out in an image of the family. If Genghis Khan originally intended to kill the heir to the throne to secure his own power, now we hear: 'Behold this child, happy in its misery, / Hereafter I will be a father to him'.[8] To Idame's and Zamti's amazed query '... what could inspire / This great design, and work this change?' the answer which so clearly and satisfactorily solves the original dilemma and at the same time concludes the play programmatically: 'Thy virtues!'[9] With this the tragic clearly appears what it mainly is in Voltaire's works: a threat which can be overcome under the banner of the Enlightenment.

II

How much Hegel's Theory of the Tragic is under the influence of the Enlightenment is shown in rudimentary fashion by the *Wallenstein* review of 1800, one of his earliest comments on our topic:

> The immediate reaction to a reading of Wallenstein is to be sadly dumbstruck by the fall of a powerful man under a silent, deaf, dead fate. When the play ends, everything is over – the realm of naught, of death has won the victory; it does not end as a theodicy, ... only death opposes life, and incredibly! revoltingly! death conquers life! That is not tragic, but shocking! This is heart-rending, one can't rise up from this with a lightened breast.[10]

By criticizing blind fate and by pleading for a theodicy, even in this early passage, Hegel draws the outline which became obligatory for his later theory of history and tragedy: the dialectically conceived self-realization of the absolute spirit as executor of a universal process both progresses and is intelligible. In Hegel's resistance to blind fate and his pleading for a theodicy, we see clearly the effective power of the Enlightenment. Theodicy, as Hegel uses the term, means not the justification of God but of history. In his *History of Philosophy* we read: 'Theodicy' is to be understood as a 'demonstration that, as I have just said, things have happened rationally in the world'.[11] Given the influence of the central ideas of the Enlightenment on his theory of tragedy, how can Hegel integrate the tragic into an Enlightenment view of the world without having to abandon the traditional dimension of the tragic with its emphasis on the destruction of order and meaning? We can put the question differently: given the conditions of the Enlightenment, how can a theory of the tragic be developed having as its models not Voltaire but rather Sophocles and Racine? The theory of tragedy, formulated in the *Lectures on Aesthetics*, can be seen as a possible answer. The most interesting aspect, to be sure, is that the influence of the Enlightenment in the final analysis keeps the upper hand over all attempts to integrate the tragic and thus paves the way for the disjunction of the tragic. The following passage shows this paradigmatically:

> However justified the tragic character and his aim, however necessary the tragic collision, the third thing required is the tragic resolution of this conflict. By this means eternal justice is exercised on individuals and their aims in the sense that it restores the substance and unity of ethical life with the downfall of the individual who has disturbed its peace. For although the characters have a purpose which is valid in itself, they can carry it out in tragedy only by pursuing it one-sidedly and so contradicting and infringing someone else's purpose. The truly substantial thing which has to be actualized, however, is not the battle between particular aims or characters, although this too has its essential ground in the nature of the real world and human action, but the reconciliation in which the specific individuals and their aims work together harmoniously without opposition and without infringing on one another.[12]

The significance of this passage is that it makes clear the twofold accomplishment of the Hegelian theory of tragedy. First, the presentation and an examination of conflict and destruction and thereby the regaining of the tragic dimensions of antiquity and the French classics, which had been lost in the Enlightenment. Second, however, the relativization of this destruction toward a reconciliation congruent to the goals of the Enlightenment. The triad of pathos, conflict and reconciliation, which constitutes for Hegel the basis for developing the tragic, illustrates beautifully the interference of these two levels. The sequence of presentation: a self-isolating individuality, the realization of such isolation in a conflict, and the mutual destruction resulting from it is overlaid by a level of meaning which is to make the tragic event clear as a model case of universal progress. In the resolution the different weighting of both elements is preserved; a tragic event in the sense of mutual destruction is a necessary prerequisite for the inherent final purpose, the removal of tragic inner strife in the 'vision of an affirmative reconciliation'.[13] If this affirmative reconciliation represents for tragedy a juncture in which the heritage of the Enlightenment is preserved then the traditional forms of realization of the tragic are preserved and asserted in the dialectically presented stages of isolation and destruction, which are a prerequisite for the goal of reconciliation.

Thus Hegel's achievement consists of assuring a realization of the tragic which threatened to be lost in the face of the trivializing intentions of the Enlightenment. At the same time he could not deny the Enlightenment its due. This becomes obvious when the various stages of his position – pathos, conflict, and reconciliation – are delineated.

Pathos is both subject and champion of the tragic process. Hegel introduces this concept of pathos in sharp differentiation to passion. Passion always signifies for him the low and insignificant, the specific, while by pathos he means 'the universal powers which ... move the human heart in its inmost being'.[14] Pathos is defined as 'essential content of rationality'; it represents 'what is essentially moral, the gods of our actual life, in short what is divine and true'.[15] By binding the tragic agent to pathos, Hegel proposes a far-reaching content limitation: the only subject for tragedy can be that which possesses the individuated form of the divine and the rational, or to put it differently, that which has a valuable place in the course of universal history. The idealistic bias on which this determination of theme is based connects in a predetermined way the binding of the tragic process to the teleologic order, which in the final analysis carries tragedy as a whole.

Conflict too is bound to such an arrangement. In Hegel's plan it retains at the same time the seriousness, the inevitability and the destructive intensity of the tragic, and to this extent restores the dimension of traditional tragedy, lost in the course of the Enlightenment. The conflict is based on the fact that pathos, as the universal and divine, necessarily splits in its historical form of realization. Hegel uses Socrates as an example of such a dialectical process of the division of the universal, which will eventually be the subject of tragedy. For Hegel Socrates' fate is at the same time 'the tragedy of Athens, the tragedy of Greece'.[16] It results from the conflict of two principles, both highly significant. The state-forming principle of the Athenians which was in effect until Socrates, is designated by Hegel as 'untrained morality'.[17] This principle of untrained morality together with Socrates' moral demand produces its own denial and thus becomes divided. Socrates postulates, in opposition to untrained morality, the determination of the good as a universal gained by subjective thinking: 'man as thinking is the measure of all things'.[18] To be sure, Socrates is 'still the hero who possessed for himself the absolute right of mind, certain of itself';[19] at the same time 'his accusation was just',[20] since he is undermining the existing laws and thus the foundation of the Athenian people. The inner necessity which belongs to the conflict between Socrates and the Athenians – as is the case between Antigone and Creon – gives the conflict a special dignity and removes the tragic end from the sphere of arbitrariness and blindness. Finally, such a conflict opens the view to the ever crucial end of tragedy: the 'vision of an affirmative reconciliation'.[21]

After the necessary conflict, the divine and the universal, which had been split in the pathos, return to their unity in the final reconciliation. Hegel regards tragedy as concluded only when this unity has been regained; thus the reconciliation becomes a component of the tragedy itself and is not – as in the Aristotelian tradition – surrendered to the effect of tragedy, the catharsis. As universal history ends in the return of the absolute spirit to itself, so tragedy must contain reconciliation as its finale or at least leave it open, in the form of a prospect. Ruin and destruction are accordingly only way-stations on the path of the absolute spirit to itself. Tragedy should so present the 'authority of a higher world-governor'[22] which manifests itself in such fashion that 'misfortune and suffering' of the individual hero on the one hand and the 'absolute rationality' on the other hand, appear together, resulting in the viewer's leaving the theater 'shattered by the fate of the heroes, but fundamentally reconciled'.[23]

In the context of our thesis it becomes clear how much Hegel disjoins the dimension of the tragic, despite his emphasis on conflict and ruin. He and his theory of tragedy are guided by the basic idea of historical progress, within which the tragic has its limited, albeit necessary, value. There is need for a tragically developing conflict between individuals so that the universally relevant progress can be completed. In the notorious formulation of the 'cunning of reason' Hegel has generally preserved the differentiation between the progress of the idea and the sacrifice of individuals.[24] We can conclude that on this basis a theory of tragedy could be developed which preserves the tie to the historical optimism of the Enlightenment. Voltaire was determined to bring in the same Enlightenment-generated idea of *'perfectibilité'* for the characters of his tragedy. As a result he paralyzed the dimension of the tragic. Hegel's dialectic statement can be read as an attempt on the one hand to regain this lost dimension by giving the protagonists a tragic field of action in the form of conflict. On the other hand it can be seen as an attempt to secure the *'perfectibilité'* on the superimposed level of the progress of the idea to itself. The priority of this latter aim is unquestionable. Thus the salvation of the tragic, as Hegel accomplishes it, always includes its relativization.

III

In many respects Nietzsche's philosophy can be understood as a negative answer to Hegel, as an attempt to lay bare and destroy the historical optimism and the dialectical thinking of progress of his predecessor in his own struggle against Metaphysics and Teleology. The outline of tragedy forms a sort of focal point of the way each viewed the universe. At the same time it reflects the opposing directions that their thinking took. While in Hegel's theory of tragedy a prospective design of a universal process is described, Nietzsche bases his affirmation of tragedy and of a tragic age modeled on tragedy, on the hope that his 'attempt to assassinate two millenia of anti-nature and desecration of man were to succeed'.[25] Thus tragedy is seen by the one as the crystallization point of cultural development, and by the other as its negation.

Nietzsche's early work 'Die Geburt der Tragodie oder Griechentum und Pessimismus' implies the negation of historical progress as the basis of tragedy. This negation was later made explicit. The tragic conflict is not seen, as in Hegel's case, in the opposition of two historically appearing, substantial powers but in the struggle between the Dionysian and Apollonian. By this is meant, that the 'Ur-Eine', a primordial principle, which existed before all historical reality, is in conflict with the forms of appearance developed from it, and is struggling for their dissolution. Accordingly Nietzsche formulates the 'Mystery doctrine of tragedy' in this early work in the following stages: 'The fundamental knowledge of the oneness of everything existent, the conception of individuation as the primal cause of evil, and of art as the joyous hope that the spell of individuation may be broken, in augury of a restored oneness'.[26] As is the case with Hegel the basic concept of tragic conflict is based on the individuation of the divine, and thus on disunion and the conflict resulting therefrom. While Hegel derives a history-making goal from this conflict, for Nietzsche, even in this early work, the fascination of the tragic conflict lies in the reconversion of the individuation to nature, to the original state, to a regressive result.

This beginning, which in the '*The Birth of Tragedy*', according to Nietzsche's later pronouncement, is still completely bound up in metaphysical speculations,[27] finds anthropological foundation and extension in the main philosophical works. The basis is the substitution of an atomistic concept of the will for Hegel's historical teleology. This is set forth particularly clearly in the famous aphorism concerning the 'will to power':

> Do you want a name for this world? A solution for all its puzzles? A *Light* too for you, you most hidden, strongest, most fearless, most benighted ones? – *This world is the will to power – and nothing else!* And you yourselves are this will to power – and nothing else![28]

Nietzsche's final solution to the puzzle, in spite of the added emphasis of the repeated negative phrase 'and nothing else', proves to be the result of reduction and a philosophical minimal position. If Nietzsche intended to reverse the metaphysical doubling of the world, he now discharges this intention by granting value only to the isolated, relationless and intentionless will for itself. The opposition between a historical philosophic concept of the world on the one hand and a vital concept of the world on the other, as it now shapes up as a contrast between Hegel and Nietzsche, finds its counterpart in the vastly different evaluation of Socrates and morality. As we have seen, Socrates is for Hegel the founder of morality 'for a mental turning-point exhibited itself in him in the form of philosophic thought'.[29] For Nietzsche too he is the founder of morality, but in being so he is the symptom of downright decadence, an example of the turning away from an unbroken ethic, symptom for an 'idiosyncracy of degenerates'[30] which is governed by 'instincts of *ressentiment*'.[31]

In Nietzsche's late writings tragedy is conceived as the counterdesign to the European development of culture. It is the sole cultural-historical reality which is able to creep in beneath the veneer of intellect and morality with which all human questions and relationships are overlaid. Tragedy is able to restore the basic text of *homo natura*[32] and, in a festival of cruelty, to assume a hypostatization of reality, which according to Nietzsche coincides with the primal condition of human beings.

It is clear that Hegel's theory of tragedy has an affinity with the

Enlightenment and takes up and extends its main concern, the *'perfectibilité'* of man and history under the banner of reason. It is equally clear that Nietzsche's attempt is directed toward voiding the values the Enlightenment imposed on tragedy, and directed toward gaining a view of tragedy which allows it to be a negation of the Enlightenment. This can be seen above all from the emphasis with which cruelty is stressed as the basis of human nature and the center of tragedy:

> We should reconsider cruelty and open our eyes. We should at long last learn impatience lest such immodest fat errors keep on strutting about virtuously and saucily, as have been fostered about tragedy, for example, by philosophers both ancient and modern. Almost everything we call 'higher culture' is based on the spiritualization of *cruelty*, on its becoming more profound; this is my proposition. That 'savage animal' has not really been 'mortified'; it lives and flourishes, it has merely become – divine.[33]

The fixation of anthropology on the one basic instinct – cruelty – illuminates in a startling way the special role, among all the cultural-historical forms, which Nietzsche gives to tragedy. A broad cultural-historical panorama – extending from the Roman gladiatorial combats and the Christian veneration of the cross through the revolutionary and the Wagnerian enthusiasm of his own time up to religious examination of conscience and the absoluteness of scientific thirst for knowledge – is also explained as a reflex of cruelty, although to be sure a reflex of secondary or tertiary degree. Tragedy is cut off from these cultural forms. In tragedy cruelty appears as the primary reflex. It stands for the time when 'mankind was not yet ashamed of its cruelty',[34] when 'the gods were conceived of as the friends of *cruel* spectacles'[35] and 'tragic terrors ... were intended as *festival plays* for the gods'.[36] According to Nietzsche tragedy realizes in aesthetic form that anthropological basis by which the human being acknowledges the bestial and does not turn it against himself for instance in the form of guilt feelings. Thus cruelty becomes the central theme in Nietzsche's theory of tragedy. The tragic hero is not – as is implied in Hegel's concept of pathos – conceived of as a historically conditioned and historically formative being but as a Hypostatization of the human primal condition. This concept of tragedy which is contrary to history finds its concrete realization in two essential characteristics: in the express denial of the guilt

question, which is traditionally important for the explanation of
tragedy and in a shocking new definition of the potential effect
which is assigned to tragedy.

That the tragic hero is active is a condition which is reflected in
the theoretical analysis of tragedy on the concept of guilt from
Aristotle to Hegel. The hero is the one who revises social and historical reality; he is the one who also brings about opposition and da-
mage. In the concept of guilt the moral-historical dignity of tragic
dispute is simultaneously perceived. The fact that Nietzsche removes tragedy from the historical process and restricts it to an ata-
vistic human province which is reduced to passions and drives
clearly renders the tradition-bound question of guilt obsolete for
him. From his vitalistic position Nietzsche defines guilt as an adul-
terating reaction to life just as he regards morality in general. Suffering is part of the inescapable reality of life. Guilt, however, by
which Nietzsche always means the feeling of guilt, is nothing more
than an excessive sensory reaction which distorts reality; it is 'not a
fact, but merely the interpretation of a fact'.[37] An interpretation
moreover that for Nietzsche is the significant sign of an ebbing life
which no longer possesses the strength for the conquest and acceptance of suffering. Because of this weakness it puts all suffering
under the perspective of guilt and is characterized everywhere by
'the *will* to misunderstand suffering as the content of life; the
reinterpretation of suffering as feelings of guilt, fear and punishment'.[38] To this vehement denunciation of guilt experience corre-
sponds on the other hand the sovereign assertion of innocence,
especially in view of the most serious crimes presented as proof of
undisguised assurance of reality. A special sign of this assurance of
reality for him is the slogan of the Assassins 'Nothing is true,
everything is permitted'[39] which he understands as the negation of
a metaphysical and moral interpretation of the world and thus hails
it as being the *'freedom* of spirit'.[40] This reality, freed of guilt and
fear, takes form in tragedy so that the tragic writer can become the
demiurge of this new world.

> Courage and freedom of feeling before a powerful enemy,
> before a sublime calamity, before a problem that arouses dread –
> this triumphant state is what the tragic artist chooses, what he
> glorifies. Before tragedy, what is warlike in our soul celebrates
> its Saturnalia, whoever is used to suffering, whoever seeks out
> suffering, the heroic man praises his own being through tragedy

– to him alone the tragedian presents this drink of sweetest cruelty.[41]

The victorious situation which is designated as the core of tragedy does not signify a cultural-historical vanquishing of pain and dread but an affirmation of this aspect of existence which constitutes human reality. By the negation of the experience of fear and guilt, which likewise function as the threshold of culture, the infection of sense and morality, resulting from the weakness of life is, according to Nietzsche, to be stopped and to be succeeded by the Saturnalia of the martial and cruel. In this guiltless festival of cruelty the question which still guides Hegel concerning the sense of tragic suffering and destruction finds a merely tautological answer:

> Saying Yes to life even in its strangest and hardest problems, the will to life rejoicing over its own inexhaustibility even in the very sacrifice of its highest types – *that* is what I called Dionysian, *that* is what I guessed to be the bridge to the psychology of the *tragic* poet.[42]

The unique special role which Nietzsche ascribes to tragedy can also be gathered from the fact that he sees the great stations and accomplishments of the history of culture as a weakening of life, as the expression of '*a will to nothingness*'[43] which works everywhere. Tragedy alone is exempted from this will. For him it is the 'great stimulant of life, an intoxication with life, a will to life'[44] so that he can finally take as a working definition 'that tragedy is a *tonicum*'.[45]

Our initial thesis was that under the influence of the Enlightenment the theory of tragedy can not avoid effecting a disjunction of the tragic. I hope to have shown that the positions of Hegel and Nietzsche, the relativization of the tragic conflict as well as its apotheosis, represent such a disjunction. Nietzsche's conjuring away of history under the sign of cruelty, does as little justice to the traditional practice of tragedy as Hegel's assimilation of the tragic to the idea of progress. Even if one could think of reading the respective disjunction historically as countercurrent phases to which the theoretical appropriation of tragedy as a result of the Enlightenment is necessarily subject, it may nevertheless be helpful, as a supplement aspect of the two positions we have sketched, to adduce general conditions to which the philosophy of tragedy is subject. The philosophy of the tragic, as it has developed from Schelling to Jaspers and whose high point probably is represented by the philosophic adaptations of Hegel and Nietzsche, continuously draws on the tragedy of the Greeks and that of modern times. Simultaneously, however, the respective design of the tragic becomes the cohesive principle of philosophy which develops it, for example Hegel not only extrapolates the principle of tragic dialectic from the tragedies of antiquity, but even more he uses this principle to profile the central point of his philosophy – the process of world history. Conversely the idea of the course of world history also determines the concept of the tragic as Hegel develops it. Similarly Nietzsche derives the principle of the Dionysian from an appeal to classic tragedy and finally posits the hypostatization of 'tragic terrors' in order to give form to his apotheosis of a world beyond metaphysics and morality. Correspondingly it is just this philosophy which stamps his view of tragedy. Thus the philosophy of the tragic, as it has developed since the nineteenth century, stands at the juncture between the reflection on tragedy and the philosophic appropriation of the world. This is to say that the philosophy of the tragic is not interpretation of tragedy, it is reflection on a specific formulation of human destruction conditioned by a specific philosophic construct of reality. Such a construct can only be disjoined; it owes its philosophic form to just this disjunction. To this extent every recent theoretical adaptation of tragedy must confront the Enlightenment. The now sketched specific causes of a philosophy of the tragic come together and intertwine. Both must be responsible for the disjunction which the positions of Hegel and Nietzsche paradigmatically show.

Notes

1. Cf. my book *Tragödie und Aufklärung. Zum Funktionswandel des Tragischen zwischen Racine und Büchner* [Tragedy and Enlightenment. On the Change of Function of the Tragic from Racine to Büchner], [Stuttgart, 1976]. I take the liberty of mentioning here some of my other writings on tragedy on which in part this article is based: 'Die Replik des deutschen Idealismus auf die Aporie der Voltaireschen Tragödien' (German Idealism's Answer to the Problem of Voltaire's Tragedies) in: *Voltaire und Deutschland* [Voltaire and Germany], ed. P. Brockmeier, R. Desne (Stuttgart: J. Voss, 1979) 439–53; 'Hegels Dramentheorie und ihre Wirkung' [Hegel's Theory of the Drama and its Effect] in: *Handbuch des deutschen Dramas* [Manual of German Drama], ed. W. Hinck (Düsseldorf, 1980) 259–72; 'Natur der Freiheit

und Freiheit der Natur als tragischer Widerspruch in "Dantons Tod" [Nature of Freedom and Freedom of Nature as Tragic Contradiction in 'Danton's Death'] in: *Der Deutschunterricht* 31 (1979) 107–21.

2. Voltaire, *Œuvres Complètes*, ed. L. Moland, 52 vols (Paris, 1877–82) II, 163.
3. *The Works of Voltaire* with notes by Tobias Smollett, Revised and Modernised New Translation by William F. Fleming, and an Introduction by Oliver H. G. Leigh (New York: E. R. Dumont, 1901) vol. XVII, p. 45.
4. Voltaire, *Œuvres Complètes*, vol.VI, p. 548.
5. *Works of Voltaire*, vol. XVII, p. 51.
6. *Works of Voltaire*, vol. XV, p. 184.
7. *Works of Voltaire*, vol. XV, p. 236.
8. *Works of Voltaire*, vol. XV, p. 236.
9. *Works of Voltaire*, vol. XV, p. 237.
10. G.F.W. Hegel, *Werke* 20 vols (Frankfurt am Main, 1971) I (Frühe Schriften) 618–20.
11. G.F.W. Hegel, *Hegel's Lectures on the History of Philosophy* trans E.S. Haldane and Frances H. Simson, 3 vols (New York: Humanities Press, 1955), vol. III, pp. 7–8.
12. G.F.W. Hegel, *Aesthetics. Lectures on Fine Arts*, trans. T.M. Knox, 2 vols (Oxford: Clarendon, 1975), vol. II, p. 1197.
13. *Aesthetics*, vol. II p. 1216.
14. *Aesthetics*, vol. I, p. 232.
15. *Aesthetics*, vol. II, p. 1162.
16. Hegel, *Werke* XVIII 447 (omitted in the translation).
17. *Hegel's Lectures on the History of Philosophy*, vol. I, p. 386.
18. *Ibid.*, p. 410.
19. *Ibid.*, p. 404.
20. *Ibid.*, p. 426.
21. *Aesthetics*, vol. II, p. 1216.
22. *Ibid.*, p. 1208.
23. *Ibid.*, p. 1215.
24. *Hegel's Philosophy of History*, trans. J. Sibree (New York: Wiley, 1944), p. 3.
25. F. Nietzsche, *Ecce Homo. The Basic Writings of Nietzsche*. Trans. W. Kaufmann. (New York: Modern Library, 1968), p. 730.
26. F. Nietzsche, *The Birth of Tragedy. The Basic Writings of Nietzsche*. Trans. W. Kaufmann (New York: Modern Library, 1968), p. 74.
27. F. Nietzsche, Introduction to *The Birth of Tragedy. The Basic Writings of Nietzsche*, pp. 17–24, and *Thus Spake Zarathustra. The Portable Nietzsche*, Trans. W. Kaufman (New York: Viking, 1954). 'At one time Zarathustra too cast his delusion beyond man, like all the afterworldly. The work of a suffering and tortured god, the world then seemed to me. A dream the world then seemed to me, and the fiction of a god; colored smoke before the eyes of a dissatisfied deity' (p. 142).
28. F. Nietzsche, *Werke in drei Banden*, ed. K. Schlechta (Munich, 1966), vol. III, p. 917 (from the literary bequest). My translation.

29. *Hegel's Lectures on the History of Philosophy*, vol. I, p. 384.
30. F. Nietzsche, *Twilight of the Idols, Portable Nietzsche*, p. 491.
31. F. Nietzsche, *Genealogy of Morals, Basic Writings*, p. 478.
32. F. Nietzsche, *Beyond Good and Evil, Basic Writings*, p. 351.
33. F. Nietzsche, *Beyond Good and Evil, Basic Writings*, p. 158.
34. F. Nietzsche, *Genealogy of Morals, Basic Writings*, p. 67.
35. Ibid., p. 69.
36. Ibid., p. 69.
37. Ibid., p. 129.
38. Ibid., p. 141.
39. Ibid., p. 151.
40. Ibid., p. 151.
41. F. Nietzsche, *Twilight of the Idols, Basic Writings*, p. 530.
42. Ibid., p. 562.
43. F. Nietzsche, *Genealogy of Morals, Basic Writings*, p. 163.
44. F. Nietzsche, *Aus dem Nachlass der Achtzigerjahre*, vol. III, p. 828.
45. Ibid., p. 829.

Translated from the German by Henry Tapp.

3
Tragic Thoughts and the Entertainments of Possibility

LEON ROSENSTEIN

Manifestly tragedy and philosophy are not the same, in as much as literature is not logic and art is not nature. Philosophy, concerning itself with the processes of reason only, is, as we have so often been told since Plato, the 'purer', the 'surer', the more internally complete and consistent in the account it gives of its subject – which is ultimately the One Reality – an account to be rendered through the medium of unambiguous and translucent language. Poetry concerns itself not only with the processes of reason, but also with emotion and free imagination. The account it gives of its subject is, on a rational plane, less complete and consistent, for it contains the impurities of *emotion* and *free imagination*; and moreover, its account of its subject is rendered through media neither unambiguous nor translucent. We see it as richer therefore in bringing into simultaneous play several human faculties and having as its aim the unification of a lush diversity of variously distributed sensuous and intellectual elements into an autonomous whole.

That philosophy is *not* poetry many literary critics and philosophers will grant, even when that 'poetry' takes the specific form of tragedy. Nevertheless, they have said, certain types of poetry, especially tragedy, *contain philosophy* or *a philosophy*. That is, presupposing their differences in structure, content, even in aim, they say that there may be extracted from the richer matrix a purely rational element, a philosophy – or, even more specifically, *the tragic philosophy* or *the tragic view of life*. Both the general claim – that the one form contains the other as an isolable subcategory – and the specific – that a *particular* philosophy is invariably expressed in those art forms called tragedy – are false. The reification or abstraction of a philosophical essence which may presumably be performed on the given tragedy is an illusion. Much as if one were to extract the chlorine from the salt in a bouillabaisse stew and call it '*the bouillabaisse chlorine*,' so, with about as much sense, does one extract the philosophy from representations of thought in a tragedy and call it '*the tragic philosophy*'. Decontextualization cannot be innocuous – it either kills or it totally transforms. Gnomic metaphysical utterances like 'little can the race of men know what future the gods plan', abstracted from a Sophoclean play, are about as trite and philosophically exciting as such moral caveats as 'do not be jealous' abstracted from *Othello* or 'do not procrastinate' from *Hamlet*.

Just as tragedy is not a truthful reproduction of the facts of reality but an imitation or 'worked world', so such thoughts as it may contain are not interpretations of reality or expressions of moral and metaphysical theses about reality (whether 'the One Reality' or any particular *Weltanschauung*), but are suggested explanations of the events of the play world, which is in each instance unique. Philosophers have 'used' tragedies. Only think of Hegel, Nietzsche, Kierkegaard, and Freud.[1] Tragedians have 'used' philosophies. Just as tragedians have taken whatever stories, characters, or facts have been ready to hand and reshaped them, or invented new ones for their particular plots, so they have done the same with philosophies – taking some here and there, reshaping them where necessary or inventing new bits. And they have then used this – actually fragments of philosophy in the form of utterances of an apparently metaphysical or ethical sort – more fully to expose, or render an interpretation of their stories, facts, or characters.[2] And this explanation or interpretation of each, and whatever interpretations of the whole, that the quasi-philosophic expressions of thought in tragedies contain need not even be consistent or complete. Indeed, as one recalls one's own examples of the best in tragedies, one is inclined to agree with Friedrich Schlegel: 'all truly great literary works must never be fully intelligible'.[3]

Leaving its presumed philosophic *content* aside, others have claimed that tragedy is like philosophy in *form*. Aristotle states that tragedy is 'more philosophical and of graver import than history', because it speaks to us not in terms of particulars but in the 'form' of probability and necessity, which is the way of knowing through the theoretical sciences; and suggests further that tragedy has a source in the natural impulse in humans to 'imitate', which itself is encouraged by the human delight in 'gathering meanings' of things and thereby learning.[4] But that tragedy is like philosophy in form because it uses modes of presentation which give its subject matter a well-connected meaningfulness, hence 'credibility', by selection and abstraction and by certifying the progression and conclusion of the action through explicitation – and that this procedure amounts to more than a mere chronicle of the particular incidents of historical actuality – this should cause us to reflect more carefully on their common categories and rules of progression and to the roles that possibility, probability, and necessity play therein. It should not lead us simply to assert (following Aristotle sometimes) that, having certain *similarities* of *form*, they *are* the *same* or that they must have a *similar* – or, for some, *identical – function,* namely, to teach us about reality.

As I have argued the fundamentals of these matters elsewhere and in greater detail before, I have no desire to repeat them.[5] It is nevertheless worth while amplifying some of the argument to illuminate several cases in point so as to be able to move on to my major issue regarding tragedy and the entertainments of possibility. In doing so, I shall use Aristotle's *Poetics* as a heuristic device. It is the most pervasive and profound meditation on the nature of tragedy; and, therefore, where possible and appropriate, I shall adopt, reinterpret, or reconstruct his argument. I do this first because it is the best account available and despite the fact that Aristotle succumbs on important occasions to the philosophical reductionisms mentioned above. That is, specifically, he sometimes treats the *content* of tragedy as if it were a mere imitative reflection of reality and thus attempts to understand it in terms of metaphysical or (more often) moral principles which are derived from there but which we know are inapplicable to the action of the worked world of tragedy; and sometimes he treats (or appears to treat) the *form* and *function* of tragedy as if they were off-shoots of or ancillaries to philosophy and thus in the broadest sense 'educative' about reality and for life generally. Where it is necessary – as in these instances – I shall reject his theory rather than distort it by misinterpretation. When Aristotle is in error, moreover, and in pointing this out, this very use of him will provide a second and further benefit – it will show us all the poisoned fruits provided by the gardener who does not tend his own garden and imagines that philosophy is tragedy.

But at least 90 percent of the time Aristotle is aware of this truth:

poiesis is not *mimesis*. And therefore there are criteria of 'rightness' in tragedy independent of the reproduction of the proportions and qualities of natural (that is extra-artistic) reality, but rather having to do with the proper structuring of its contents' proportions and qualities, the rules for which the form of the worked world supplies. So while Aristotle does go 'off track' on occasion, he himself points out: 'there is not the same kind of correctness in poetry as in politics, or indeed in any other art'. He thus can recognize 'poetic license' with respect to the metaphysics and morality of the actual *contents* of a tragedy's characters and events and can accept 'likely impossibilities' so long as they are 'convincing' and 'depravities of character' when 'use is made of them'.[6] Similarly, he is capable of recognizing that *'invention'* – that is creation of a convincing, i.e. meaningfully articulated, sequence of action – is the essence of the tragic *form* and what enables it to function as form, and that this is what makes the poet a 'poet' – not his versification of or his adherence to traditional or historical actualities or his philosophizing about them.[7] So, too, his calling music the 'most imitative of the arts' has nothing to do with that art form's copying natural sounds but with its work upon emotional states of the soul: it transforms them (or the feeling we get when experiencing them) through a different medium into a new experience elicited by the new invention.[8] Hence, after all, the title of his work on tragedy – *Poetics*, not *Mimetics* – for the tragedian does not merely collect the facts and hold a mirror to the world, but invents new facts suited to the world of his invention.[9] In this way, he does what Aristotle says all fine art must do – not only imitate, but bring into being new realities which nature does not provide.

Aristotle further believes that there is a 'special pleasure' or 'special effect' appropriate to the experience of tragedy and that this pleasure is different from that experienced with comedy or epic.[10] He believes that this special pleasure has something to do with pity and fear. In fact in one place he says this pleasure *'is* that of pity and fear'.[11] Now much has been written about his claim – and especially the problem it creates of how and why anyone should choose to experience these essentially unpleasant emotions (Aristotle says they are 'painful') by witnessing a tragic performance for its 'special pleasure'. Even more has been said about Aristotle's cryptic term 'catharsis' which is supposed to explain how this should occur.[12] (This usually means trying then to account for how catharsis works upon, or does something with or to pity and fear, and thus converts the painful in us to special pleasure.)

Now Aristotle states in the *Rhetoric* that *pity* – fear is treated quite similarly – is a 'feeling of pain' caused by the apprehension of 'painful destruction' which 'befalls one who does not deserve it', especially 'persons of noble character'.[13]

Let us look for a moment at 'undeserving noble characters' and at 'painful destructions' which elicit pity and thus come to the 'special pleasure' which catharsis is supposed to provide by somehow working on this pity.

The moment Aristotle begins to apply ethical criteria to tragic persons his argument begins to fall apart. Unwilling ethically to allow tragedies to represent 'good men passing from happiness to misery' because it is 'simply odious', he requires an ethical legitimation of catastrophe and thus introduces the infamous 'some error of judgment' (*hamartia*).[14] But using such a legalistically defined term from the *Nicomachean Ethics* never gets very far – precisely because his subject is tragedy and not life, its agents are *dramatis personae*, not real people.

'Hamartia', if it is a term ever to be used in poetics at all, is merely an aesthetical device, not an ethical criterion; for in no sense can it justify ethically the consequences of a character's actions, but merely unifies the action from a selected point of view. A character possessing this trait (the 'tragic flaw') does not thereby become an ethically 'intermediate type of personage' for such a conception is inconsistent with Aristotle's own requirement for tragedy's subject – that it have noble characters, which makes it differ from comedy, whose personages fall on the other side of the line dividing the whole of mankind.[15]

Aristotle's use of the legalistic term *hamartia*, introduced by the inconsistent phrase 'intermediate kind of personage', is a red herring. As we follow it down the ethical stream looking for a *reason why* (or a set of criteria to be established for determining *how*) some character is sufficiently 'noble' and 'undeserving' for our pity and yet 'intermediate' and 'flawed' enough to deserve his calamitous fate, we will find ourselves awash with inconsistencies until we debouch into the ocean of critical nonsense. Better to avoid hamartia fishing expeditions to which serious ethical inquiry inevitably impels us. Not some philosophical system of morality but the tragedy itself makes its characters 'deserving' and 'undeserving', just as it provides its own criteria of 'nobility'. It is not really their 'moral goodness' or 'freedom from villany' that makes them 'win pity' from us at all. It is because they are *heroic* (that is *'spoudaios'* in the pre-philosophic sense – seriously to be dealt with because they are impressive by their magnitude and terrific in their power) that they evoke in us the *special tragic pleasure*, a pleasure only 'akin' to pity, as tragedy is akin to philosophy, and art to life generally. That is why Shakespeare's Richard III is as tragic as his Richard II or his Othello and why Euripides' Medea is as tragic as his Hecuba in *Trojan Women*. As far beyond our ordinary reality as the hero's character is, so different from our ordinary pity is the emotion evoked by the aesthetic experience of tragedy. We shall explain this more fully in a moment; but now we have seen how far Aristotle's moral preoccupations have led him astray.

If we leave aside looking for the moral worth of individuals in tragedy and look for a metaphysical exposition of reality to be called 'the tragic philosophy', we need also to take a look at the other requirement for pity noted above besides 'noble character' – a 'painful destruction' brought about by an ordered progression of incidents manifesting irresistable forces so as to take characters 'from happiness to misery'.

There are two instances where in the *Poetics* Aristotle comes to discuss painful destruction and the fateful death of tragic heroes. In the first he speaks of Euripides' tragedies which, however 'faulty in other respects', are 'the most truly tragic' because he gives so many of them 'an unhappy ending'.[16] And for the same reason he praises the *Oedipus Tyrannus* – which seems in most respects to be his paradigm of excellence in plot construction – that it has the 'finest form' of discovery, which attends reversal by way of making each recognition a further step in the calamity.[17]

This sounds perfectly reasonable and consistent – with the rest of Aristotle's argument and with our own experience of tragedy. The death of the tragic character is the incarnation of tragic action. It terminates the plot and transforms thematic thoughts into destiny or fate. Death functions so as to render unalterably significant the life of the tragic personae (pregnant at every moment and in every word and gesture), creating a sort of Heideggerian 'being-towards-death' in the vision of tragic characters whose ownness and completeness is achieved in their anticipatory resoluteness. Death in tragedy, not in real life, concludes the character, because it realizes the metaphysic of the worked world he inhabits, a world whose laws require his death and *vice versa*. That is why in tragedy every death is a 'convenient' death and 'the good death', for it 'proves' the character and his fate.

The occasional difficulty of a known tragedy which does not end in this way (e.g. *The Eumenides* or the *Iphigeneia in Tauris*) is nothing compared, then, to the difficulty Aristotle himself proceeds to generate within his own theory. He does not, we noted earlier, make the mistake of trying to isolate in tragedies 'the tragic philosophy'. On the contrary – almost to the other extreme – he introduces a new preference. Without reconciliation or justification with the forementioned requirement (regarding death and painful destructions' elicitation of pity), he offers the judgment that 'the best' type of play will have a recognition scene which occurs before, and so as to prevent, the painful and destructive act, leading to a happy conclusion. It is hard to know how pity can come from this. It is easy to see again how moral and metaphysical preferences extraneous to the typical tragedy's world incline one to finding them there, or in the 'best ones'.

The second instance where death and painful destruction are spoken of by Aristotle's theory is in his account of the marvellous. There Aristotle observes that fearful and pitiable incidents have

the very greatest effect on the mind when they occur unexpectedly and at the same time in consequence of one another; there is more of the marvellous in them ... if there is an appearance of design as it were in them; as for instance the statue of Mitys at Argos killed the author of Mitys' death by falling down on him when an onlooker at a public spectacle: for incidents like that we think to be not without a meaning. A plot, therefore, of this sort is necessarily more beautiful than others.[18]

We ought first of all to note carefully several things said here and *how* they are said. The 'appearance' (*phainetai*) of design – not 'reality' of design. Not 'meaningful' he says, but 'not without meaning'. Such a plot is more 'beautiful' (*kallious* is his word, rather than Bywater's 'finer') – not 'truer' or more 'just'. Tragedy is a worked world. We know that in real life the statues of victims do not slay their murderers. They do not fall in accordance with the 'natural law of irony', but with the law of gravity, which does not discriminate. In real life the 'design' of the world is not very clear and justice does not often prevail. In tragedy we have *apparent* reality in which such things do occur – and, given the proper conditions, must occur! Each tragedy establishes its own conditions. Here justice is always 'poetic'–even if it isn't 'just'.

It is this sort of understanding that Aristotle has and of which we must approve – even if he cannot remain faithful to it. In this way we see how the improbable and unexpected of life become the necessary and anticipated of art. These events suggest meaning. And it is this intricate working out of the quasi-metaphysical principles operating in the worked world of tragedy – principles made concrete and human in the form of fate – that make the work beautifully satisfying.

And this brings us to the satisfaction of tragedy – the special pleasure it provides. As we have been discussing the causes or conditions of this pleasure we have been arguing along with the case presented by Aristotle: that this pleasure is that of pity and fear, as he says. But *is* it? These are *painful* emotions, as Aristotle also says, so why should we choose to experience them at all? Or is it actually the catharsis of them which is the final cause and special pleasure of the tragedy, and not pity and fear themselves, which are only emotional *means* to this end?

In truth, as I have already intimated above, we do not really feel pity and fear when experiencing a tragedy. (Or, if we do, we are not experiencing *the tragedy*.) We would be as much in error to *pity* tragic characters as we would be to take expressions of thought from their mouths and project them upon the real world as its 'philosophy' or as an interpretation of extra-artistic reality from the perspective of 'the tragic philosophy'. Conversely, if we *really* pitied them we would walk on stage to aid them, and if we *really* feared we would flee from our seats. To attempt to mollify this response by suggesting that in the theatrical context this pity and fear become 'milder' or 'intellectually constrained' or 'aesthetically distanced' emotions misses the point. Aristotle's belief that as an audience we in fact experience pity and fear and his claim that the tragic pleasure '*is* pity and fear' run counter to his own assertions regarding the poet's invention. Only by failing to recognize this fact, by confusing art with reality, by piercing the imitational veil of the art form, by totally disregarding the art form's material and efficient causes (its vehicles for presenting its subjects to us), by ignoring the art object altogether, could we vicariously experience fear for, and masochistically feel pity in, ourselves. We perhaps respond with hunger when we see a basket of fruit on a table. We do not have this emotion when these become subjects represented in, for example, a painting by Cézanne. And should the art object that is a performance differ? The pity we may feel for the sufferings of good people whom we know from life is not the emotion we experience when observing *Oedipus Tyrannus* or *King Lear*.

But if we do not really experience pity and fear at all, then what of catharsis and the 'special pleasure of tragedy' it presumably confers? There is no pity or fear. Catharsis cannot operate upon what is not there – to increase it, to remove (purge) it, or purify it, or balance it in us, or enlighten us with regard to it.

Catharsis is a function of the imitation/invention. That is its antecedent in the definition sentence in which Aristotle uses the word. The term does not refer to a transformation of the psycho-physiological condition of the spectator. It refers to a process of the invention whereby events of life and the emotional responses appropriate to them, are transformed into the subject of a type of art work and the responses appropriate to it. I am not saying that, for example, Richard III's painful evil becomes a pleasant good because we cannot believe that anyone who speaks so beautifully is all bad. I am not saying that the sonorous harmonies heard as Hecuba speaks in the *Trojan Women* enable us to ignore or make light of the pity and fear we really feel. I am not saying the beauti-fully ironic constructions of fate we see operating in the *Oedipus* give us a kind of pleasure in themselves beyond the painful des-truction they wreak and the dreadful 'wisdom' they bespeak. I am saying we do not experience pain at all because we do not experience pity and fear; and we do not because the work does not elicit them from us. They do not themselves need to be transfor-med *in* us because in making the work the tragedian has *already* done all the transformation *for* us. Like the transformation of chlorine into the salt of a bouillabaisse, of the tart apple-taste of the fruit into the vibrant green form of a still-life painting, of the mar-ble mass of Mitys' statue into the fateful hand of vengeance, of the emotion of frenzy into a tune on the Pan flute in the Lydian mode – like all of these, pity and fear are transformed already by the invention's catharsis. And whatever Aristotle *may* have meant by the word, this is what he *should* have said. Catharsis produces the prime effect – the special pleasure – of the art form. The term denotes the accomplishment of the task undertaken by the transformative abilities inherent in the art work's imitative/inventive techniques: that is, in this case, the speech, melody and spectacle wherein and whereby the tale is told in a worked world invented for it.

But if the painful and destructive events represented in a tragedy are not for the purpose of provoking pity and fear in us, then what do they do and what are they for? If the quasi-philosophic thoughts expressed in tragedy are not about reality and the lives we must lead in it, then what are they for? In both cases the answer is: to stimulate our attention and thereby entertain us with possibility.

If our rational faculty can be attuned by the thoughts in the work and our emotions stimulated by the events in the work, then, insofar as this is an art-work, this attuned stimulation is accomplished ('catharsis') by the media and performance. It is they – and *not merely* the interior message or content, i.e. the progression of plot line, characters' lives, thoughts and themes – which engage and bring our various faculties into play.

It is obvious that the account we give of any experience must always remain a function of the particular attitude – our expectation and disposition, our attunement – towards the object we experience. We must be sufficiently concerned to take the work seriously by responding to it in its own terms and by being concerned enough about its subject and its mode of presentation to certify its presentation to us as significant.

And yet it seems that in the account given of tragedies – at least as these are usually presented by philosophers – only the interior, the message, has seemed to matter. It is as if a summary of its plot-line and its themes was all that was really there to be experienced, as if we were like Kant's Iroquois Indian, Sachem, who noticed only the pastry shops in Paris,[19] or as if we were to be satisfied and done with a Titian altarpiece once we had recognized the figures of Christ, Mary, John the Baptist, etc. We must, rather, expect the whole and be attuned to the whole as a whole. This is how we attend to all art works. So must we remain attached and captivated by the corporeal structures of its medium (its language, sounds and metaphors, its actors, their gestures and expressions, its staging) and, at the same time, be continuously attuned by these corporeal sensuous elements to the cognitive forms of the unique worked world which they generate (the story and its themes, the characters and their thoughts) – an artificial world with its own objectively given actualities, the possibilities to be continuously interpolated upon them, and its own values and interpretations. This is the illusion of the tragedy – indeed of any art object – that it opens up its own space and time and 'puts into play' there the creatures of its own reality.

What is fully 'in play' before us is a unified whole and it is this whole which stimulates and entertains. This unification is effected by both the inherent properties of its content (plot, character, thought) and of its means and manner (speech, melody, spectacle)[20] – each of which is coordinated with the other. The unification takes place, then, on many levels and in innumerable ways – settings, recurrent moods and words, symbols, auditory, verbal and visual images, etc. To take just one example: Lear's naked ranting on the barren heath amidst the torrent – seen on a stage whose lighting is alternately glaringly harsh and dim and heard in words spoken in tones cracked and rough and alternately full and empty of emotion – is an instance of the demonstration of significant action not only as the consequence of Lear's precedent abdication but becomes the mirror of abiding division and rage, elucidating such statements as his last distracted request ('Pray you undo this button') – all of which is reaffirmed by the perpetual verbal image of negation.

We must go even further and recognize that for tragedy *fully* to be 'in play', it must be the unique engagement of a performance which constitutes 'the work'. Unlike philosophy the text (if not the interpretation) of which endures continuously unmodified forever, tragedy, even unlike painting and sculpture, but like music, exists fully only in existentially intermittent performance, each instance of which is a variation of the others. It is in the intricate intersticies of this play that the imagination is set free and we are entertained with possibility.

As possibility is freer than actuality, so imagination provides a more expansive world than perception. Philosophy is bound to perception and its reasons. Tragedy – like all art – touches perception with imagination and transforms it for imagination. Philosophy's task is finally to delimit the given orders of and relations in the actual world; in this procedure imagination considers possibilities only so as to conform them to, or to confirm therewith, a system of perceived actualities circumscribed by philosophic understanding. Tragedy's task is to propose new relations of possibility in imitation of the limited orders of reality by creating new and only vaguely commensurate worlds; in this

process the actualities of perception are expanded into a plenitude
of possibilities by the imagination simply to 'occasion much
thought' (to put it in a Kantian phrase).

To continue in the Kantian mode of expression, in tragedy, as in
all art, 'the understanding is at the service of the imagination, and
not *vice versa*'; and indeed therefore tragedy as poetry is nothing
but 'the art of conducting a free play of the imagination as if it were
a serious business of the understanding'.[21] But whereas for Kant, as
for philosophers generally – as we noted above – the pleasures of
entertaining ourselves with possibilities thus generated ('aesthetical
ideas', he calls them) are intellectual pleasures only, we must add
the whole realm of emotion and the physical vehicles upon which
the play world is erected. Tragedies create not only a plenitude of
ideas and images, but of interrelated feelings and sensuous
stimulae.

This, then, is that complex and special pleasure of tragedy – that
it entertains us with possibilities. These are not merely possibilities
as stimulants to imagination through thought – for example,
variable or alternative interpretations of the action – but also
possibilities which concern the affective stimulae and our infinitely
variable emotional responses to them as they create and relate to
thought and its reasons. Moreover, if we keep the term 'catharsis'
and interpret it as the taking of actualities (things and persons,
events, philosophies, emotions) of the extra-artistic world and
creating a new actuality of the worked world, then such 'thoughts'
as may be present in the world of a tragedy stimulate us not only to
consider the possibilities of its own reality but also enliven the
imagination to ponder the relations of that reality and its 'thoughts'
to reality and its philosophy, to explore further the interrelations of
the worked and extra-artistic worlds. To say that the world of
tragedy is its own world is not to deny its *relation* to the real one,
any more than to insist on the distinction between art and nature is
to deny their relationship.

Our main concern has not been the entirety of tragedy but
essentially its 'thoughts'. Thoughts are but a portion of its interior
worked world. And the interior itself is but a portion of the whole
work. Consequently, our expectations for the entirety of the
affective response to tragedy cannot – as we have noted – be
reduced to our intellectual response. Insofar as 'tragic thoughts'
have some modal relation to that response, however, we hope to
have clarified one of its aspects. If we properly interpret 'tragic

thoughts'to mean nothing but 'thoughts in tragedy' then we have come some way to understanding the pleasure of tragedy.

Notes

1. For example and analysis see my 'Metaphysical Foundations of the Theories of Tragedy in Hegel and Nietzsche', *Journal of Aesthetics and Art Criticism* (vol. 28, no.4) Summer 1970, pp. 521–33.
2. Aristotle, for example, with what *appears at first* to be uncharacteristic vagueness, only requires that thought in tragedy be present to show character, or prove or disprove or enunciate general propositions on matters 'not indifferent' to the plot. There is not a hint in any of this of the 'tragic philosophy'.
3. Friedrich Schlegel, Lyceum Fragment, no. 20.
4. *Poetics* 1451b 5–10 and 1448b 5–20.
5. Leon Rosenstein, 'On Aristotle and Thought in the Drama', *Critical Inquiry* (vol. 3, no. 3)., Spring, 1977, pp. 543–65; 'Rethinking Aristotle's 'Thought', *Critical Inquiry* (vol. 4, no. 3), Spring 1978, pp. 597–606; and 'The Ontological Integrity of the Art Object from the Ludic Viewpoint', *Journal of Aesthetics and Art Criticism* (vol. 34, no. 3), Spring 1976.
6. *Poetics* 1460a 26–8; 1460b 14–16, 23-7, 32-5; 1461b 9–22.
7. *Ibid.*, 1447b 18–20; 1451b 20–30.
8. *Politics*, 1339–1342.
9. *Physics*, 199a 15–16.
10. *Poetics* 1450a 30; 1459a 20; 1453a 34-40.
11. *Ibid.* 1453b 12; also stated in the definition of tragedy at 1449b 26-8 and at 1452b 2–3.
12. See my article, 'The Last Word on Catharsis', forthcoming in *Annales d'Esthétique*.
13. *Rhetoric* 1385b–1386b.
14. *Poetics* 1452b 33–5 and 1453a 9.
15. *Ibid.*, 1448a 1–5 and b 24–6; 1453a 5–10; 1454b 8–10; and Gerald F. Else, *Aristotle's Poetics: The Argument* (Cambridge, Mass., 1957) pp. 77–82.
16. *Poetics* 1453a 14–30.
17. *Ibid.*, 1452a 21–33.
18. *Ibid.*, 1452a 2–11.
19. *Immanuel Kant, Critique of Judgement*, trans. J.H. Bernard (New York: Hafner Publishing, 1951), Sec 2. p. 38.
20. For clarification see my 'Ontological Integrity of the Art Object', p. 325.
21. *Critique of Judgement*, see sections 22, 49, and 51 especially pp. 79, 157, 165. pp. 79, 157, 165.

4
Tragedy: Its Contribution to a Theory of Objects and the Emotions

RICHARD F. KUHNS

> *The sense of what is real*
> *...the thought if after all it should prove unreal,*
> *The doubts of daytime and the doubts of nighttime...*
> *the curious whether and how,*
> *Whether that which appears so is so ....*
> *Or is it all flashes and specks?*

Walt Whitman

I

We have survived the death of positivistic, analytic, linguistic philosophy in the era of modernity; we emerge now, we tell ourselves, into the realm of the post-modern – wondering just what that refers to. One consequence of our uncertainty has been a broadening of the professional subjects thought proper to the practice of philosophy, or as we had become proud to say, 'doing philosophy'. So that in the post-modern era, presumably *ours* for the next several years, philosophy has looked about for enriching sources to ingest, to fatten out a meagre and narrowing body. One source has been tragedy, about which much has been written; more goods are displayed on the 'tragedy' counter than most others, and the attention given to tragedy is far more intense than anything it demanded for itself.

What can philosophy learn from tragedy? Beyond the great texts *on* tragedy – by Aristotle, Nietzsche, Freud – philosophy in the post-modern era has lectured tragedy on what *it* really is about;

and so we have had lessons in French tragic cookery, serving up a ten-course meal, complete with human sacrifice.

Can tragedy tell *philosophy* anything at all? If so what? I shall develop the thesis that tragedy has a lot to tell philosophy about the emotions, and I shall make the case through specific passages in tragedies we all know.

Tragic action presents deep conflicts between persons on the level of that affective domain of words and images that the psychoanalytic theory of mind refers to as 'primary process thought'. To be sure, there is no primary process thought, at least where artistic enactments are concerned, that is not represented by secondary process thought: in the theatre characters present themselves through language, gesture, physical movement. Yet it is not in the representational exhibition – what we witness as we watch – that the deep emotional conflicts are encountered. They are in part hidden, to be inferred. In short, there is a *manifest* and a *latent* content in all tragedy.

Of course, all interpretative methods postulate a manifest and a latent content in drama, for the whole strategy of interpretation is to reveal or uncover the deeper, the inner, the 'real' meaning of an action. The latent thus made manifest is in part a function of the theory in terms of which the inquiry and interpretation were carried out. And that is why the later moments in modernity resisted interpretation; for there was a static moment – it now seems to be the dividing line between modernity and the post-modern – when interpretation tried to rid itself of accumulated theory. But we are back, today, with theory, more extreme, bizarre and outrageously inventive than ever before.

Ambivalence towards theory remains; I run a risk, then, in basing my discussion of emotion in tragedy on the psychoanalytic interpretative theory, for there is today much scepticism towards it. But I have found that the psychoanalytic theory of maturation and development and the affective life is the best we have, and so I use it, not with the conviction it will stand for all time, but simply that it is the best of *our* time.

My thesis, then, is simply this: philosophy can learn about the emotions from tragedy, that from tragedy we can find a way to a more adequate and complete theory of the emotions.

As the discussion on feeling, suffering, and 'catharsis' in the *Poetics* makes clear, tragedy has thought hard about the place of emotion in the *representation* of human actions. By 'human actions', the phrase used by Aristotle, is meant deliberation and choice regarding an end to be aimed at. So when human actions are *represented* there is a degree of distance from everyday, real-life situations of choosing and aiming at a goal. The degree of distance is marked by plot, character and the modulations of poetic language. As we sit in the theatre we watch characters on the stage, but we are never confused about their 'reality'. The are dramatic personae, whose mythic origin and aesthetic distance keep them out of our experience *except* as we meet them on the stage. Part of growing up in culture is to learn to mark the boundaries between the *agora* and the *orchestra*. But *cultural reality* is a presence as much part of experience as everyday *agora reality*! And therefore we must understand the contribution to culture of the tragic drama.

Where a culture draws the boundaries between representations and everyday activities – between the cultural tradition, and the natural conduct of community life – differs in time and place. It is far more difficult for us to participate in dramatic festivals, and in the total communal commitment of mythic plots than it was for the Athenians in the fourth century. In many cultures – ours has its limitations in this respect – the tradition of enactments is a powerful influence, a source of learning, a pedagogical necessity, a way to shape belief and modulate affect. The ways feelings work – how aroused, how directed, how modified, how judged, how welcomed or shunned – is shaped, disciplined, rewarded and punished through representations of actions, as in the tragic drama. Enactments that tell a story are cultural constants; the use and interpretations of such enactments are cultural individualities.

I shall assume in this discussion that tragedy is one of a whole class of objects (cultural enactments) whose purpose is to shape, direct, and assess, to punish and reward, the life of feeling as it is represented on the stage. Thus I regard the representational inquiries into feeling to be a central interest and purpose of tragedy.

Classical philosophers thought a lot about the *paideia* of tragedy; their arguments and disagreements have been thoroughly researched.[1] And we must ask the same questions they did, beginning with our native scepticism: do either philosophy or the arts have any consequences in the realm of human affect? Is one's emotional profile, as it were, shaped by these cultural objects? Do they form the person in the life of feeling? Or is that a maturational trajectory launched and completed long before one sits in the theatre? Are feelings, objects of feelings, control over feelings so biological-genetic, or tied so firmly to early experience that later cultural factors simply do not count? If the answer is 'yes', then Hamlet's question, 'What's Hecuba to him or he to Hecuba?' is easily answered: cultural enactments, such as tragic drama, are formative to us only momentarily, in the heat of the passions of the enactment and the *acting*, in the sympathy drawn forth there and then, but nothing more.

Yet we are reluctant to assent to that conclusion; for we undergo such passion, are not only so moved, but also so adoring, that we cannot believe the enactment has so little long-run effect. Certainly *outside* the performance we continue to experience deep feeling; but that expresses a conviction about the importance of art to life, an ideological *idée fixe* of academics, some artists, and a host of professional purveyors of 'culture'. More often than not, I find that the enthusiasm in witnessing performance is no more than the defense of the object as *an important object*! And yet, we insist, there is so much evidence to support the view that the arts shape feelings, character, beliefs; can we not defend the position here of such importance: that the experience *in the theatre* of a tragic performance, when well done, to be sure, has a lasting effect?

Let us begin with cultural conditions we rely upon in answering the question, but conditions that lie furthest from us, that of Classical Athens, where evidence suggests beliefs are forcefully held about the character-shaping of experiences in the theatre.

In both *The Persians* and *Seven Against Thebes* violent emotions are summoned up throughout the action; deafening noise of combat, of wailing, of mourning, of strife within and without the characters sounds throughout the plays. We are forced to watch through the din. The sounds arouse feelings in the audience, and while sounds are 'objects', and important dramatic objects, sound alone does not fix the emotions and focus them. For that, additional objects such as human facial expressions – in Greek drama, masks – gestures and postures are needed, and we shall see that the sounds are always coordinate with a dramatic visual or linguistic focus.

Although the 'object' in each play is complex, simplified presentations can be made here in this introductory analysis. In both cases, it is the dead and dreaded father whose presence in the plays is given various object-ifications: in the *Seven* through constant references to Oedipus, and through the formulation of seven riddles, all of which direct us back to the underlying Oedipus story; in the *Persians*, through conjuring up the shade of the departed Darius, to whom supplication is addressed, and from whom advice solicited. The *Seven* also builds its structure around the mother, represented and symbolized by the city itself, and the homeland, 'mother earth'. Confronted with the rites of mourning, the fighting, the noise, the references to the fathers and the mother, the audience suffers an affective coercion, for here are situations that are immediately filled with high emotion for each witness. Throughout the dramas, ambivalence towards the dead is generated as the feelings coalesce around dead parents; the spectacle elicits responses that have been oftentime rehearsed in family and communal life. To be sure, as Yeats said, 'Mirror on mirror mirrored is all the show.' We, the audience, are mirrored on the stage, as the stage mirrors the city in all its agony of fear and loss.

Let us leave the audience, for a moment, *in* the theatre to which I shall return in a moment to rescue them from an overlong exposure to dramatic stress. And let us turn for a moment to reading (or 'doing') philosophy. Is there anything similar in the parallel I am about to draw, between feelings aroused and 'shaped' in the theatre, and feelings discussed, analyzed, theorized about in a philosophical text? We are audience to the text as we are audience to the dramatic spectacle.

From the earliest considerations of emotion in classical writing, the assumption has been that philosophy tames, directs and orders the emotions on behalf of living well, self control, and political stability. Yet we philosophers, in our own lives and in our observations of *the* philosophic life as it exhibits itself in those we live among and work with, recognize the weakness of the claim, for it would be hard to defend the position that philosophers (i.e. those who 'do philosophy') are any more controlled, reasonable and emotionally developed in terms of the goals set out by Plato and Aristotle than are others. To be sure there are many examples of 'the philosophic life' as defined by Socrates, but not necessarily exhibited by philosophers. There is a disappointing disjunction between 'doing philosophy' and living 'the philosophic life'. Might there be a closer fit of the two if the philosopher spent more time in the theatre?

Let us return to the theatre now.

Dramas come to an end; there is a final scene, and it is there that Aristotle centered 'catharsis'. Conclusions are supposed to leave the witness in a state of emotional closure, resolution, granting to the suffering protagonist the acceptance and communal integration that the plot denies. Is there an emotionally and cognitively satisfying *resolution*? Aristotle argued there was, that the experience with tragic drama in the theatre is philosophically sound, realizing goals that philosophical theories of the emotions set as desirable. We the audience, for example, grant Oedipus the accommodation denied him by the city, through internalizing the character and according to Oedipus (in the *Seven*) the mourning he was denied in dramatic 'reality'. Yet at the end of the theatrical performance the audience moves back into the everyday reality of city life; just as the reader of the philosophic text must go on to faculty meetings, committee work and family, if not, in any self-conscious way, into political life.

Theatrical undergoing taps deeper levels of emotional life than reading and 'doing philosophy'. That can be used as an argument for or against the relevance of tragedy to conduct depending upon one's view (and here enters philosophy) of how the emotions are aroused, directed, controlled.

What is it that goes on in the theatre? Psychologically, the resolutions of tragedy take a long time and extend outside the actual performance – we work through tragic endings long after they are witnessed on the stage. In comedy, by contrast, where conclusions are often represented by marriage, or a problem solved, there is a life-affirming realized ending that is also a resolution, *in the theatre*. While in tragedy, ending and resolution are separated in time. (The close affinities, however, between tragic and comic endings and resolutions are studied and explored in *Hamlet*.)

As philosophers we maintain that endings should yield truth and conviction; we ought to be somehow changed by tragic denouements as we say to ourselves we are changed by reading philosophical arguments. We ought to 'believe' differently at the end of tragedy as we ought at the end of the *Critique of Pure Reason*. And with new belief and changed knowledge should come a development in the affective side of life: we ought to *feel* differently after exposure to drama and to philosophy. But that does not seem to happen. What does happen is this: the experience in the theatre is deeply moving, sometimes painfully so. And we are sufferers, yet joyful sufferers on some occasions. The experience with philosophy when it talks of living well, rarely arouses feeling at all. It remains on the level of argument, and might use as example a tragic drama or a work of art to illustrate a point. But it would not aim to arouse strong feeling. Might it be useful to philosophical argument to recommend a visit to the theatre?

Since Aristotle argued that tragedy is more philosophical than history, we might press that a bit to ask, in what does catharsis enter into one's emotional response as one is a witness to tragedy? 'Catharsis' has a root meaning of 'separating out', clarifying, keeping the worthwhile element, discarding the useless or the contaminating element. With the root meaning, 'catharsis' has many metaphoric applications, all of which are in the *Poetics* in one way and another. But most important in the extended metaphoric application of 'catharsis' is that which fits it to be both an artistic and a philosophic term. Thus we can say that in both plot and argument there is a 'catharsis' achieved through the process of separating out, and keeping some worthy part and discarding some unworthy part. In argument the process is supervised by the 'rules' of logic and rhetoric; while in the tragic drama, the process is dependent upon not just a manipulation by the dramatist, or the performance, but upon a proper response in the audience which goes along with, as an internalization of, the dramatic presentation.

To grasp the truth of tragedy the audience must have a certain set of emotional responses in a certain sequence, and those responses are stimulated by a complex set of represented events. They are: natural or physical reality; communal or political reality; and internal or psychological reality. The total presence, then, to which the audience responds can be referred to with those now commonly yoked terms, 'nature' and 'culture'.

The process of dramatic catharsis involves two processes in the representation which is the drama, with all its mythic and aesthetic references: the first is the cultural tradition that interprets nature; the second is the artistic tradition that interprets culture. Thus any individual drama, in its performance, provides two interrelated interpretative presentations to the audience, one is a deep and almost unconsciously centered way of seeing the universe; the second is a more self-conscious way of seeing other dramatic and mythic representations within the tradition of objects. The first is realized in that which philosophers in the idealistic tradition referred to as a *Weltanschauung*, however barbaric that may sound; the second is realized in the stylistic individuality of a culture whose very being is established through a tradition of cultural objects, works of art, of engineering, of dress, manners, linguistic structures, and consciousness of themselves in a tradition.

To convey such real yet hard-to-pin cultural endowments, highly charged emotional objects are brought into the performances. It is the mode of function of these objects that shall concern me in the remainder of this study.

II

By 'objects' I refer to cultural objects, and they range all the way from things such the aniconic *omphalos* at Delphi, to the heroic names that fill the tragedies, to the objects, such as a handkerchief whose presences both conjures and incites, to bodies, parts of bodies, thoughts, references to other scenes, and the stuff of making itself, which can be roughly divided among the material, the tonal, the linguistic.

By bringing objects forward and endowing them with great affective potency, the presentation to the audience focuses feeling on presences that assume metaphoric powers. The evidences I have in mind are Philoctetes' wound; Clytemnestra's body; Oedipus' name; Othello's handkerchief; the broken jug in Kleist's drama of that name; Lady Macbeth's hands; and so on. In each case the 'object' accumulates references, meanings, and calls forth interpretations, many of which are given in the dramas themselves. Tragic drama presents and interprets objects in a way very different from the treatment accorded objects in philosophical thought and writing. In tragedy, objects are dynamic, referential on all the levels I mentioned: natural, cultural, psychological, and are always objects *for me* in the sense, *for* the character, *for* the individual members of the audience, *for* the network of developing metaphoric meaning which will call for interpretation, both within the drama, and without the drama. Whatever their provenance – be they taken from nature or created by an artist working in a cultural tradition – the objects in tragic drama are *cultural objects*, that is, unrealizable and unthinkable and uninterpretable except as they relate to and are bound up with individuals who participate in the cultural tradition.

Audiences become or are disposed to be so sensitized to cultural objects that the name or term alone is sufficient to mobilize strong affect. Twice in Shakespeare's deepest tragedies the name of Nero is invoked; and both times the reverberations carry the name out into the action as both a metaphoric cluster of meanings and as an interpretative device.

Hamlet, Act III, scene ii. When Polonius tells Hamlet his mother wants to see him, Hamlet thus muses on himself:

> 'Tis now the very witching time of night ...
> 　　　　　　　　　　　 ... let not ever
> The soul of Nero enter into this firm bosom;
> Let me be cruel, not unnatural:
> I will speak daggers to her, but use none...

Lear, Act III, scene vi. Edgar appears, as a wild, mad man, to Lear.

> Nero is an angler in the lake of darkness. Pray innocent
> and beware the foul fiend.

'Nero' is spoken in order both to arouse strong feeling and to offer an interpretation of the action.[2] Hamlet obviously entertains sexual wishes towards his mother, and alerts the audience to that psychological reality; while the very name 'Nero' conveys as well a whole train of actions as possible consequences to the feelings Hamlet suffers as he goes up the staircase. We are all aware of the Nero model as an incestuous, violent ruler whose evocation startles as it reveals.

So too in *Lear*: the sudden, unexpected reference to Nero in the setting on the heath provides instant interpretation, as it were, for compacted into that name and the definite description attached to it is the whole of the Lear action. 'Nero is an angler in the lake of darkness' both identifies Lear with Nero, and gives an interpretation of Lear's search: it is both a sexual search, powerfully conveyed by the term 'angler', and a philosophical search, mysteriously conveyed by 'lake of darkness'. Here the complexity of Lear's motivation, and the deep conflicts that generate his overwhelming outbursts of passion are 'explained', that is, made clear to the audience if the compacted sense and feeling of the language are interpreted. Of course, the interpretation is not the work of a moment, but the feelings aroused are instantaneous and endow all the actions in the scene with a nimbus of affect that carries on through to the end of the play.

In contrast, emotion can be stifled, aborted, a dramatic technique that works as a complement to the use of an object as a means to focus feeling. In *Hamlet*, as Hamlet addresses the players he is overwhelmed with emotion; but as he finally attends the play, when the 'mousetrap' is sprung, he does not let the feeling overwhelm him. As the 'murder' is done on the stage, Hamlet interrupts the full force of it by saying to Ophelia:

> He poisons him i' the garden for 's estate. His name's Gonzago; the story is extant, and writ in very choice Italian. You shall see anon how the murderer gets the love of Gonzago's wife.

The audience therefore is not allowed to respond to the action as a full measure of dramatic reality, but has the building of affect diverted by the commentary, as Hamlet is using that himself to dampen his strong affect towards the action. The object in this case is the entire play within the play as a highly charged emotional object to which we respond as audience, and in so doing are directed in our feelings towards *Hamlet* itself, the proper 'object' of our experience in the theatre. We are conducted on a search for the *proper response* to the enactment by the play itself, and thus within the theatrical experience we undergo a developmental maturation in the life of feeling.

And that brings us now to the basic differences between objects philosophically considered and objects in tragedy. In the arts generally, and in tragic drama in particular, the relationship between perceiver and object is a dynamic, developmental, ever changing relationship in which both object and perceiver travel through, as it were, stages of 'growing up', of becoming mature in the cultural reality that we inhabit as communal beings. In contrast, the philosophical way of treating objects is as static, fixed, 'out-there' and always the same external realities; while the perceiver perceives from a fixed point at an unchanging time. There is no 'growing up' in modern philosophy; only being-there-forever as a perceiver stuck in time.

The reality of cultural life is much more faithfully, completely realized by tragic representations in which the maturational and developmental trajectory of feeling as it coalesces around objects is portrayed. The audience therefore undergoes a developmentally complex affective 'growing up' in the theatrical experience, and this helps us to understand the full meaning of 'catharsis', that process which lasts throughout the play – it is not confined to the end – and is the descriptive term for a clarifying of, separating out of, a getting centered upon the right emotion. There is the *right* way to feel at the action, and the well-constructed play will induce the *right* feeling at each stage of the enactment.

Tragedy has a psychological goal that ties it into cultural reality, for the growing up in culture is the central task of every member of a society, and tragedy participates in that end through its deep understanding and control over emotion. Philosophy, for its part, can at best make use of and attempt to draw tragedy into its own vision as a realization of argument, but by itself philosophy has little power to mold character, and far less influence in bringing about cultural integration.

The 'ancient enmity between poetry and philosophy' of which Plato speaks, represses the genuine and determinate and unchanging differences between poetry and philosophy by pretending that philosophy has at its disposal as many affective instruments as does poetry; it does not. And in the contest so gleefully sponsored by the dialogues, the cultural reality drops away, and is replaced by a philosophic fantasy. That is the fantasy I believe we still inhabit, we philosophers, who continue to spread over ourselves the mantle of character insight as we express in our actions childish immaturity.

I think there is a renovation of the millennial denial that has so limited philosophy with but occasional diversions, in the period we now enter, a period in which philosophy seeks counsel in allied inquiries and in affined cultural enactments. The most important of these is tragedy, and the inter-inanimation of philosophy and tragedy may yet allow philosophy to realize a full theory of the emotions. Tragedy, a cultural enactment, offers to the philosopher a range and a spectrum of objects and emotions that simply are not to be found in philosophic thinking.

The reason for this has already been stated by reference to the model of static-object-static-perceiver that has dominated Western thought. The philosopher, accused of such limitations in the conceptual model, might well reply that philosophy has no interest in the maturational trajectory of the individual, but rather deals with fully developed persons. So far as philosophy carries out its program in those confined terms, it is cut off from consideration of such things as social reality and cultural tradition, for which it must substitute the model of modern science and modern (Cartesian) philosophy.

However, there is a cultural problem for us today. Tragedy, as a cultural event, has specific locations in history that make it difficult to assimilate into our contemporary interests. We think of ourselves as inhabiting a world beyond the mythic, as dominated, especially in philosophy, by the scientific outlook of modernity, and for modern philosophy to turn to an ancient art form, however revived in more recent times, demeans philosophy, suggesting that it lacks resources of its own to cope with problems of growing up. Yet over and over again our most persuasive and important artists make the point: experience, as described by philosophy, is simply inadequate, and the full complexity of experience is given only through the arts, as we have seen in the discussion above of tragedy.

How, then, is philosophy today, in its exploration of experience, to accept and work with sources of interpretation other than the scientific? By concentrating on *objects* as I have, I think some few tentative suggestions may be made about the appropriation of tragic insights by philosophical inquiry. Tragic drama, in both its classical and in its more recent enactments, knew all along, and made manifest in its representations, much that psychoanalytic theory won through painstaking clinical study. The theory of objects that tragedy contributes to philosophy can be given a rather dry clinical description; that then ought to be followed by an example from tragedy.

The deepest conflict explored and represented in tragedy is that between private psychological need and public political obligation. Because of this deepest preoccupation, tragedy stands at the intersection of the political and the psychological, where individual instinctual actions intersect with group behavior and organization. Tragedy demonstrates the universality and inevitability of the conflict, and therefore never 'solves' the problem represented in the dramatic plots, but rather provides a deep and fully sensitive awareness of the complexity characterizing the conflict. Of course, tragedy accomplishes much more than this, but I am simplifying for the purposes of the discussion.

In order to encompass the conflict, to make it evident, available, and to pull it out of latent unconscious thought into manifest conscious thought, tragedy relies upon the representation of *objects* in their special function as both psychological and political realities to which every individual must establish a relationship in the process of growing up. Objects therefore function on both latent and manifest levels, and engage both primary process thought and secondary process thought.[3]

I have already mentioned in earlier examples some of the kinds of object representations that tragedies rely upon. Both the wide range of objects, and the establishment of intimate object relations on the part of the characters, provide the plot with essential articulations. Thus objects tie together plot, character, language, and spectacle, the essential elements of tragedy analyzed in the *Poetics*. How each character relates to the essential objects becomes a central concern for tragic knowledge, and it is here that philosophical theory can gain some complementary contributions to its own concern for objects and object relations.

Two tragic dramas provide insightful illustrations to exemplify the thesis. The first is Aeschylus' *Seven Against Thebes*, already referred to. The second is *Othello*. Both of these tragedies have received less thorough study than they deserve, and each has received excellent recent interpretations that I shall refer to in my brief closing remarks.

The long descriptive passage in *Seven* beginning with the Scout (lines 380 ff.) introduces a set of emblems and objects, functions of fighting gear and political strategies, yet closely interwoven into the psycho-sexual realities of the Oedipus story. A penetrating interpretation of the seven fighters and the seven riddles each one poses is given by Helen Bacon in her translation of the *Seven*.[4] Each fighter carries a shield, with a device painted on it. And each fighter carries an emblematic figure representing himself and the meaning of his presence, on both a latent and a manifest level. Names as well as devices are meaningful and demand interpretation. Here the whole emotional force of the play is woven before our eyes as we watch, and as we are introduced to each fighter we must interpret the objects whose complex presence relates them back to earlier events and characters, to the present action, and anticipates future outcomes.

Each object and fighter generates a riddle whose solution opens up both manifest and latent meanings; and in addition there is one great central riddle having to do with the meaning of the name Eteokles, son of Oedipus, defender of the city. Matched to Eteokles is the fighter Eteoklos, whose name so closely imitates Eteokles that we suddenly realize, as Helen Bacon states it, that he is 'the attacking double of the defender; Eteokles, by this extension, is both outside and inside the city, and therefore it is folly to fear, to observe, to take precautions chiefly against the danger of what is outside. Here is a representation of Eteokles as his own worst enemy ...' And with this 'double' we realize that a process of *splitting* has occurred, in which one object is split into its different aspects. This is a common mode of object relations, and is explored with great depth in this play.[5]

Through the objects and fighters the whole of the psycho-sexual tragedy of Oedipus from its origin through all of its stages to the present violent conclusion is slowly revealed; only we, the audience, know the truth thus represented, for the city defenders are not only driven by denial, but cannot reconstruct their own history. In that way, that which is latent in their defense of the city is manifest through the interpretation of the objects.

In representing the inner struggle between psycho-sexual need and political obligation through the relationship of persons and objects, tragedy presents – here better than does philosophy – a fuller, more adequate, epistemology and politics because it generates a theory of human action, and explains how objects work in the development of the individual – the development of growing up in the family, and the development of political life in culture.

My last example is drawn from Shakespeare's *Othello* , the object of an interpretative analysis by the psychoanalyst-critic André Green,[6] One object dominates the play, the handkerchief given Othello by his mother, and by him to Desdemona. Close reading demonstrates the psycho-sexual and political force of the object, whose 'reality' differs for each character, and whose presence, in actual display and possession, or whose absence (it is then thought about and referred to) enters into every scene, every action, and the terrifying scene of suffering at the end. Throughout the play there is an emphasis on body parts: eyes, lips, nose, head and their magnetic power to attract affect. All of these 'parts' are highly charged with feeling, and it is the handkerchief that brings the feeling out to the surface. The handkerchief, as André Green writes, poses the deepest questions of the drama: 'what do the gods say of this union between Othello and Desdemona'; and 'who guarantees the awakening of desire, and by what means?' Othello loses consciousness in an epileptic fit when he finally believes he has come to understand (mistaken though he be) the way the handkerchief enters into language and the sexual fantasies he has been unconsciously entertaining. Green interprets the handkerchief in its psycho-sexual presence: 'The attack seizes him when he has grasped the relationship of speech ("It is not words that shake me thus"), the function of the handkerchief as a link ("Pish! noses, ears,

and lips") and the dual role of the mouth as the organ of speech
and the organ of the kiss.' We the audience witness Othello's ever-
increasing preoccupation with objects as they become metaphoric
expressions of the unconscious conflicts that determine his
interpretation of character and action. He suffers from the extreme
scepticism of the child for whom the world may be, in the words
that began this reflection, 'all flashes and specks', an epistemological subjectivism generated not by an autonomous philosophic
doubt, but by the kinds of conflict that underly and lead to
philosophic doubts, because of instinctual conflicts that are
unconscious, and that tragedy is able to study, interpret, and allow
us in the audience to realize *consciously*. Tragedy makes manifest
much of philosophy's latent conflict, conflict that philosophical
argument tries to resolve, but cannot because it is not able to reach
the primary process thought that formulates the instinctual drives
upon which the secondary process thought of philosophy is
superimposed.

Here, in the two tragedies so briefly regarded, are interpretations
of objects and their function in psycho-sexual-political conflicts that
fill out and complete the rigid and limited philosophical entertain-
ment of the political of life. In calling for the reliance upon tragic
dramas in philosophy's coming to understand action and character,
an exchange must not be neglected: philosophy has its own mode
of interpretation to give to our understanding of tragedy. And the
most enduring philosophical thinkers have always denied, *in
practice*, as did Plato himself, that there could be an ancient enmity
between poetry and philosophy. Let our philosophical practice
today continue that alliance and affinity, so recently lost, so deeply
a part of our tradition.

Notes

1. My contribution to the views of Plato and Aristotle on these questions
    was made in *The House, The City, and The Judge. The Growth of Moral
    Awareness in the Oresteia*. (Indianapolis: *Bobbs Merrill*, 1963).
2. It is worth noting as a bit of cultural history that Nero was the
    Elizabethan model and standard for the incestuous character with
    designs on his mother, while in our own era, the character who suc-
    ceeds in that role is Oedipus. A whole interpretative story of cultural
    relativity and constancy could be generated out of that succession.
3. For a full discussion of objects in art, see my *Psychoanalytic Theory of
    Art*. (New York: Columbia University Press, 1983).

4.   Aeschylus, *Seven Against Thebes*, Trans. by Anthony Hecht and Helen Bacon. (New York: Oxford University Press, 1973). Introduction and notes by Helen Bacon.

5.   For a discussion of splitting, see Freud, *An Outline of Psychoanalysis*; 'Splitting of the Ego in the Process of Defense'. Standard edn, vol. XIII, pp. 2O5–7; 271–8.

6.   '*Othello*: A Tragedy of Conversion: Black Magic and White Magic', in *The Tragic Effect, The Oedipus Complex in Tragedy*. André Green. (London: Cambridge University Press, 1979). Translated by Alan Sheridan.

7.   Ibid., p. 126.

5
The Role of Philosophy in the Development of Tragic Drama

E.F. KAELIN

I

Originally a celebration of the mysteries of the Dionysiac cult, tragedy developed into another artform in which the human predicament was represented as exhibiting the moral values of character and action. Such artistic representations were susceptible of generating a response in an audience made up of sensitized human beings who were capable of understanding the necessity of suffering the consequences for one's own personal actions. That the Greek gods had ordained such retribution for the mere act of being human seemed only to harden the force of the necessity. Any excess here, any expression of human *hybris,* was visited with swift and painful destruction. That a sympathetic audience could find such spectacles uplifting needed further explanation. How did the act of contemplating human suffering end in determining a positive response in the dramatic audiences? Answer that question and you will have described the phenomenon of tragic art. How, indeed, does tragedy induce us to transevaluate the apparently negative values of pain and suffering?

There have been three distinctive answers to this question: the earliest, by Aristotle;[1] and two more in the 'modern' age of our Western culture. The first of these is by Friedrich Schiller in the eighteenth century,[2] and the second by Friedrich Nietzsche, in the nineteenth.[3]

In his answer, Aristotle argued that the effect of the tragic representation was the catharsis of the original feelings of pity and fear,[4] and contemporary Aristotelians continue to repeat the argument, even when they disagree concerning the mechanism of the catharsis or even concerning what it is that eventually is purged in

86

the minds of an attentive audience.[5] One recent aesthetician has even argued for three different interpretations of the Aristotelian catharsis in three differing moments of his career.[6]

But if talk of a catharsis of feeling has become otiose in our own time, the reason would seem to be the fact that there is no essence of tragedy, neither in its representation of the conflicts in the lives of good or evil men, nor in its purgation of the feelings or ideas aroused by witnessing such events. At certain stages of its history, tragedies have functioned in different ways: as religious celebrations, as representations of mythical truths, or of moral ideas, and as creations of new myths; but whichever of these functions has dominated at a particular time, they all have served by being tied to the artistic institutions of a given society. For without such a tie, without forming a significant part of a work of art, the end effect of which was the creation of a positive value, there was no understanding how contemplating pain could culminate in a pleasure – should one be charitable enough to assume that dramatic audiences have never been either sadistic or masochistic in temperament, nor even, at their worst, the slightest bit sadomasochistic. The phenomenon of tragedy is one thing; it cannot be found outside the realm of art; and its theoretical explanation is quite something else, whether that explanation be cast in terms of the purgation of feeling (Aristotle), the representation of sublime human being governed by freedom rather than by necessity (Schiller), or by the assimilation of pain as a catalyzing, Dionysiac, element in the intensification of our sense of life (Nietzsche).

Aristotle's account is 'naturalistic'; Schiller's, 'idealistic'; and Nietzsche's 'romantic'. Considering the differences in these accounts of the tragic experience may help one appreciate just what the phenomenon itself has been in the various periods of interpretation.

Aristotle had already informed us that Aeschylus enlarged the number of characters in the plays from one to two. Sophocles introduced a third, the better to complicate the dimensions of the dramatic intrigue, to strengthen the tensions of the expressive power inherent in the medium. And Euripides, enamored of feminine psychology if not of women, introduced an element of realism unknown in the medium before. They all used myth to structure the events of their representational worlds. And where the effects of representing the negative values of human life are perceived to constitute a positive value in the life of the persons having an aesthetic experience governed by such representations, the mystery as well as the challenge of tragedy was to officiate this transmutation of the negative into a positive value. I shall refer to this phenomenon as 'the tragic lift'.[7]

Can the tragic lift we experience in contemplating the evil of human suffering be given a rational, naturalistic explanation? Is it because our god has suffered, as Nietzsche claimed? Or because the effect of art is to intensify our feeling of being alive, as Nietzsche and most other romantic theorists maintained? Or, because that feeling is all the more intense the more it is threatened to be extinguished, even if only within the bounds of imagination, as Schiller maintained?

Surely an interpreter of this and associated phenomena will be excused the impertinence of explaining the historical changes in the medium from the earlier satyr plays staged in honor of Dionysus and the later dramas of Aeschylus, Sophocles and Euripides – on the grounds that the second represents a positive development within the institutions of art. That Aristotle thought this assessment of the situation to be true, while Nietzsche denied it, is of no impelling significance here. What is not so clear, and what does suggest some import for further investigation is why the ancient Greeks, of whichever epoch, excelled in the art to a degree unsurpassed since.[8] But if that contention is true, the clue for an understanding of the reason may be found in the worldviews of the different cultural moments – as long as we take the precaution of examining just how such worldviews are expressed in a specific dramatic context.

Therefore, it seems natural to speculate that an age's commitment to the dominance of one artform over another depends upon the importance of the worldview expressed in those artforms, as upon that expressed in any given state of our culture. As the old saying goes, a culture is expressed in its artworks, and philosophy, whether it be predominantly metaphysical or moral, is a part of a culture's definition. When the naturalism of the early Greeks became supplanted by the supernaturalism of the Christian era, for example, the necessary and probable events of a tragic plot could only be interpreted in a different light. In effect, it could be argued that the daily Mass of the devout Christian replaced the Dionysiac revels: the God is still represented as having suffered, but that suffering was for the good of mankind.

Ironically, the sacrifice of Jesus, in taking away the responsibility for personal atonement, also took away any tragic significance in the fact of sin (or crime) and its punishment: it was no longer fashionable to suffer the condition of being human; suffering itself was a physiologically determined event, not the badge of our courage in accepting the conditions of life. He who has been born again may have been saved, but in the process has lost any claim to moral dignity. In the Christian worldview there is only one tragic hero, and that is Lucifer himself. Faust is only that one's plaything.

I shall argue below that as the myths of an earlier cultural stage give form to later representations of the human predicament, and so become reinterpreted in these later expressions, this process of embodying, and surpassing, the myths of our culture is continuous. As the Attic tragedians interpreted human suffering as transcending the Dionysiac celebrations of an earlier culture, the significances embodied in their own plays may be changed when they are filtered through succeeding levels of philosophical interpretation. But in measuring out these differences we must attend to the poetic techniques of the dramatists as they work upon the preconstituted meanings of their culture.

II

Where the ancient myths provided some kind of explanation for the existence of the evil we experience in some forms of suffering and death, it is not the office of art to offer explanations for natural or moral phenomena. The ancient artists merely used pre-existent myths – even those expressed in another artform, such as the epic poems of Homer, or in another institution such as the ambient religious culture – to structure the events of their stories, presumably because one way of accentuating the positive in their art was to begin by displaying the negative characteristics of human life already expressed in the available myths. And they were equally convinced that the only way to achieve the positive response they desired was by the artistic control they could display over their medium. Whence, the notion that art may actually deliver us from evil. The three explanations of 'the tragic response' given in the aesthetic theories of Aristotle, Schiller, and Nietzsche all make this same claim.

But, rather than seeking a theoretical explanation of the tragic response, as aestheticians of every stripe have traditionally done, we may find it more profitable to consider an example of one myth, and to trace its transformation of significance through successive re-interpretations. For this purpose, I have chosen the myth of the curse upon the house of Atreus, as it is used by the three principle Attic tragedians, and as it is reinterpreted by Jean-Paul Sartre in *The Flies*.

To shorten the myth we need only hold on to the immediate facts of the story: Orestes and Electra kill their mother, who killed their father, who killed her daughter for a favourable wind to launch the siege of Troy.

III

The Oresteia myth was presented by Aeschylus as a trilogy of dramatic representations including the *Agamemnon*, *The Libation Bearers*, and *The Eumenides*.[9] The first play presents the action as set in Argos (Mycenae) immediately after the Trojan War. Clytemnestra welcomes her returning husband, feigning to do so with pleasure, along with his living booty, the Trojan princess Cassandra. She invites them into the castle, and kills them both forthwith.

Agamemnon's murder is no surprise: he had sacrificed his and Clytemnestra's daughter, Iphigeneia, to placate Artemis, offended by his having wounded a sacred stag, to allow the Greeks to leave Calchis for the invasion of Troy. If this personal vengeance on her husband were not enough, there was the affront of Cassandra, and the jealousy she provoked. In addition, Clytemnestra had already become the paramour of Aegisthus, Agamemnon's cousin, who had waited out the war. Once the deed was done, Clytemnestra explains her action as avenging Atreus' crime upon his brother, Thyestes, Aegistus' father, Agamemnon's uncle. That crime, we recall, was the murder of the brother's children and the banquet where they were served to their unsuspecting father as food. Thyestes' provocation was the seduction of Atreus' wife Aethra, an action repeated in the relationship between Aegisthus and Agamemnon. The audience has been forewarned: like crime will produce like punishment. Aegisthus will die for his crime, and along with him, Clytemnestra, for hers. The *Agamemnon* closes with Clytemnestra urging her lover to quit the violence: they have the power of state.

But human law us not the only determinant of the tragic bind. Zeus' power, as king of the gods, ordains justice in the affairs of men. Zeus, of course, was the reputed father of Clytemnestra and Helen, out of Leda. Apollo, his son, had had a similar unfortunate relationship with Cassandra. He had given her the gift of prophecy, out of his infatuation with her; but she refused him the son he so desired. In vengeance for her refusal, he placed a curse upon her, making it impossible for her prophecies to be accepted as true. It was for this reason that her prophetic description of the fall of Troy was refused by the Trojans.

Within the subplot of Aeschylus' *Oresteia*, Apollo is the tragic hero. His fault: the infatuation with a mere mortal; his crime: the word of his oracle to Orestes to avenge his father's murder by murdering his mother and her lover. His punishment: himself not to be believed as bearing the truth of Zeus' will on the affairs of human contrivance. More on this subplot in the denouement of Aeschylus' trilogy.

The Libation Bearers opens at the tomb of Agamemnon, with the returning Orestes placing a lock of his hair on the tomb. He and his friend Pylades, are returning from Phocis, where Orestes had been spirited after Agamemnon's murder to protect him from the customary family retribution. Electra discovers the lock of hair, and Orestes' footprints – both of which match her own, a fact to be later satirized in Euripides' *Electra*. At her discovery of Orestes' presence in Argos, she proclaims that by 'force, right, and Zeus almighty' Clytemnestra and her lover are to die. And the chorus agrees with her judgment.

But the prey is weak. Clytemnestra had just had a dream of having given birth to a snake, and fearing some evil omen, sent offerings to Agamemnon's tomb. Orestes, apprised of this fact, decides to become the snake of his mother's dream. He and Pylades plot her murder, by stealth, entering the palace as visiting foreigners with news of Orestes' death. Again the chorus agrees that the decision is right. Aegisthus is killed first, and Clytemnestra thereafter. Orestes proclaims the rightness of his action, and manfully awaits the reprisal of the Furies, always unleashed by Zeus at the willful spilling of human blood. But was the action right? And if it were, why would the Furies demand their due?

The Eumenides answers both these questions. But to do so, the overt, principal plot of human crime and punishment must recede into the background, while the subplot of Phoebus-Apollo's crime and punishment comes to the fore. The first scene is laid in the sanctuary of the Pythian Apollo, where Orestes had taken refuge in his flight from the Furies. Apollo puts them to sleep until the ghost of Clytemnestra appears to remind them of their duty. As they awake the scene changes to the temple of Pallas-Athene, where, on Ares' hill, Orestes' murders are to be judged. Athene herself serves as judge, Apollo, as character-witness for Orestes. Athene promises to break any tie in favour of the defendant, even before the votes are counted. Apollo cites his advice to Orestes as a mitigating circumstance to the crime, but even then cannot gain a clear victory for his protégé. In the judgment of men, his decision is not to be accepted – the same curse he had visited upon his dead, beloved Cassandra.

That Athene should support Orestes' case is not a divine vote in favor of Apollo's credibility; for she votes as she does to make it clear that questions of guilt or innocence must be determined by human decision, with the presumption of innocence where no clear majority of opinion exists to the contrary. Euripides has Athene make the same revelation in his *Iphigenia in Tauris*.[10] The law of the talon was to be broken by the law of the land; the law of nature by constitutional law. Orestes is freed from the Furies by Athene's support for human law.

Yet she has to use all her persuasive powers – and she is the goddess of wisdom – to persuade the Furies to relent, and to accept her designation as goddesses – older than herself – in service of the Earth. Promised no diminution in their divine powers, and, incidentally, in their respect from humankind, the Erinyes take up residence under the earth as the Eumenides. In this way, laying myth upon myth, Aeschylus explains how the humanly malevolent goddesses were transformed into those benevolent agencies working in service of earthly replenishment and growth.

Human tragedy is avoided at the end of this trilogy in that Orestes is saved from the reprisal of the Furies, but only with the reversal of plot and subplot. Apollo's reversal of fortune is complete, his word discredited before the human court. This reversal of plot and subplot, of human and divine heroes, is no more than an advertisement for the tragic circumstances to begin with: human beings find themselves in the conflict between human and divine law, and the law of nature exacts that they suffer for making the wrong choice. Such is the philosophy that Aeschylus wrenched from the myth of the house of Atreus. But we can know of it only in tracing out the patterns of the events related in the tragic plot.

Sophocles' *Electra* is a tighter narration of Clytemnestra's murder.[11] The play opens following the death of Agamemnon, at the court of Clytemnestra and Aegisthus, where Electra and her sister Chrysothemis have taken opposed attitudes to their situations. Electra, mourning her father, prays for the arrival of Orestes to perform the act of vengeance. Chrysothemis, more pragmatic, is reconciled to the earthly power of the tyrants. She is sent by her mother to bear offerings to her father's tomb, but is persuaded by Electra to replace their mother's gifts with some of their own: each leaving a lock of her hair, and Electra, her belt.

As Chrysothemis takes the gifts to the tomb, Clytemnestra comes out of the palace and is confronted by Electra. The mother claims her murder of Agamemnon was justified, owing to his having murdered their daughter – he was killed for his own murder; Electra responds that it was unseemly for her mother to marry one of her enemies, even if it were for the sake of a murdered daughter. Orestes' tutor enters and falsely announces Orestes' death, suffered during an accident at a chariot race. Electra is defeated; Clytemnestra, truly ambivalent, sorry to hear of her son's death, but relieved that he can no longer take out his revenge upon her.

But Chrysothemis returns from the tomb with news that Orestes is alive. She found his flowers, and traces of his libations at their father's grave, along with the customary lock of hair. After begging for Chrysothemis' help in a plot to undo her mother and stepfather, Electra learns of another conception of justice: the laws of the state whose rightness does not depend upon the morality of its administrators and whose imperium over its citizens supersedes the vengeful law of natural retribution that may be felt by an angry citizen. The two girls cannot agree where their allegiance should lie. And Electra loses the natural attachment to her sister.

The foreboding evil is brought to a head when Orestes appears with an urn full of ashes claimed to be his own. Electra is further crushed by the deception, until, after one of the longest scenes of discovery in ancient drama, Orestes admits his identity. His pedagogue enters to inform them that Clytemnestra is alone, preparing the ashes for burial. Orestes strikes her down, and covers her body with a cloth. As he enters, Aegisthus is led to the same spot where Agamemnon was killed, and is slain there by Orestes, who ends by proclaiming:

Justice shall be taken directly upon all who act above the law –
justice by killing. So we would have less villains.[12]

So wrapped up in the rightness of his action, he fails to recognize
that his words apply to his own deed – or could be interpreted to
be so, had not the audience been assured by the Chorus that justice
had been done:

O race of Atreus, how many sufferings were yours before you
came at last so hardly to freedom, perfected by this day's deed.[13]

But this Chorus does little more than to highlight one of the
claims made for justice: the appeal made to the 'natural' law of
vengeance for the death of one's kin, in effect Electra's appeal. The
claims made for the opposing appeal, that of Chrysothemis, having
been ignored since its last airing, leaves the philosophical matter
unsettled. Yet, the necessary commitment to an act – Electra's and
Orestes' – to which they are pushed by the admonition of Orestes'
tutor, becomes essentially tragic as the consequences of such action
puts them in jeopardy of acting unjustly. The relation of men and
women to the binding power of their laws, both human and divine,
has taken on a newer significance, not so easily to be explained by
the institution of courts and trials by jury.

Sophocles said what Jean-Paul Sartre would later say more
clearly – that being a self is a value to be won by a personal
decision to act in spite of the circumstances that would defeat the
enterprise. The bind is felt by the 'tragic' personality, and the
solution to the tragedy is the decision to act. Or, as Sophocles'
Chorus has already informed us: freedom is won at the price of an
act. In this scheme, the morality of the situation takes the
subordinate role to the dominant role of metaphysics; and as in
Aeschylus' trilogy, where plot and subplot are reversed as the
image and ground of an optical illusion, here morality and
metaphysics change relative positions in the determination of the
tragic situation. Electra is too weak to define herself in action;
Orestes is forced to perform her deed. Whichever view of earthly
justice prevails, Electra cannot succeed in determining the
conditions of her own existence, as Chrysothemis had forewarned.
Her tragedy is to have her brother act in her name, with the
ambiguity of the morality of the act, its justice, left undetermined in
the context of the play's represented action.

Euripides' concern for the fate of the house of Atreus expressed itself a number of times: twice with an account of Iphigenia (at Tauris and at Aulis), once with Helen, and once each with Orestes and Electra. For sheer dramatic inventiveness, i.e. for his ingenuity in discovering a means for presenting or for varying the details of the original myth, Euripides has had no equal. I have chosen his *Electra* [14] as continuing the investigation begun with Aeschylus' *The Libation Bearers* and continued in Sophocles' *Electra*. What was for Aeschylus a drama of personal revenge in a world governed by universal law, whether human or divine, became in Sophocles a drama of personal self-determination in the face of the moral forces opposed to such a phenomenon. Finally, in Euripides, Electra's tragedy becomes the drama of the psychological person internalizing the conflicting demands of personal revenge and universal justice against the realistic self appraisal as a woman with uniquely womanly needs.

As the play opens we discover Electra, after the slaying of her father, married to an old farmer who protects her in a condition of honorable poverty, while 'respecting' her virginity out of the recognition of their difference in civil station. Orestes and Pylades show up, looking for her. They find her expressing desires for vengeance – and, behold – jealousy of her mother, fulfilled in love. The Old Man, who had raised Orestes after the murder of his father, recognizes him by a youthful wound suffered in play – the occasion which allows Euripides to mock Aeschylus' use of the hair-lock and footprint resemblances of Orestes and Electra to permit the discovery of Orestes' identity. As he does identify him, the Old Man advises Orestes to kill his father's murderers. And, the deed is done, while Aegisthus prepares a sacrifice of an ox in a religious ceremony in honor of some nymphs.

This reference to the sex of the goddesses is not completely fortuitous, since sex hangs over this tragedy with the force of a Jovian thunderbolt, such as the one which, from a swan's thighs, laid Leda low. Not only has Electra been imprisoned in a sexless marriage, when Orestes first meets her, she reacts to his touch with the outraged decency that is identical to sexual frustration: 'Get out; don't touch. You have no right to touch my body.'[15]

Not knowing that he was her brother, she could not understand his impulse for bodily contact. She has been too self-consumed with the images she has conjured of her mother in Aegisthus' bed. And when Orestes kills Aegisthus, Electra berates the corpse with her sexual ambivalence, praying for a mate with something more than looks to recommend himself to her approval. A mighty warrior, at least, as Aegisthus was not.

At the sight of his mother, following his murder of Aegisthus, Orestes loses his courage – the theme of Euripides' *Orestes*,[16] where the effect of the Furies is depicted as the remorse of a bad conscience. The confrontation with Clytemnestra – the obligatory scene – is left to Electra, who hears her mother admit that 'Women are fools for sex.'[17] After all, Leda was her mother.

Electra had objected that the killing of her father was not for the sake of justice, as maintained by Clytemnestra, but a terrible deed performed against God and love alike. But when Clytemnestra is slain, after having been tricked to make her appearance at the Old Farmer's hovel to assist Electra after a falsely announced birthing, Electra reciprocates her mother's considerate reaction to the news of a new grandchild with an equally human reaction of remorse for her mother's death.

Granted Clytemnestra could be suspected of desiring to identify the child who might later want to murder her in vengeance for her own murder, just as Electra's natural moment of conscious remorse could have been for herself rather than for her mother: she admits as much, as she expresses the thought. Who would want to marry her now, an unnatural matricide? What man take her as bride to his bed? As for Orestes, he is incapacitated for further action, consumed in his own remorse. Asked by Orestes to cover their mother's body, Electra sums up her psychological plight:

> Behold! I wrap her close in the robe, the one I loved and could not love.[18]

And the Chorus comments, as in Sophocles, 'Ending your family's great disasters'.

To get himself out of the dramatic impasse, however, Euripides makes final appeal to a *deus ex machina*, in effect, to two gods at once. Castor and Pollux, the Dioscuri, born of Zeus out of Leda, twins from a single egg, call down to Orestes. Justice, they say, claimed their sister, Clytemnestra; but *his* act was not just: he killed his mother, an unjust and quite unnatural act. Apollo knew the truth of the matter, but his oracle had lied. How then were the claims of justice to be fulfilled?

In answer the Dioscuri decree:

— that Electra be given as wife to Pylades, who shall lead her away to a life in Phocis;
— that Orestes go to Athens, to be judged on the Hill of Ares, and to be acquitted by a jury's split decision;
— that the Furies lose their fury, to be changed from the avenging Erinyes to the benevolent Eumenides;
— that the Argives bury Aegisthus' body in a secret and concealed spot;
— that Menelaus and Helen bury Clytemnestra's body.

Helen, in this decision, was disculpated from involvement in the Trojan War, since she did not go to Troy, but only her Zeus-made image, carried there in her stead, so that men might 'die in hate and blood'.

For its part, the Chorus asks forgiveness, and receives it; as does Electra: only the falseness of Apollo's oracle is to blame for Clytemnestra's death. And for her punishment, Electra receives nothing more serious than exile from Argos, and separation from the physical presence of her brother Orestes. And so Electra and Orestes are freed from their tragic situation by divine intervention in the determination of their fates.

Euripides 'psychological' interpretation of Electra's ambivalence towards her mother and of Orestes' moral inanition in the face of guilt are natural enough explanations of their behavior. But the philosophical resolution of the painful incidents of a tragic action that depends upon the will of the gods will seem unsatifactory to a contemporary humanistic audience. How a tragic circumstance will become somehow less painful to us with the supposition that this suffering has been ordained by a divine power is hardly comprehensible.

Moreover, all three of the Attic tragedians whose works are still extant have considerably hedged their bets. Aeschylus and Euripides have one divine form testify against another: Athene vs. Apollo and the Dioscuri vs. Apollo; and Sophocles makes the tragic situation depend upon the necessity of acting in ignorance of the reassuring circumstances of moral certainty.

IV

If it is fair to describe Aeschylus' treatment as moral or ethical, Sophocles' as metaphysical, and Euripides' as psychological, each aiming at a tragic effect through the emphasis of a different aspect of the original mythical situation, there should be as many manifestations of the tragic 'essence' as there are ways to modify the dramatic representations of the original myth. My last example, *The Flies*, of Jean-Paul Sartre,[19] will show how the original philosophical idea of the myth – retributive justice in crime and its punishment – alters its significance depending upon the change of dramatic techniques for representing the characters of the original myth.

Characteristic of Sartre's handling of the theme is the reversal of the original myth's significance in a single developing dramatic sequence of represented events. The phenomenon is similar to the depth expression of a philosophical idea, in which the idea – whether metaphysical or moral – serves as the deep structure underlying the narration of first order, surface, events.

On the surface of the representation, the basic myth of the curse on the house of Atreus undergoes a transformation that owes something to all three Attic tragedians: to Aeschylus the intermingling of plot and subplot; to Sophocles, the definition of the dramatic conflict in ontological terms as the necessity of action for the self-determination of character; and to Euripides, for the 'naturalization' of the punishment by the Erinyes as the remorse for one's guilty acts.

What is new in Sartre's treatment of the myth is its transformation from the naturalism of the Greeks to the existentialism of his own philosophical orientation.

Following the dramatic action of the 'classical' three act drama, the spectator is led through a rising action to the murder of Clytemnestra and Aegisthus by Orestes in Act II, scene ii, and his Electra's flight into the sanctuary of the shrine of Apollo. At this stage – the highest point of the developing classical myth – the action falls into a resolution of the conflict between competing myths with the final obligatory scene in which Orestes confirms his tragic character by assuming the responsibility for the murders that Electra had already repudiated. If my reading is justified by the text, then the reversal of fortune undergone throughout the dramatic action is not that of a single character: neither Electra who is defeated out of her own moral weakness, nor Orestes, who triumphs over the moral dilemmas surrounding his action by the willful act of accepting the responsibility for having done so; but the original myth itself, being relegated to the background of the replacement myth which arises to take its place. We shall discover, within the structure of this play, the same sort of transevaluation of values already found in Aeschylus' reversal of plot and subplot in the three plays of his *Oresteia*.

As always in deep, phenomenological, readings, the narration of the surface events of the drama cannot be ignored.

Act I opens with a depiction of life in Argos following the murder of Agamemnon by Clytemnestra and Aegisthus fifteen years earlier. Since that time, the people have developed a morbid self-indulgence of their own remorse, made palpably effective by the mordant presence of the flies. Once a year, on a day to honor the dead and Zeus, their patron, a ceremony takes place in which a great stone is rolled back to allow the dead egress from Hades. Orestes and his tutor (a philosopher with a humanistic bent) appear, to witness the curious religious ceremony. Zeus appears in *propria persona* tracking the progress of Orestes. Only two individuals escape the otherwise universal self-indulgence in remorse: Aegisthus for whom the murder of Agamemnon was just, considering the treatment of his father Thyestes by his uncle Agamemnon; and Electra, whose guiding passion is the mourning of her father and the longing of his death to be avenged. Even Clytemnestra engages in the popular sport of confessing her crimes in public.

Act II is in two scenes. In the first, Electra refuses to don black for her part in the rites of the dead; instead, she appears in her finest white costume, exhorting the public to refrain from participating in the rites. Only the miraculous action of Zeus prevents her success in separating the populace from the conspiracy of state and religion to enslave them into the role of repentant sinners. The almost litanic refrain of the men, 'Forgive us for living while you are dead', is broken into by Electra's appearance in white; she even dances to show her disdain for the dead of the others: her dead are her sister Iphigenia and her father Agamemnon. After Zeus' miracle restores the normal order of the place, Orestes reveals himself to his sister, and they plot the murder of their mother and her lover.

In the second scene of Act II, Zeus conspires with Aegisthus (religion with the state) to prevent the latter's murder. While the two discuss their respective responsibilities as spiritual and temporal leaders of the people of Argos, Zeus warns Aegisthus that Orestes knows that he is free and that under the circumstance the gods can do nothing against him. Justice, says Orestes, is the affair of men, not of the gods. As Zeus cannot strike Orestes with a thunderbolt, Aegisthus cannot defend himself against Orestes' attack, as he is fascinated by the prospect of witnessing a guilty act for which there would be no remorse. Following Clytemnestra's murder, brother and sister flee into a sanctuary to protect themselves from the attacks of the avenging flies.

Act III opens within the sanctuary of Apollo's temple, where Electra finally succumbs to Zeus' admonitions for her to repent. Overcome with the natural feelings of remorse for the murders, prompted by the attacks of the Furies and the flies, she is vanquished when she accepts repentance as the way out of her guilty conscience. Zeus and Orestes contend for the allegiance of the suffering girl, and Orestes loses her to her act of repentance. Alone, against the king of the gods, without seeking his succor to avoid the stings of the flies, he leaves the sanctuary, drawing the flies after him and away from the people of Argos.

Revisiting these events displays the following pattern with the intertwined myths of divine justice – in this play supported by the justice of the state – and of human freedom. At the beginning of the play, where the first myth dominates, the flies and the Furies are natural and supernatural symbols for human remorse; the tragedy is the necessity of acting either for justice and against oneself or for oneself and against justice; the hero is Orestes, the expected avenger of his father's death; and, his freedom, to act in accordance with necessity.

Each of these significances changes, however, at the height of the rising action. Once the murders have been committed, the original values have been transevaluated. The replacing myth is that of freedom through transcendence. The flies and Furies lose their sting as the hero refuses to feel remorse; the tragedy becomes the necessity of acting not with or for a certain motive, but in spite of any external claim that would set a standard for judging the act in question. Orestes, in the second myth that comes to replace the first, achieves this reversal of values only by his decision to assume personal responsibility for his act; he does not avenge his father, but frees his father's subjects from their repentance for their part in his father's murder. And, lastly, Orestes' freedom is measured by the self-determining action to transcend the limitations of naturalistic or spiritualistic determination.

His reward? Existential solitude.

What new philosophy have we here? Not the obvious statement of an existentialist's worldview, but rather a still more basic claim which may be made clearer still by descending one more level into the depth of Sartre's dramatic representation.

The first level, we recall, was constituted by the events in the lives of the characters that presented a picture of the original myth of the doomed house of Atreus. That myth was covered over by the naturalistic philosophical biases of the earlier tragedians, each of whom embodied the myth in a different manner, to express his own philosophy. In those philosophies, we found the third level of depth, just below that of the myth itself, which was already an account of a well-known moral phenomenon. The fourth level is the transformation of the naturalized myth into the existentialized myth of Sartre himself. And, in the transevaluation of the former by the latter, we were led in the end to discover a 'truth' facing all valuing individuals: that any existing value thought to be determinant of human behavior can be so only if the acting individual wills it to be so, and that when this happens the value is no longer customary, or socially sanctioned, or even institutionalized, as it would have been made personal by choice, and realized in an action for which one has assumed the responsibility.

More important than the substance of philosophical idea, however, is the indirect manner of its expression – an idea already familiar within existentialist aesthetics as *le langage indirect* to which Merleau-Ponty compared the 'voices of silence'.[20] For us, who have worked within the movement, it matters little whether we refer to the 'obliquity' of metaphorical expression or to a philosophical idea as giving form to a dramatic work of art.

Expressed in a literary work of art, a philosophical idea lends its structure to the events of the literary narrative. That this process should be so complicated in the case of Sartre's *The Flies* is perhaps explained by the length of the dramatic tradition and the number of accumulated versions of the original myth that must be read under before discovering that level of depth in which the original narrative finally comes to rest.

V

Sartre's *The Flies* not only illustrates the thesis of the indirect expression of a philosophical idea; the philosophical idea it expresses is doubly Nietzschean: the reversal of the mythical significance that constitutes the single developing dramatic episode of the play – of the subplot underlying the obvious plot of the first-order events presented in the dramatic representation – is itself an instance of the transevaluation of values, which, if Nietzsche is right, constitutes one determinant of the tragic experience. And the effect of viewing this higher-level 'reversal of fortune' allows one, in the second instance, to participate in the joy of creating the newer, replacement value.

In this way, it might be argued that an exegete can avoid the Socratism Nietzsche so deplored in the Attic tragedians (Euripides only being the worst) without appealing to the structures of another artistic medium for an explanation of the tragic effect, which still seems to me to lie somewhere between the Nietzschean and the Schillerian accounts of the phenomenon – between the celebration of life-sustaining force on the one hand and, on the other, being transported beyond nature into the realm of the sublime.

And where, pray tell, is this to be found?

Within an experience of the plays themselves, when we leave ourselves open to the tensions of their texts. Surely it is there, rather than in anyone's aesthetic theory, that the phenomenon appears in its clearest manifestation.

Notes

1. Aristotle, *De Poetica*, trans. by Ingram Bywater, in *Introduction to Aristotle*, ed. Richard McKeon (New York: Modern Library, 1974), pp. 622–67.
2. Friedrich von Schiller, 'On Tragic Art', *Aesthetical and Philosophical Essays*, no trans., Nathan H. Dole, ed. (Boston: Aldine Publishing, 1896), vol. II, pp. 61–85.
3. Friedrich Nietzsche, *The Birth of Tragedy from the Spirit of Music*, trans. Clifton Fadiman, in *The Philosophy of Nietzsche* (New York: Modern Library, n.d.), sec. 1.
4. Aristotle, *De Poetica*, 1449 b.
5. See the translation by Leon Golden, *Aristotle's Poetics* (Englewood

Cliffs, NJ: Prentice-Hall, 1968), where the standard pagination is maintained.

6. See Paul Ricoeur, *La Symbolique du mal*, (Paris: Aubier, 1960), 216–17; *De L'interprétation: essai sur Freud* (Paris: Editions du Seuil, 1966), p. 328; and, finally, citing Professor Golden's translation of *The Poetics*, *La Métaphore vive* (Paris: Editions du Seuil, 1975), p. 57ff.

7. Borrowing from Prosser Hall Frye's 'tragic qualm'; see his *Romance and Tragedy* (Boston: Marshall Jones, 1922). For some paradoxical reason, tragedy does not depress its audience; it uplifts. The phenomenon seems secure; only its explanation is in dispute.

8. This assessment is offered by Stith Thomson and John Gassner, eds, *Our Heritage of World Literature*, revised edn (New York: Dryden Press, 1946), p. 135.

9. See Aeschylus, *Oresteia*, tr. by Richmond Lattimore in Aeschylus I (Chicago: University of Chicago Press, 1953).

10. *Iphigenia in Tauris*, trans. by Witter Bynner, in *Euripides II* (Chicago: University of Chicago Press, 1952, 1956), p. 186.

11. Sophocles, *Electra*, trans. David Grene, in *Sophocles II*, ed. David Grene and Richard Lattimore (Chicago: University of Chicago Press, 1957).

12. Ibid., p. 187.

13. Ibid.

14. Euripides, *Electra*, trans. Emily Townsend Vermeule, in *Euripides V* (Chicago: University of Chicago Press, 1959).

15. Ibid., p. 16.

16. In *Euripides IV*, trans. by William Arrowsmith (Chicago: University of Chicago Press, 1958).

17. Ibid., p. 53.

18. Ibid., p. 61.

19. Jean-Paul Sartre, *The Flies*, in *No Exit and Three Other Plays*, no trans. (New York: Vintage Books, 1958), pp. 49–127.

20. See Maurice Merleau-Ponty, 'Le langage indirect et les voix du silence', *Les Temps Modernes*, VII (June 1952), 2113–44; VII (July 1952), 70–94.

6
Tragic Action

N. GEORGOPOULOS

Whether or not it is true, as many believe, that the *Poetics* was Aristotle's answer to Plato's criticism of tragedy, it is indisputably true that the *Poetics* laid the groundwork for all subsequent discussion on tragedy. And this because Aristotle's was the first attempt to treat tragedy in its own terms. With a few bold and characteristic taxonomic strokes, he separated tragedy from the theoretical and the practical. As a *poietic* enterprise, tragedy was further distinguished from the rest on the basis of the nature of its imitation. Focusing on its distinct kind of imitation, Aristotle organized his discussion in terms of the six elements he discerned as constituting tragedy.[1] He expanded his discussion by making further delineations within these elements.

One may disagree with Aristotle that tragedy has six and only six parts. One may further disagree with the specific distinctions he made within these parts. However, one has to agree that these parts are constitutive of tragedy. By viewing tragedy in terms of its structural elements and by defining it in terms of action,[2] Aristotle was the first to attempt to treat tragedy as art.[3]

There are those who find Aristotle's approach too formalistic. Herbert Muller, for example, complained that 'Aristotle's concentration on a formal aesthetic analysis is so surprising that we forget his rather strange neglect of the philosophical and religious implications of tragedy'.[4] Walter Kaufmann's *Tragedy and Philosophy* intends to take care of this neglect. If the *Poetics* was concerned with 'form' alone, his own 'New Poetics' explores 'the historical dimension', the poem's relation to the poet and his times, and, above all, 'the philosophical dimension'. By the latter he has in mind 'the poet's thought which can be different from all the ideas of his characters' or the meaning in the tragic poem.[5] Thus, while he insists on calling the tragedies he examines 'works of art', he finds their significance in specific meanings they are supposed to convey.

Speaking of *Oedipus Tyrannus*, he concludes by saying that the play raises doubts about justice on the cosmic and human level. 'At one level, *Oedipus Tyrannus* raises the question of the justice of men's fate and their suffering. The noble fair worse than those who are less admirable'. At the other level, through Oedipus' desire to punish Teiresias and Creon, the play questions human justice.[6]

Kaufmann's approach is typical of those of many others who, while purporting to treat tragedy as art, reduce it to some sort of intellectual or moral enterprise,[7] thus erecting a parapet that prohibits entry into the extraordinary domain to which a tragedy may otherwise lead.

An attempt to consider tragedy as irreducible to specific intellectual and moral significations was made by Susanne Langer.[8] Langer went out of her way to argue against what Kaufmann called 'the philosophical dimension' of tragedy, and, for that matter, against the 'historical', 'psychological', 'religious', and 'political' dimensions as well. For her, the stated or suggested significations have import only insofar as they are means to an artistic end: the construction of the tragic image or semblance. Moving from representation to presentation, she focuses on the structure of the heroic action – the tragic form. In tragic drama, the growth–maturation–decline pattern of life, what she calls 'the tragic rhythm of life', is abstracted from its actual context and is imprinted on the dramatic action which is graphed in terms of the hero's growth, efflorescence and exhaustion. Thus the heroic action, i.e. the tragic form, is a symbol that captures in a direct, presentational way the unfolding of the felt meaning in the organic, personal pattern of human life in its entirety as it arises, grows, accomplishes destiny and meets doom.

Through her notion of tragic drama as semblance and presentational symbol, Langer bypasses the difficulties that attend those who respond to tragedy in terms of its represented and expressed meanings and values. At the same time this notion provides her, at least implicitly, with a criterion on the basis of which she can distinguish between tragedy and philosophy. Philosophy, Langer admits, is often concerned with human life and experience. However, while the language of philosophy is conceptual and referential, tragic drama presents the meaning of life directly and concretely. Even on those occasions where philosophy makes 'the tragic sense of life' its explicit theme, as with Schopenhauer[9] and Unamuno,[10] that sense escapes us because, in Langer's way of thinking, it is diluted in the distinctions of conceptualization and the generalizations of rational discourse. For Langer, this sense can only be captured in the symbolic form that is the tragic drama. Symbols are not foreign to philosophy. But whereas philosophy constructs its meanings by synthesizing simple and independent symbols, tragic drama is a single, complex symbol – 'a prime symbol'. In its unity it captures the meaning of human life as a whole.

But is it true that human life can be caught by a symbol? Can human life, which in essence is contingency and possibility, be captured by a form which, in Langer's own words, is 'closed and final'? Can the meaning of life be projected in a single symbol? Does not such a symbol force life into a closure, falsifying it? And what about the uncanniness of the events depicted in a tragedy, their impenetrability and darkness? Tragedy, Langer is right, cannot be captured by the discursivity of traditional philosophy; can it, however, be captured by the unity that a symbol is? Don't we have here a 'disproportion of form and essence' – to borrow a phrase from Gadamer's own discussion of the symbol.[11] Do not the uncanny events of a tragedy, its totally non-human aspects, break up, break open, this unity? The non-human aspects of tragedy not only render inadequate all efforts to reduce it to specific intellectual or moral significations, to characteristically human meanings and values; they also make it impossible for any symbol to capture it. Tragedy, Langer is right, is not a sign. But neither is it a prime symbol. It thwarts the straightness of the former and explodes the unity of the latter.[12]

Aristotle defined tragedy in terms of action. Following him, Langer went on to find in the action the structure she did. Both refused to locate the significance of the action in the individuation of the hero or heroine – his or her personality.[13] Hegel, too, avoided this temptation. Hegel's contribution was the recognition that the tragic action has the structure of an *agon*. However, Hegel understood the tragic struggle as one between two agents who represent equal but opposing aspects of the spiritual essence of man – 'the ethical substance'.[14] If Hegel's characterization of the tragic action as struggle marks, as we believe, an advance over Aristotle and a corrective to Langer, it is limited by the way he understands this struggle. By seeing it as a struggle between *two* agents, he removed the *protagonist* from his or her right place at the center of tragedy.

By seeing it as one between two *spiritual* powers, he denied the protagonist his or her *human* status. And by seeing the struggle as involving *equal* powers, he was not true to the radical inequality, the irreducible difference, the unmediated opposition, between the protagonist as human, and the other-than-human circumstances in the midst of which he is placed and by which he is confronted. Hegel was truer to his own metaphysics than to the nature of the opposition in tragedy. His notions of Spirit, dialectic and mediation could not allow him to recognize the tragic circumstances as totally non-human, as radically other, not amenable to mediation.[15]

If all three philosophers recognized the importance of action, they did not take seriously that in the face of which this action is the kind of action it is it requires the structure it does. In what follows we will turn our attention to that. We will maintain with Hegel that the tragic action is a struggle, but we will see it as a struggle of the protagonist as human facing that which is non-human, other. We will agree, therefore, with Langer that it is the hero's action that structures tragedy, that gives it its tragic form. However, we will see that structure not along Langer's lines and certainly not as a symbol that captures the meaning of life as a whole, but as a form that brings to awareness that which is on the other side of what is characteristically human, an awareness that qualifies the tragic structure of action as an art action. First we will turn to the action within tragedy and see what makes it tragic. Then we will speak of its significance.

II

A tragedy opens into a terrifying set of circumstances. A curse from the gods has fallen on Thebes. Racine's Phèdre lies possessed by a love as potent as it is illicit. 'Othello's occupation's gone.' In Denmark 'The time is out of joint'. Moby Dick lurks beneath each lowering in Melville's novel. These circumstances make claims on the human agents involved in them. The protagonist is the agent to whom these circumstances pertain the most and on whom they make their greatest claims. What makes him a tragic protagonist is the way he comes to relate to them. Finding himself in their midst the protagonist neither avoids, evades nor dismisses them, nor yet does he accept them, but stands forth, opposing them, refusing to yield. What a tragedy does is to present, orchestrate and develop this opposition and its effects on the protagonist from an incipient or abrupt beginning, vertically and cumulatively, to a culminating confrontation and catastrophe. The catastrophe is not something that merely befalls the protagonist. It results from his stance of defiance to the circumstances that oppose him. These circumstances, it should be stressed, are depicted in such a way that they are taken by the protagonist himself as extraordinary – beyond human comprehension, on the other side of the human nature the protagonist brings to them, outside the ordinary personality we ourselves, viewers or readers, initially bring to the tragic goings-on.[16] These circumstances need not be an 'objective' state of affairs, external as it were, to the protagonist. They may be sentiments or aspects of inwardness, as in *Othello* or *Phèdre*.[17] In either case their non-humanity is emphasized. In fact those dramas, novels or poems that fall short of developing a tragic mode or action do so either because the author presents circumstances that are not radically different and as such opposed to the protagonist as human, or because the appreciators fail to consider them as such.[18]

The protagonist and the catastrophe are tragic only when they are presented or considered in relation to such circumstances. More specifically, the protagonist's actions, sufferings and death are tragic when they are seen to be determined by his insistence on facing in human terms and on the basis of human resources circumstances that are non-human. By this insistence the protagonist is brought to the outermost periphery of his human self, a periphery he cracks, and in so doing abandons himself to what lies on the other side of it – the non-human circumstances in the midst of which he found himself and which he was forced to confront.

Kenneth Burke found in tragedy a 'dialectic' which he articulated in terms of *'poiemata, pathemata, mathemata'*.[19] Francis Ferguson, translating this as 'Purpose, Passion, Perception', and adopting it as the criterion of what he called 'the tragic rhythm of action', agreed that the hero, through suffering, comes to a new perception of his situation.[20] Although such dialectic is to be found in some tragedies, it can hardly be taken as typical. But even where it occurs, as for example in *Oedipus the King*, Burke's and Ferguson's paradigm, the hero's perception of his situation is a by-product of the action; it does not define it. This perception may enhance the emotional effect of the play, as Aristotle speaking of Oedipus' *anagnorisis*[21] thought it did, but it does not determine it as tragic.

Others have found in tragedy the manifestation of the protagonist's greatness. It has been repeated that the distinct function of tragedy is to present events through which there emerges the greatness of the protagonist, events that make us rejoice in his or her grandeur and therefore in the 'grandeur of man'. Thus we have been told that the importance of the great tragedians lies in their ability to celebrate the greatness of the human spirit which rises superior to the calamities they recount,[22] that 'the sublimity of the hero's spirit is superior to the sublimity of the power that overwhelms him', that 'tragedy exalts man. . . . Its creed is humanistic'.[23] It is true that in many tragedies the protagonist is painted in powerful colors, and his actions and passions are depicted in such a way as to endow him, particularly at the moment of the catastrophe, with great stature. However, it is not true that the 'essential nature', even of such tragedies, lies in the greatness of the protagonist; it is not his grandeur that turns him into a tragic agent. Below any dialectic that leads to the protagonist's knowledge of the situation, and deeper than his possible grandeur, cuts the developing action that brings the protagonist to confront those extraordinary circumstances in the midst of which he initially found himself. In the course of this action, as we have seen, he extends his human nature to its utmost, to the point beyond which it cannot go and remain what it has been. This point at which the protagonist is brought to the edge of his human self, and standing there affirms his humanity as he moves beyond it and is destroyed, is the highest point of tragedy – its culmination and epitome. The development of an action that brings a human agent to this point, and incorporates it, is the development of a tragic mode of action; it is this action that defines the protagonist as tragic. This kind of action is perhaps best developed by Sophocles in *Oedipus the King*, by Shakespeare in *Othello*, by Racine in *Phèdre*, and also by Melville in his most famous novel.

In *Moby-Dick* Melville depicts circumstances that are clearly opposed to anything human. He sets out this opposition gradually and builds on it. He begins by contrasting the land and the sea. The land stands for 'safety, comfort, hearth-stone, supper, warm blankets, friends, all that's kind to our mortalities' (ch. 23). The land is fixed, one-leveled and already formed by 'the marks of slavish heels and boots' (13). On the other hand, the sea is multi-leveled, 'limitless and unchartered'. As the *Pequod* reaches the whale grounds, leaving far behind 'turnpike earth' and 'slavish shore',

Melville stresses the immensity of the sea, its terrible power, 'the full awfulness which aboriginally belongs to it'. The sea is 'an everlasting terra incognita' and 'a foe to man who is alien to it'. However much man's science and skill may develop, 'yet for ever and for ever, to the crack of doom, the sea will insult and murder him, and pulverize the stateliest frigate he can make' (58). Listening to its stirrings, the unceasing rise and fall, they 'seem to speak of some hidden soul beneath' (111). Exposed to its depth and immensity, little Pip loses his mind. It is in this sea that the leviathan roams.

Melville, with irony and even humor, tries to give an 'appreciative understanding of the leviathan'. But all the adjectives and finite qualities do not add up to its inscrutability. Ishmael's initial taxonomy of 'the whale in his broad genera' becomes 'the classification of the constituents of chaos' (32). Later, he is 'horror struck at this antimosaic ... which, having been before all time, must needs exist after all humane ages are over' (104). Distinguishing the sperm whale from the other species, he can speak of its ferociousness, its ponderousness and profundity, but not of the sperm whale itself. This 'mystic-marked whale remains undecipherable' (68): its head 'the Sphynx's in the desert' (70), its motions unaccountable, its face non-existent.

Moby Dick gathers on the 'colorless all-color of its hue', and surpasses the inscrutability of the sea and the undecipherability of the sperm whale: ghostly, nameless, faceless, ineffable – mystery chiseled on mystery. Melville in so many ways stresses that the nature of Moby Dick is not to be found within the domain of human meaning and value, that it lies outside the horizon of human categories, moral or intellectual: 'morbid hints of half-formed foetal suggestions of supernatural agencies' (42), 'glimpses into polar eternities' (104), 'unsourced'. Only to an ignorant trimmer such as Flask, the white whale would be 'a magnificent mouse' or 'a water-rat' (27). Only to 'a soulless thing ... and as mechanical', as Ahab calls Stubb, whose eleventh commandment is 'Think not', would the white whale be an occasion for jokes. By the same token, only 'ignorant landsmen might scout at Moby Dick as... a hideous and intolerable allegory' (45). And only 'a staid, steadfast man', such as Starbuck, for whom 'duty and profit' go hand in hand, would see Ahab's pursuit as 'a vengeance on a dumb brute' (36).

Ahab, to be sure, had his reason to be vengeful. His vengeance, however, is but the motive that sets Ahab once again on his course to fathom the unfathomable, to finitize the infinite. Elijah's cryptic allusions 'about the thing that happened to [Ahab] off Cape Horn, long ago' (9), etc., identify Ahab with this very course. This time, this course becomes concretized and explicit – the undecipherable is gathered on the hump of the albino whale, it wears the mask of Moby Dick, and Ahab 'must strike through the mask' (36). On this voyage, one legged, his drive turns into a monomania that can only be matched by his sense of pride and self-sufficiency. On board the *Pequod* he writhes, paces the deck, raises the doubloon, throws his still-lighted pipe into the water, smashes his quadrant, tosses aside Starbuck's entreating arm. Ahab's vengeance pushes him to extremities. His behavior in 'The Quarter-Deck', his speeches invoking the primordiality of the elements, his long soliloquies which often break into incoherence, the baptism of his harpoons in the name of the devil, his refusal to help Captain Gardiner in search of his lost son – all register the ministrations of his vengeance. But they also make clear that these extremities are the extremities of his powers, the limits beyond which even Ahab, a man with 'a globular brain and a ponderous heart' cannot go, or rather, beyond which he will insist on going, even if he is destroyed. If, within the story, Ahab's vengeance is a justification of his monomania, it is also the means by which Melville structures an action, the development of which brings his human protagonist, inevitably, into a direct confrontation with the non-human in the midst of which he has placed him, a confrontation in which the protagonist, in his human insistence, lays his humanity bare at the threshold of the non-human. Melville presents this confrontation starkly and powerfully in the last and penultimate chapter. The line of the action that was threaded by the incidents and events in the previous chapters brings Ahab, in this chapter, 'Forehead to forehead' with Moby Dick. And in the last gesture of the action, 'Thus, I give up the spear', Melville brings that line, now the line of that spear fastened on Moby Dick, to catch Ahab around the neck, shoot him off his whaleboat and pull him down.

Probably in order to soften the 'dire' way Ahab's drama ends, or to absorb 'the shocking nature of the book',[24] some commentators have concluded, in the spirit of those others we have alluded to above, that 'the end of Ahab is not unrelieved defeat, but victory in defeat', and that 'the tragic point of *Moby-Dick* is Ahab's discovery, in his last soliloquy, that 'the only compensations for his fate are to be found in himself, in the nature that is capable of an exaltation exactly equal to his grief'.[25] Such a response forces a reconciliation that simply is not there. There is no exaltation here, no victory – only human finitude, and the adumbration of what lies beyond it and defines it. The 'creed' of this or any other tragedy is not humanistic. What, if anything, is 'victorious', what remains and endures, is the white whale still roaming, after 'all collapsed', under 'the great shroud of the sea [that] rolled on as it rolled five thousand years ago' (135). 'The tragic point of *Moby-Dick*' is not the equivalence that Myers, for example, found above, nor, for that matter, the moral ambiguity that Sewell[26] presents as a corrective to Myers' view. Rather, it is embodied in that moment when, having been brought face to face with what now, for the first time, Ahab calls 'unconquering whale', raises his harpoon arm for what he knows to be the last time. In '*Thus*, I give up the spear', Ahab stands fast by his humanity in the face of the non-human – the exigencies of his nature do not allow him to do otherwise. In 'Thus, *I give up* the spear', he, in the face of these very exigencies, opens to the non-human, even though he knows he will be destroyed in doing so. Ahab's gesture and the words that accompany it culminate an action the development of which brought Ahab to stand at the limits of his humanity, limits he cracks, opening himself to what lies beyond him. Ahab's tragedy is defined by this action, and is epitomized in this gesture, his last.

Ahab's end, however, does not end Melville's novel. As the opening of the novel is not merely a technical device, so its epilogue is not a mere appendage. Its function is not to tell us, as it does, that 'the drama's done'. In telling this, it also tells of another drama which is about to begin, the drama that takes its point of departure as Ahab lowers his harpoon for the last time – the drama of art. The epilogue reverts us back to the beginning where Ishmael, himself drawn by 'the image of the ungraspable phantom of life', 'opens the great flood-gates of the wonder-world' (1) and is carried over into a happening that develops as Ahab's pursuit develops – a development that originates in and is sustained by Ishmael's activities which open him to that which destroyed Ahab. Ishmael survives to retrieve Ahab's quest for the unfathomable. The end of the represented action signifies the beginning of the art action, the death of the protagonist, the birth of the artist – Melville, who, according to Hawthorne, always speaks 'of everything that lies beyond human ken' and wants 'to be annihilated'.[27]

In asking us to call him Ishmael, Melville asks us to see him as an exile, an outcast, standing at the boundary between what is and what is not of human ken, between land and landlessness, and beckons us to follow him as he returns to begin from there. In following him we too leave behind the hearthstone, the warm blankets and all the assurances and assuagements of our ordinary self, our 'insular Tahiti', and on board *his* ship, the ship of fiction, come, as orphans, to participate in an occurrence of emergence in which what is non-human also participates.

Not many tragedies end or begin the way Melville's novel does. They do not juxtapose to or intertwine with the figure of the protagonist, the figure of an Ishmael. The advantage of considering *Moby-Dick* is that it makes evident the significance of the catastrophe and the events that culminate in it – the significance of the tragic action. The closing and opening of *Moby-Dick*, that is, Ishmael's participation, leaves no doubt that this action is an art action. It makes evident that the movement that structures a tragedy is a movement into art. If it is the case that it is the action that defines a tragedy, the significance of that action is to be found not in its representational allusions, its presentational illusions or its metaphysical embodiments, but in that it is an action that leads to art, a structuring activity in which emergence occurs, an emergence that originates in what is non-human. In and through the action that defines the protagonist as tragic, the tragedian, and possibly and subsequently we, in activities that open to the other, take part in the happening of such emergence.

III

Such a happening does not occur only in tragedy. Dramas, novels and poems we call tragic are not the only ones through which we come to be involved in activities that open to what is other. All involvement in art is constituted by such activities. That this is so, however, is witnessed most in those examples from the arts which accentuate aspects that clearly cannot be accounted for in human terms, aspects that block the humanity we bring to them. Many of Caspar David Friedrich's paintings and Blake's drawings; paintings depicting mythical themes; Van Gogh's pictures; music using old melodies such as Mahler's, Stravinsky's and Bartok's; Michelangelo's 'unfinished' statues; novels that recount uncanny events – all these can be taken as examples. The myths, the uncanny situations, the 'starkness' in a painting by Wyeth, the 'emptiness' in Friedrich's 'Monk by the Sea', the unworked stone in a sculpture by Michelangelo or Noguchi, are irreducible to human meanings and values. Yet, that such aspects arrest us and ellicit a response indicates that the working of art in these cases is due to factors other than characteristically human ones. The stream that is art and in which the painter, the sculptor, the musician and the appreciator enter is fed and sustained by currents that have a non-human source. In the above examples, that which cannot be accounted for in human terms serves the function of pointing to such transcendent source, and of providing the awareness that the happening of art is due to human openness to what is other than human. What distinguishes a novel, a drama or a poem we call tragic is that it enlarges such awareness.

Perhaps we can shed more light on this by turning to an art-object other than a tragic drama, novel or poem – a plastic art-object such as Van Gogh's *Starry Night*. The painting hanging on the wall is static. But, as Croce said of all art-objects, this one too is a memorial, a monument commemorating activity. The configurations and the still colors are remnants of work. They are the frozen testimony of the painter's activities. We get a clue about the nature of these activities from the extraordinary elements that predominate in this painting, elements that set limits to the self we bring to them, elements that make *Starry Night* unlike any other starry night we may have witnessed. The activities that crystallized in this art-object cannot be seen as having their source in Van Gogh's ordinary experiences, his acquired professional expertise, his familiarity with the materials of his craft, in short his humanity or subjectivity. The violence of the brush strokes, the use of paint that is often worked with the thumb or brush handle, the green conflagrations of the cypress in front, the ferocity of movement and the excruciating colors above that coil together the moon and the individual stars into a single blaze, are evidence of this, contrasted as they are with the peacefulness, and, what is more, the ordinariness of the village – the human habitat – below. Such aspects evidence Van Gogh's confrontation by the night and register its effect. In his effort to capture the night, he gets caught in its depth, its luminescence. He gets caught in a process where ordinary images and colors, learned devices and techniques, give way to activities that are determined not by them but by the depth and darkness of the night, the commotion of its genesis, its mystery. The thickness of paint, the force and crudeness of brush stroke, the vortex of light, the hues that rupture the color-spectrum, evidence activities that draw their energy and gain their essence by opening to that in which the night itself has its source. They evidence activities that are at the same time passivities, responsive activities that bring about an emergence whose occurrence is due to Van Gogh's participation in a process in which what is non-human also participates.

Obviously there are differences between *Starry Night* and *Moby-Dick*. The former has nothing to do with whale-hunting. Its blues move us in one emotional direction; Captain Gardiner's searching for his lost son in another direction. The values and meanings expressed in the former are different from those expressed in the latter. Such differences exist among all works of art, which in their various represented or directly presented significations enrich our human world. However, the differences among works of art disappear when we see them from the perspective of the activities that constitute them, activities that open the painter, the sculptor, the poet, etc., and the appreciator, to what is other, an opening that lets what is other occasion the emergence that takes place there. From this perspective what distinguishes *Moby-Dick* from *Starry Night* and therefore a tragic novel or drama from other works, plastic or not, is that in the former such activities become more evident, placed as it were in relief. Unlike many paintings, sculptures, poems and musical pieces, a tragic drama, novel or poem is the representation or narration of human action. Unlike a novel or drama in general, the action in a tragedy has, as we have seen, a definite structure. It is in this, in the action it depicts, in the context it places it, and in the way it structures it that tragedy occupies a distinct place in the arts – enlarging and deepening the awareness we spoke of above. If in a sculpture the other is suggested by the presence of unworked stone; in an abstract painting by the opacity of pigment; in a musical composition by an old melody; in the case of tragedy it is forcefully pointed to by the circumstances which oppose the protagonist as human. And if a painter's openness is suggested, for example, by Van Gogh's activities or by Jackson Pollock's characteristic movements on the canvas; a poet's, for example, by Wallace Stevens' use of words and lines that crack conventional meaning; a sculptor's, for example, by Noguchi's rough textures, irregular and minimally carved surfaces, the gouges, incisions and drill holes in works such as *Myo, The*

Seeker Sought and *Euripides;* the tragedian's openness is powerfully reflected in the protagonist's violence and suffering, i.e. in his vulnerability, and above all in the fact and manner of his death. In the action of the protagonist, the tragedian enacts the action of art, the action that defines him as creative. And as it is the protagonist's response to the non-human circumstances that defines his actions and qualifies him or her as tragic, so it is the tragedian's response to his uncanny themes and his openness to the other to which they point as their source that defines his activity as artistic and qualifies him as creative. In and through the tragic action the tragedian and possibly and subsequently we, in activities of openness come to be engaged in a happening of emergence that originates in the other.

Psychologists, aestheticians and theoreticians of art often address the issue of creativity, purporting to explain it. They speak of it in terms of the artist's unique capacity to form or transform reality; of the artist's ideas and how they germinate and grow in the mind. They speak of the discovery of new values and meanings and of how the artist succeeds in conveying them by molding chosen media. They refer to the artist's psychological make-up, history and times. Many of these views can be easily dismissed for being theoretical constructs, extrinsic to art. But even those accounts of creativity that reflect concerns intrinsic to art, more often than not share with these views the basic misconception, a legacy of Kantian aesthetics, that the art-work originates, is grounded, in the artist's subjectivity.[28] Our consideration of the tragic action provides us with an awareness of the tragedian's activities, i.e. the creative process, that runs counter to these accounts. In tragedy non-human elements dominate, elements that cannot be seen as being reflections of the tragedian's or our ego, aspects that set limits to subjectivity.[29] As the circumstances in the midst of which he is placed, in their extraordinariness, block the protagonist's efforts to relate to them in characteristically human terms, so the myths, stories or situations that constitute the themes of tragedy, in their impenetrability, block efforts to be vehicles of the tragedian's ordinary self. They demand his transmutation, as the tragic circumstances demand the tragic protagonist's absolute transmutation – his death. The protagonist's death reflects the death of the tragedian's ordinary self as the latter opens himself to what is other, thus coming to take part in the process of creation.

The significance of *Moby-Dick* as well as that of other novels, dramas or poems we call tragic is that they make us aware of such a process. It is this that makes tragedy the 'ground-phenomenon',[30] as it were, of the arts. Thus although we do not say, as some have said,[31] that tragedy is the highest form of art, we can say that it occupies a privileged position among the arts. In a way that is more articulated, forceful and engaging than works in other media and with different thematic materials, tragedy makes us aware of human beings' participation in a process in which what is other also participates, a process that originates in that.

IV

Those who respond to tragedy simply in terms of the emotions it evokes or treat tragedy in terms of the meanings and values it is purported to convey or embody close off such awareness. What is puzzling is that the reduction of tragedy to emotional, moral or metaphysical significations has been, at its origin, the work of philosophers. Did not philosophers sense in tragedy aspects that are not amenable to rational intelligibility, aspects that set a barrier to explanation, an impasse? More generally, did not philosophers, in their thinking, and *not only of tragedy*, sense a radical otherness lurking in the interstices of their ratiocinations, an inexplicable residue in their explanations? Could it be that having sensed that they, like Hegel, spent their energies in eliminating its traces in well-wrought thought or, like Descartes, leveled it to the ground with the bulldozers of clarity and distinctness so that nothing remained indeterminate, nothing aroused wonder? But were they doing justice to philosophy whose *arche*, as it was stated at its inception, is wonder? Could it be that philosophers having sensed an impasse to which their reasoning brought them backed off and, like Hume, decided not to go on, returning to enterprises other than philosophy or, like Kant, who, having made reference to the unconditional ground which reason cannot think, went on, falling back on well-known ground? It is as if Ishmael stated that the 'phantom of life' is 'ungraspable', and remained on shore without going on that journey that almost drowned him. Do not philosophers dare 'own the whale'? Have they no 'itch for things remote?' Are they afraid of being left orphans? Are they afraid of shipwreck?

Yet, was it not a philosopher, Jaspers, for whom philosophy, in posing limit questions, has to do with shipwreck? Was it not Plato who was led repeatedly to shipwreck, showing that shipwreck is essential to thinking, to philosophizing? Does not Heidegger's language in his later essays lead him and us to the limits of perplexity? It not the Wittgenstein of the later essays on ethics led to shipwreck, to a language 'beyond significant language'?

What is the significance of such shipwreck? Why does Plato, for example, return repeatedly to the beginning, starting once more by placing his protagonist in the midst of yet different interlocutors, commencing the Socratic logos anew – the logos that will be brought to yet another impasse? Why does Heidegger insist, almost monomaniacally, on the course in which language as communication or expression breaks down again and again? Is not such shipwreck analogous to the tragic shipwreck? And is not its significance found in the vicinity of the significance of the tragic catastrophe, in the openness that is registered there? In each Platonic dialogue, the Socratic logos is brought to an impasse. But at this impasse, thought opens to what thought cannot grasp, what the Socratic speech cannot say. It is this openness that makes each Platonic dialogue more than the undeniable failure with which the corresponding Socratic logos closes, an openness to what evokes wonder, signaling the beginning of philosophizing. It is this openness that justifies Plato's return to begin anew, each beginning being a beginning from out of what brought the Socratic logos to ruins; each dialogue a response that opens to that.

An analogous response marks Heidegger's later essays. Heidegger, to be sure, has no Socrates. And there is no Ahab and Ishmael to symbolize his action. The action of these essays is the activity, as he himself said, that is thinking. And the nature of the activity in these essays is reflected in the language that constitutes them. Forced, coerced, stretched, cracked, language here comes to an impasse, revealing its limits. The bending of syntax, the constant breaking-up of ordinary locutions, the stammering, the breaking down of its supports, record the failure of this language to communicate or establish a meaning. But at the same time they also record an openness to what this language does not and cannot say – what is unsaid but needs to be said, the unsaid, what evokes wonder. Unlike Kant, for instance, Heidegger does not allude, as it were, from afar to what is beyond thought and language. The activities of these essays record a direct engagement with and register a human need to be related to what is other, not unlike the need reflected in the action that defines the tragic hero, a need that results in the hero's catastrophe. Clearly, language in these essays fails to transcend its limits. But in its very failure, in its cracking, as in the tragic catastrophe, language opens to what transcends it, letting the unsaid permeate what is being said, contributing to the emergence that takes place there. It is this openness that makes these essays more than the failures they are, as it is the tragedian's openness that makes tragedy more than the human catastrophe with which it ends. In responding to these essays we come to be involved in a process that originates in sources other than the speaker, sources which in tapping, we, too, following Heidegger, can become creative. In this sense and from this perspective there is no difference between a Platonic dialogue and one of Heidegger's later essays. In the same sense and from the same perspective there is no difference between these and *Moby-Dick*.

In the previous sections of this essay we have tried to show that when seen from the perspective of the activities that constitute them, all art-works are tragic. What we have been trying to suggest in this section is that, when philosophy drops its pretensions to systematic coherence and complete intelligibility, and, acknowledging the mystery it is confronted by, expresses the human need to be related to it by opening to its wonder, its activity, like the activity that involves artist and appreciator in art, is not unlike the activity that involves the tragedian and ourselves in tragedy.

Notes

1. Aristotle, *Poetics*, 1450a.
2. Aristotle defines tragedy as 'mimesis of a praxis ...' 1449 b24. At the same time he considers the plot as 'the soul of a tragedy' 1450 a38, and speaks of it as 'a mimesis of the praxis' 1450 a34. I agree with John Jones' resolution of this 'awkward doubleness of praxis and muthos', when he takes 'muthos to mean the fully realized praxis' and sees the action as the 'form' or principle of tragedy. See *On Aristotle and Greek Tragedy* (New York: Oxford University Press, 1962), pp. 24–6. Also, Leon Rosenstein, 'On Aristotle and Thought in Drama', Critical *Inquiry*, Spring 1977, vol. 3, no. 3, p. 553.
3. Elsewhere I have argued that in fact this attempt failed. See 'Plato and Aristotle: Mimesis, Tragedy and Art', *Homage to Evangelos Papanoutsos*, vol. 1, eds K. Boros *et al.* (Athens: Center for Neohellenic Research, 1980), pp. 199–212. I disagree, therefore, with Roman Ingarden who, in interpreting *mimesis* the way he does, argues that for Aristotle the world of tragedy has no real reference to the world outside tragedy.

See his 'A Marginal Commentary on Aristotle's *Poetics*', Part I, *Journal of Aesthetics and Art Criticism*, 20:2 (Winter 1961), pp. 163 ff.

4. Herbert Muller, *The Spirit of Tragedy* (New York: Washington Square Press, 1965), p. 9.

5. Walter Kaufmann, *Tragedy and Philosophy* (New York: Doubleday, 1968), pp. 93–4.

6. *Tragedy and Philosophy*, p. 130.

7. Martha Nussbaum, for example, while all along purporting to treat (Greek) tragedies 'in all their poetic complexities', and 'be responsive to the poetic features of the texts', from the very outset, reduces them to the ethical insights she finds in them. *The Fragility of Goodness: Luck and Ethics in Greek Tragedy and Philosophy* (Cambridge: Cambridge University Press, 1986), pp. 14, 394.

8. Susanne Langer, *Feeling and Form* (New York: Scribner's, 1953). See chapters 13, 19 and 21.

9. Arthur Schopenhauer, *The World as Will and Representation*, trans. E.F. Payne (New York: Dover Publications, 1969), Vol. I, p. 322 and Vol. II, pp. 435–6.

10. Miguel de Unamuno, *The Tragic Sense of Life in Men and in Peoples*, trans. J.E.C. Flitch (London: Macmillan, 1921).

11. Hans-Georg Gadamer, *Truth and Method*, 2nd rev. edn, translation revised by Joel Weinsheimer and Donald D. Marshall (New York: Crossroads, 1989), p. 78. Gadamer's discussion is related to Langer's since she borrows from Schiller and Schelling, the very people whose ideas about the symbol Gadamer examines.

12. For a fuller presentation of Langer's ideas on tragedy and for a lengthier critique see my 'The Tragic Form', *Man and World*, Vol. 10, No. 2, pp. 137–51.

13. Aristotle repeatedly subordinates character to action. 'The purpose of action on the stage is not to imitate character, but character is a by-product of the action'. 'The Poetics' in *Aristotle: On Poetry and Style*, G.M.A. Grube (New York: Library of Liberal Arts, 1958), pp. 13–14.

14. G.W.F. Hegel, *Phenomenology of Spirit*, trans. A.V. Miller (Oxford: Oxford University Press, 1979), p. 445.

15. Although in a context very different from ours, Jean-Pierre Vernant too refers to the radically other in tragedy. In his discussion of *Antigone* he speaks of the Law of Zeus as totally non-human. Aside from his overall interpretation of *Antigone* and his particular identification of the non-human with the *nomos* of Zeus, Vernant is on the right track in his recognition of the radically other in tragedy, and therefore of his criticism of Hegel: 'I would point out right away, to indicate my disagreement with the Hegelian position, that this *nomos* of Zeus cannot be [mediated] because it is absolutely incomprehensible and impenetrable from the human view-point.' 'Greek Tragedy', *The Structuralist Controversy*, eds Richard Macksey and Eugenio Donato (Baltimore: Johns Hopkins University Press, 1979), p. 281. Speaking not of tragedy as such but of Hegel's view of art in general, and of Hegel's idea of inwardness in romantic art in particular, William Desmond also recognizes and makes much of an otherness that resists Hegel's total

self-mediation. 'Art, Origins, Otherness: Hegel and Aesthetic Self-Mediation', *Philosophy and Art*, ed. Daniel O. Dahlstrom (Washington: Catholic Universities of America Press, 1991), pp. 209–34.

16. More than anyone I know of, John M. Anderson thematizes what he calls the 'negative elements' in comedy and tragedy, showing the centrality of the 'alien' in art. In obvious opposition to Hegel, he stresses the importance of the unmediable in tragedy. My understanding of tragedy has been greatly influenced by insights first presented by Anderson in his remarkable book *The Realm of Art* (University Park: Pennsylvania University Press, 1967), particularly pp. 95–129 and 131–61.

17. Heidegger goes out of his way to make the same point in his analysis of the first choral ode in *Antigone* in his *Introduction to Metaphysics*, trans. Ralph Manaheim (New York: Doubleday, 1961), p. 131.

18. *Tess of the D'Urbervilles* exemplifies the first case; *An American Tragedy* may be taken as an example of the second case. Living in a capitalist society we may find nothing extraordinary in the world of wealth Dreiser depicts and by which Clyde is destroyed.

19. Kenneth Burke, *A Grammar of Motives* (Berkeley: University of California Press, 1966), p. 39.

20. Francis Fergusson, *The Idea of a Theater* (New York: Doubleday Anchor Books, 1969), p. 31.

21. *Poetics*, 1452 a32–b2.

22. Aside from Nietzsche, the classic expression of this view in English is found in Joseph Wood Krutch, 'The Tragic Fallacy', *The Modern Temper* (New York: Harcourt, Brace, 1929), p. 128.

23. D.D. Raphael, *The Paradox of Tragedy* (Bloomington: Indiana University Press, 1960), pp. 27 and 31.

24. Richard B. Sewell, *The Vision of Tragedy*, new edn (New Haven: Yale University Press, 1981), p. 104.

25. Henry Alonzo Myers, 'The Tragic Meaning of *Moby-Dick*' in his *Tragedy: A View of Life* (Ithaca: Cornell University Press, 1956), pp. 72–4

26. *The Vision of Tragedy*, p. 102.

27. Nathaniel Hawthorne, *The English Notebooks*, ed. Randall Steward (New York: Russell & Russell, 1962), p. 432.

28. Along not very different lines William Desmond writes that 'Man is not 'creative'. Man cooperates in creation …. Art testifies to our imaginative power and participation in the universe of otherness'. For his notion of the other and 'our openness to what is other' in connection to art in general and in connection to tragedy and comedy, see chapters 2 and 5 of *Philosophy and Its Others: Ways of Being and Mind* (Albany: State University of New York Press, 1990), p. 91.

29. Joyce Carol Oates in her book on tragedy speaks of 'the violent loss of self that signals the start of artistic effort: an appropriation by destruction, or an assimilation into a self of a reality that cannot be named.' *The Edge of Impossibility* (New York: Vanguard Press, 1972), p. 3.

30. The term is Gadamer's. He refers to the tragic as 'a ground

phenomenon'. His context is different from the one in this essay. Still, I agree, but for different reasons, with Gadamer's view that tragedy provides the best example of the incapacity of (Kantian) aesthetics to comprehend Art. *Truth and Method*, p. 129.

31. Schopenhauer, for example, refers to tragedy as the 'highest poetical achievement'. *The World as Will and Representation*, vol. I, p. 252. F.W.J. Schelling speaks of it as 'the most sublime art'. *The Philosophy of Art*, edited, translated and introduced by Douglas W. Scott (Minneapolis: University of Minnesota Press, 1989), p. 259.

7
Philosophy and Tragedy in the Platonic Dialogues

DREW A. HYLAND

The very suggestion that there might be a connection between Platonic philosophy and tragedy might seem at first strange. If the severe criticisms of tragedy in Books III and X of Plato's *Republic* are taken as Plato's literal teaching on the subject rather than, say, a 'provocation'[1] to the thoughtful reader, then it is hard to imagine how the question of whether there is a 'tragic' dimension to Platonic philosophy could seriously arise. Unless we invoke explanations from psychopathology, how could a writer so harshly critical of tragedy knowingly include a tragic dimension within his own conception of philosophy? And indeed, many commentators, from very different schools of Platonic interpretation, have argued that the portrayal of philosophy in the dialogues is not tragic, and, according to some authors, even thoroughly anti-tragic. Thus Allan Bloom, in the 'commentary' to his edition of Plato's *Republic*, characterizes that dialogue (it is less clear whether he would say the same for the dialogues altogether) as a 'divine comedy'[2] and more recently, Martha Nussbaum, in her *The Fragility of Goodness*, devotes the central part of the book to arguing that Plato's philosophical standpoint abandons the tragic insight of his predecessors which only Aristotle restores.[3]

Yet clearly, the issue is more complex, for a number of authors have argued that notwithstanding the occasional surface teachings of the dialogues, Plato was much more sensitive to the tragic element in human life than might at first seem, and indeed, that there is a tragic element to his very conception of philosophy. David Roochnik, for example, argues the point superbly in his response to Nussbaum, and John Harman has recently argued that the portrayal of the philosopher in the *Republic* is a tragic one.[4] In this essay, I would like to contribute to the debate by arguing, initially by appeal to the account of eros in the *Symposium*, that the

account there of the human condition is indeed one with a strong
tragic element, and then appeal to the portrayal of philosophy in
the *Republic* as confirmation of this interpretation.

I begin, strange as it may seem for one seeking tragic elements in
philosophy, with the hilarious account of eros presented in the
Symposium by the comic poet, Aristophanes (*Symposium*, 189c–193e).
He begins his speech not with an account of the origins of eros but
with an account of the origins of human nature. We were originally
very different than we are now. We were, by contrast to our present
condition, double beings, with two heads, four arms, four legs, and
more rounded bodies which enabled us to roll along the ground with
great speed. We came, moreover, in three varieties, a double female,
a double male, and a male/female pairing, divisions which
Aristophanes will presently use to account for the three forms of
sexuality in our present condition (189e–190c).

About this initial portrayal a number of points need to be
observed. First, in an obvious sense, our original condition was
'superior' to our present one; we were much more powerful and in
a sense more 'complete'. Our present condition is thus in some
sense a 'fall'. If we keep in mind that Aristophanes begins his
speech with a religious emphasis, arguing that Eros is both a god
and the one who loves mankind the most, and moreover, that he
emphasizes throughout the importance of our piety toward the god
Eros (else we shall be punished by being split yet again!), we can
see how thoroughly Plato has had Aristophanes present a
fundamentally religious portrayal of eros. For, as it turns out,
though our original condition was indeed superior to our present
one, it was not perfect.[5] We were characterized by a flaw, the
familiar religious flaw of *hybris*, overweening pride. We desired, in
what might be called the pagan version of original sin, to
overthrow the gods (190b ff.). The gods, once again consistent with
the Judaeo-Christian teaching, punished us by reducing our
condition and thereby rendering us as we are now; Zeus, with the
consultation of Apollo, split us in two, and tied our skin in a knot at
the front (now called the navel), so that we may look down upon it,
be reminded of our former condition, and be humble (190e).

As Aristophanes tells it, Zeus' initial efforts to punish us were
not entirely successful. He wanted to punish us, render us weaker
so that we were no longer a threat to the gods, and double our
number, thereby increasing the number of sacrifices to the gods
(190c: the Greek gods, somewhat more obviously than in the

Judaeo-Christian tradition, are motivated strongly by self-interest). However, instead, we were dying off, since we spent our time doing nothing but trying to join together again with our original halves. Zeus, hardly omniscient, is portrayed as something of a comic fool. A second operation is necessary; Zeus moves our genitals around to the front so that when we attempt to join together we will procreate (at least, the male/female pairings will) and the race will be continued (191b–c).

There are a host of themes present here, some of them quite hilarious, which we can mention only in passing since they bear only indirectly on our theme of tragedy. Aristophanes here gives an account of the origins of the three forms of sexuality; depending on what sort of original whole we were, we will, in our split condition, be either homosexual, lesbian, or heterosexual; sexual orientation is a function of genealogy, not of environment! Moreover, given the significance of the episode where a second operation was necessary to insure procreation, we can even see implicitly the traditional conservative bias in favor of heterosexuality.[6] It is only the unions of heterosexual pairings which will contribute to the continuation of our race. As for the homosexual pairings, says Aristophanes, '...at least they will become satiated from the union, and stop, and turn to their work and the other concerns of life' (191c). Perhaps somewhat counter to this, it might be noted that Aristophanes, in opposition to what Diotima will later teach (206c), suggests that the urge to procreate is clearly subordinate to and, at least originally, an unconscious derivative of, the more primordial desire to join together (a priority, one might note, whose phenomenological accuracy is well-attested).

Most importantly, however, Aristophanes has given us an account of the origins of eros and of our present human condition which makes them virtually identical. Eros is born out of our 'fallen' condition as split, incomplete beings, and has three aspects or 'moments'. First, in what might be called the 'ontological' moment, it is our condition as incomplete, partial. Humans are erotic because we are incomplete. But stones are incomplete too, and we do not call them erotic. The second moment in the structure of eros is that we experience our incompleteness as such, we recognize it, and third, we strive to overcome that incompleteness, to return to our original state of wholeness.

Because Aristophanes is Aristophanes, he wants us to think of this triadic structure of eros primarily in terms of the sexual act itself, and so considered, it is ribald good fun. We take all those funny positions and get so passionately excited because we want to overcome our physical incompleteness and become whole again. That is what the sexual fuss is all about. But it is not difficult to see that the core of Aristophanes' teaching goes much deeper than that. In principle, all the myriad ways in which we are incomplete, experience that incompleteness, and strive to overcome it, are manifestations of our erotic natures. All human aspiration to become more than we are, whether physical or spiritual, is erotic. This would certainly include (although for obvious reasons, Aristophanes does not emphasize this) political aspiration and, decisively, philosophy itself; precisely as Socrates understands it, philosophy is a paradigm case of being incomplete (in regard to wisdom), recognizing that incompleteness (the clear pedagogical point of much of Socratic elenchus), and striving to overcome it. Long before Socrates' speech, Aristophanes offers us the foundation for the erotic basis of philosophy.

Eros is not eternal; in our original situation before being split we were, presumably, not erotic. Eros is born out of the rendering incomplete of human beings. It is our nature as human. This is in clear tension with Aristophanes' explicit teaching, at the beginning and end of his speech, that Eros is a god, a god who loves mankind, and one toward whom we should be pious (189c–d, 193b–d). Implicit within this religious presentation is a position which we today would call secular humanism. Eros is not a god but 'alienated' (that is, incomplete) human nature.

One more episode in Aristophanes' speech needs to be considered before we shall be prepared to elicit the tragic elements in Aristophanes' portrayal of the human situation. At 192d–e, we are asked to suppose that Hephaestus were to ask us, as lovers, what we truly wanted. At first, we are told, we would not know, but would 'speak cryptically and in riddles' (192d). If he inquired whether what we wanted was to be welded together so that we would live and die as one, we would reply that that is what we wanted all along, but could not articulate. The profound pessimism of this characterization, which Socrates' subsequent speech will take steps to qualify, should be noted. Human beings cannot articulate their situation. We are not self-conscious; we do not have self-knowledge. We need the gods, and so religion, as a replacement for our inability to understand ourselves.

We can now turn to a consideration of the extent to which Aristophanes presents us with many of the elements of a tragic portrayal of human being. I begin with four dimensions to the human situation which are often associated with tragedy, and shall use the Oedipus story as my operative example.[7] First, a situation is tragic insofar as one is subject to a fate which is outside one's control and for which one is not directly responsible. Oedipus is fated to kill his father and marry his mother, and as so fated, he can hardly be held straightforwardly responsible for those events. Second, part of what we are fated to is that we fight against, or strive to overcome, that destiny to which we are determined. Oedipus goes to extraordinary lengths, once he discovers his destiny, to avoid it. He leaves what he believes is his homeland and his parents, thereby assuring, he supposes, that he will be able to avoid the horrible prophecy. Third, the very activity of striving to overcome that fate in fact condemns the tragic figure to it. By leaving his 'foster' home, Oedipus in fact returns to his true homeland, and the tragedy begins. Fourth, we do not understand this situation adequately. We understand our situation only darkly, at least, until the very end, when our fate becomes manifest. Oedipus' slow, utterly painful awakening to self-knowledge is the substance of the ensuing tragedy.

A consideration of the human condition as Aristophanes portrays it shows at once how clearly it conforms to the tragic dimensions so far outlined. First, all humans, from the first generation of split people on, are fated to our situation as erotic: incomplete and experiencing that incompleteness. That situation is not one we can control, nor is it something for which we are directly responsible; it is the consequence of the 'original sin' of our forefathers. Moreover, second, part of what we are fated to is that, as erotic, we are bound to strive to overcome the incompleteness which we experience. That is precisely what the energy of eros is, according to Aristophanes. Third, the nature of this erotic striving is such that it will never be finally successful. This is again fully obvious after the first generation of split people. The progeny of the original split generation, born split or incomplete, do not even have a true 'other half' with whom to join. We are thus condemned not only to incompleteness but to a striving to overcome that incompleteness which is itself bound to fail. In a subtle but decisively pessimistic remark toward the end of his speech, Aristophanes says:

Our race can become happy if we satisfy eros, and if each can
find his proper beloved and return to his original, natural state. If
this is the best thing, then, by necessity, what in our present
circumstances comes closest to it is best for now. That is to find a
love who is of like mind to oneself.[8]

Clearly, it is necessary (*anangkaion*) for us 'in our present
circumstances' to settle for a second best because our true
aspiration, to achieve our original wholeness, is no longer possible.

Fourth and finally on this point, we do not fully understand our
situation, but can only 'speak cryptically and in riddles' (192d), as
the episode concerning Hephaestus makes clear.

The preceding considerations have established, I would hope, the
remarkable extent to which Aristophanes' portrayal of eros is
presented within an account of the human situation which contains
many of the elements of tragedy. That the comic poet presents a
portrayal which is in certain ways tragic is perhaps part of the
meaning of Socrates' insistence toward the end of the *Symposium*
that it is possible for the same man to write comedy and tragedy
(223d).

However, I have spoken cautiously of 'elements' of tragedy in
Aristophanes' speech because we cannot say simply and
straightforwardly that Aristophanes' understanding of eros is
tragic. We cannot, because other elements of tragedy, and one
decisive one in particular, are missing from his portrayal. I am
thinking of the dimension of nobility. In Greek tragedy, it is not
simply that the tragic figure is fated to a situation wherein the
hero's efforts to overcome his or her fate are bound to fail; it is
further the case that the very effort to overcome that destiny,
notwithstanding and indeed in the midst of its failure, is
nevertheless an effort which ennobles the hero. This is usually
portrayed symbolically by making the tragic hero be of royal
lineage. But in a deeper and more significant sense, the Antigones
and Oedipus' of Greek tragedy exhibit noble character. And it is
this reference to the nobility of erotic striving which is missing from
Aristophanes' account. For obvious reasons, he is much more
impressed with how foolish, how comical, eros, and so human
nature, is. Notwithstanding the clear presence of tragic elements,
then, Aristophanes' speech remains a comic portrayal of the human
situation because he fails to see the element of nobility in our tragic
erotic striving. To find that element of nobility, and so to fulfill the

tragic portrayal of human eros, we must turn to the speech of Socrates.

To a remarkable extent, Socrates' speech constitutes a proto-Hegelian *Aufhebung* of the previous speeches. In the case of Aristophanes' speech, Socrates clearly goes beyond the comic poet's account and thus, as I shall presently argue, shows its inadequacy as a 'complete speech' regarding the erotic nature of human being. But it is no less true that Socrates' speech lifts up and preserves crucial elements in Aristophanes' presentation, although, to be sure, in a different manner from the comic myth that Aristophanes sets out. Socrates begins his speech with a brief dialogue with Agathon, questioning Agathon's claim that eros both is beautiful and loves the beautiful (199c ff.). The crucial premise in Socrates' refutation of Agathon establishes that eros is always eros of something, and moreover, of something which it lacks. The clearest formulation of this aspect of the argument occurs at 200e:

> And now, said Socrates, are we agreed upon the following conclusions? One, that Love (Eros) is always the love of something, and two, that that something is what it lacks?

It is not difficult to see that this point, established 'logically', has its origin in Aristophanes' myth regarding our incompleteness. The core of Socrates' position here is that eros is founded in a 'lack' or incompleteness, an incompleteness which, second, is experienced as such, and third, that eros is the impetus to overcome that lack; these are, of course, precisely the three 'moments' of Aristophanes' portrayal of eros.

But Socrates goes further. Abandoning the elenchus with Agathon and turning to a recounting of the teaching which the priestess, Diotima, gave him when, as a young man, he went to her to learn about eros, Socrates extends the significance of the essentially Aristophanic points established so far in a way which fulfills the tragic dimension to erotic striving. Indeed, Socrates, following Diotima, characterizes that manifestation of eros with which Aristophanes seemed exclusively concerned, personal love between individuals, as but a first, albeit necessary (210a) and decisive step. Human eros is too complex, too multi-directional, to be exhausted or satisfied by one person, although love of an individual can certainly be part of the eros of a rich life. Still, there are other manifestations of eros, of experienced incompleteness and the striving to overcome it: the creation of laws, artistic creativity, and philosophy itself. By limiting the explicit manifestation of eros to individual love, Aristophanes, as we saw, construed eros primarily as a source of consolation for humans, and thereby failed to see in it the source of nobility. Socrates, by making explicit that eros has many other manifestations in addition to personal love, also makes more explicit than Aristophanes could the way in which erotic striving can be a source of nobility.[9] The desire for creativity or generation which eros inspires (206c ff.) is the source not just of human children,[10] but of the creation of great legal traditions (Solon and Lycurgus are cited: 209d), of the creations of the great poets (such as Homer and Hesiod: 209d), and of philosophy itself, as the famous 'ascent passage' at 210a ff. makes clear.

What is the source of this more positive, potentially noble dimension to human eros? We are shown the source in a passage where Diotima seems to respond to Aristophanes' myth with one of her own. In answer to Socrates' strikingly strange question, 'Who are eros' parents?', Diotima replies that eros is the child of Poros and Penia, of 'Poverty' or 'Lack', but also of 'Plenty' or 'Resourcefulness'.[11] She goes on to describe how the child eros takes after its parents, and so participates, however paradoxically, both in incompleteness or lack, and in a kind of overfullness or resourceful power. If we contrast Diotima's myth to Aristophanes' (as we are clearly invited to do by the very fact that Diotima presents a myth of eros' origins), we could say that Aristophanes was far more struck by eros' maternal inheritance and failed to pay sufficient heed to its paternity. He emphasizes, and by its exclusiveness even exaggerates, the element of incompleteness in eros, but fails to recognize in the element of overfullness the source of creativity (206c ff) and nobility. Eros' parentage, according to Diotima, shows that there is something paradoxical about it; it is at once incomplete and overfull, the true child of Poros and Penia. That paradoxical character does not deny but rather makes it possible that human erotic striving could be, on the one hand, fated to fail, yet on the other hand, a revelation of the nobility of human aspiration; in a word, genuinely tragic.

We can thus formulate the crucial point for our argument. Human eros is not just a source of consolation for foolish humans; in its multiple manifestations, it is the source as well of the noblest of human aspirations.[12] As I have already suggested, this makes the human situation not less but more fully tragic. Not only are humans fated to a condition of incompleteness which they will never fully overcome, not only are they therefore fated to aspire toward a goal to which they are doomed not to attain, but this aspiration, notwithstanding its fated failure, nevertheless can be a failure which, in the striving, ennobles human being. The portrayal of eros in the *Symposium* therefore sets out in full richness the potentially tragic character of the human situation.

I know that this interpretation is controversial. Perhaps the most controversial point is my claim that the project of completeness, precisely in its manifestation as the love of wisdom, is itself incompleteable. Could one not, after all, point to the 'ascent passage', which culminates in a sudden vision of 'Beauty Itself' (211a–b), and which Diotima claims is our achievement of immortality 'if ever it is given to human being to be immortal' (212a) as clear evidence that the project of wholeness in the pursuit of wisdom is by no means incompleteable but fully attainable? Could not one then turn to the *Republic*, in its development of the conditions for training philosopher-kings who would be wise, who would comprehensively know the Forms and rule in light of them, as further confirmation of this possibility of completeness? If so, what could possibly be tragic about a project of wholeness which is in principle fully achievable?

Such a position could be taken and has been taken, most recently by Martha Nussbaum.[13] Before leaving our consideration of the *Symposium*, then, I want to take up her interpretation of it briefly and indicate why I disagree with it so fundamentally, why, *contre* Nussbaum, I hold that the account of eros in the *Symposium*, and indeed Plato's account of the human situation, is deeply sensitive to its tragic dimension.

Nussbaum's interpretation of the *Symposium* concentrates on the speech of Alcibiades.[14] This is already noteworthy, since orthodox interpretations of the *Symposium* usually turn directly to the speech of Socrates, assuming that it will, of course, contain the core of 'Plato's position'. This, for example, is the strategy of Gregory Vlastos in his 'The Individual as Object of Love in Plato's Dialogues',[15] an article which, as so often is the case with Vlastos, establishes the prevailing opinion on the subject. His almost exclusive concentration on Socrates' speech, and his implicit assumption that whatever is contained in that speech must be 'Plato's view', leads him to criticize Plato for ignoring the significance of uniquely individual love in his concern with 'universalizable' and therefore impersonal attributes. Nussbaum's recognition of the greater complexity of the dialogue form in ascertaining 'Plato's view' enables her to call Vlastos' interpretation into question convincingly. Alcibiades' speech, which concentrates on the very personal, individual love of Alcibiades for that unique individual, Socrates, shows clearly (as does Aristophanes' speech), that Plato was aware of the issue of, and the importance of, individual love.[16]

Nevertheless, in the final analysis Nussbaum virtually capitulates to Vlastos' central contention. While she insists that Plato was clearly aware of the attraction of personal love, she concludes that Plato in the *Symposium* is actually presenting us with the choice between his own view, embodied (here she concedes to Vlastos) in the speech of Socrates/Diotima, and the attraction of personal love with which he knows that he must contend:

> We see two kinds of value, two kinds of knowledge; and we see that we must choose. One sort of understanding blocks out the other. The pure light of the eternal form eclipses, or is eclipsed by, the flickering lightning of the opened and unstably moving body. You think, says Plato, that you can have this love and goodness too, this knowledge of and by flesh and good-knowledge too. Well, says Plato, you can't. You have to blind yourself to something, give up some beauty.[17]

Having glimpsed something of the significance of the dramatic form of the dialogue, Nussbaum gives it up too soon and returns to the orthodox assumption that 'Plato's view' is of course located in the speech of Socrates.[18] I would contend that she needs to take her insight one massive step further, and see that 'the Platonic view' is not contained in the speech of any single person in the dialogues, but is located in the elaborate tapestry of the dialogue as a whole. To which it may be objected with some plausibility that surely Socrates ought at least to have pride of place in our interpretations, even as he does in most (but again, not all) of the dialogues. To be sure. But then what are we to make of those dialogues, of which the *Symposium* is a good example, in which Socrates rather quickly departs from his characteristic mode of speech (his brief dialogue with Agathon – 199c–201d) and instead reports what he has heard from someone else (in this case, his instruction on eros under

Diotima)? At the very least, we ought to consider who it is whose speech Socrates is reporting and what effect that personage might have on our construal of the speech. Who, then, is Diotima?

First and foremost, she is a priestess.[19] She speaks, therefore, with the authority of, but also from the finite standpoint of, religious revelation. Now this perspective is without doubt an important and thought-provoking one; but it is not identical with the philosophical standpoint. Perhaps, then, we should not facilely identify the two. We need to ask what modifications we might have to make in order to render this dominantly religious presentation into a more straightforwardly philosophical one. That in turn forces us to ask, what is there about Diotima's speech that seems paradigmatically religious, perhaps even, from a philosophic standpoint, exaggeratedly so? One obvious candidate is the very strong 'otherworldly' tendency of Diotima's position, her tendency to recommend that we 'leave behind' (although she never puts it in exactly these terms, it is an easy inference from her position) the love of individuals, of the body, even of individual souls, in the name of more 'universal' objects, and ultimately, of 'Beauty Itself' (210ff). What is part of the exaggeratedly religious standpoint of the priestess Diotima's position, what needs to be modified in order to arrive at a more genuinely philosophic position, is precisely what Vlastos (and, finally, Nussbaum) take as Plato's own view.

The speeches of Aristophanes and Alcibiades, therefore, are not 'alternatives' to Plato's own view but clues as to the direction in which Diotima's 'otherworldly' tendencies need to be modified. And one thing that they both emphasize, as Nussbaum correctly sees, is personal, individual love, including, certainly, love of the body. I hasten to add, this is not to recommend going to the other extreme, repudiating entirely Diotima's position and opting instead for, say, an 'existentialist' interpretation of Plato. Plato rather invites us, provokes us, to hold the positions together, to recognize and pursue the 'higher' more 'universal' objects of knowledge while at the same time preserving our concern for and even our love of individuals and the bodily. But, it will be objected with Nussbaum, is not preserving both concerns impossible? Precisely! The philosophic enterprise, through and through erotic, seeks to hold the whole together, as one. Without doubt that enterprise is doomed to failure. Yet even in the failure and precisely by striving to achieve the impossible, the pursuit may be the most noble of lives. And that is why philosophy, like the human erotic condition of which it is a high manifestation, is tragic.

But even if the portrayal of philosophy and the human situation in the *Symposium* is tragic, is not the portrayal in the *Republic* a clear and decisive refutation of a tragic element in philosophy? At very least, will we not have to appeal to a 'developmental' hypothesis and say that Plato 'changed his mind' between the *Symposium* and the *Republic*? After all, the *Republic* presents us with an elaborate proposal, on the surface quite serious and straightforward, to educate a class of philosopher-kings who will be not philosophers in the Socratic mode, lacking wisdom, recognizing their lack, and always seeking to overcome their *aporia*, but rather, wise men and women, who comprehensively know the Forms and who, however reluctantly, will rule with perfect justice in the light of their comprehensive wisdom. If such an education is possible, if such wise people are possible, if such a perfectly just city is possible, has Plato not decisively overcome the conditions which might lead us to view human life and philosophy as tragic? What could be tragic about living in a perfectly just city ruled by perfectly wise rulers?

In other publications, I have participated in the controversy regarding whether the portrayal of the 'city in speech' of the *Republic* is to be taken as a real possibility, and to what extent.[20] With crucial qualifications (regarding primarily the 'first wave' of Book V: equal treatment and education of women and men), I conclude that the perfectly just city is not intended by Plato as a real possibility. To cite in review only the most striking evidence, the necessity of the successful implementation of the preposterous 'noble lies' of autochthony and the metallic constitution of souls (*Republic* 414b ff.), the demonstrable incoherence of the arguments for the 'second wave' of Book V (the communality of wives and children, parents not knowing their true children, the bizarre sex laws, etc.), the manifestly ironic acknowledgement at the end of Book VII that the city can in fact be established 'quickly and easily' – by getting rid of everyone over ten years of age (541a), and the concluding remarks, at the end of Book IX, that not only will the city not exist as a real city but that it does not even finally matter that it will not (592a–b), all make clear enough that whatever the complex intentions of the *Republic*, its success does not depend on a claim that such a city is in fact possible. If I am right, then the *Republic* does not contain, as a serious teaching, the anti-tragic optimism regarding the real possibility of a perfectly just regime. Indeed, part of the implausibility of such a regime is the necessity of hypostacized 'philosopher-kings', who are portrayed not as philosophers in the literal sense elsewhere insisted upon and exhibited by Socrates, people who lack wisdom, recognize that lack, and strive for wisdom (and so are exemplars of our erotic nature), but who are portrayed instead as wise people, with a comprehensive knowledge of the Forms and how such Forms are to be applied in governing. If such comprehensive wisdom were genuinely possible, philosophy would hardly be a tragic enterprise; but as the preceding considerations indicate, there is no reason to believe that such a possibility is real.

Why, then, present it? The concluding remarks at the end of Book IX point to the answer:

> "But in heaven," I said, "perhaps, a pattern is laid up for the man who wants to see and found a city within himself on the basis of what he sees. It doesn't make any difference whether it is or will be somewhere. For he would mind the things of this city alone, and of no other." (592b).

Even though impossible, such a city is worthwhile as a goal to be striven after, within the soul of the philosopher. And this is just to confirm the tragic nature of the philosopher, pursuing a goal impossible of full realization, but in doing so, indeed in ultimately failing, living the best possible life.[21] The erotic, and therefore tragic, portrayal of the philosopher in the *Symposium* is preserved in the *Republic*.

In our contemporary epoch, steeped as we are in various forms of 'pragmatism', steeped as well in an acute sensitivity to, perhaps even an obsession with, the dangers of 'frustration', the idea that it might be rational and best to pursue goals known in advance to be impossible is not easily welcomed. We are more likely to recommend, to our children and to ourselves, the pursuit of clearly achievable goals as the surer path to happiness and contentment. Perhaps that is but an indication that we are losing our taste for the tragic. If so, Plato especially challenges us, issues us a provocation, by his presentation of a life recommended as the best life, a life destined to fall short of its goal, a life, as I have tried to show, paradigmatically tragic: the life of philosophy.

Notes

1. I borrow this wonderfully apt term from Mitchell Miller's 'Platonic Provocations: Reflections on the Soul and the Good in the *Republic*', in Dominic J. O'Meara (ed.) *Platonic Investigations* (Washington, DC: Catholic University of America Press, 1985), pp. 163–93.

2. Allan Bloom, *The Republic of Plato* (New York: Basic Books, 1968), p. 381. See also pp. 407–8.

3. Martha Nussbaum, *The Fragility of Goodness: Luck and Ethics in Greek Tragedy and Philosophy* (Cambridge: Cambridge University Press, 1986). See, for example, page 134, where the dialogues are characterized as 'anti-tragic drama'. Nussbaum's interpretation of Plato on this issue is successfully refuted by David Roochnik, 'The Tragic Philosopher: A Critique of Martha Nussbaum', unpublished manuscript.

4. John Harman, 'The Unhappy Philosopher: Plato's *Republic* as Tragedy', *Polity*, vol. XVIII, no. 4, Summer, 1986, pp. 577–94. Stanley Rosen has argued consistently and persuasively that the Platonic portrayal of philosophy is somehow both tragic and comic. See for example his *Plato's Symposium* (New Haven: Yale University Press, 1987), p. 286.

5. *Contre* Nussbaum, *op. cit.*, who characterizes our original condition as 'perfect and self-sufficient physical beings' (p. 172).

6. This is not contradicted by Aristophanes' later claim that 'the best' of these types are the homosexual pairs, of whom the boys enter into politics when they grow up (192a). One need only look quickly at Aristophanes' plays and note the low opinion he generally has of politicians, to see how thoroughly ironic this 'praise' of homosexuality is. Note that in his plays, tyrants are regularly portrayed as homosexuals.

7. I emphasize that I am not hereby claiming a 'definition' of tragedy. I believe there is altogether too much emphasis by scholars on the supposed importance of definition in the Platonic dialogues. It should be noted that, with the bizarre and very superficial exception of the definitions of the four cardinal virtues in the *Republic* (428a ff.), the attempts at definitions – of piety, courage, friendship, *sophrosyne*, knowledge – nearly always fail. The real intent of the regular failure to 'define' the virtues may well be to finally drive us away from an obsession with the closure of definition.

8. *Symposium*, 193c. I follow, with some alterations, the translation of Suzy Groden, *The Symposium of Plato* (Amherst: University of Massachusetts Press, 1970).

9. I emphasize that eros can be a source of nobility, not that it is somehow noble 'in itself'. One of the ways in which Diotima establishes the status of eros as 'in the middle' is that it is in the middle between nobility and baseness (202 ff.). The point is that erotic striving can be noble, and therefore can take on this important dimension of tragic experience.

10. Although even of this creation Diotima insists there is 'something divine' (206c).
11. *Symposium*, 203b ff. It is instructive that 'Poros', in another of its possible meanings as 'way' or 'path', is the root word of the privative, *'aporia'*, that recognition of his lack of knowledge so characteristic of Socrates' philosophic stance.
12. Diotima does not emphasize what is clearly compatible with this claim, namely, that eros can no less be the source of the worst of human aspirations. Plato shows his full cognizance of this by emphasizing in the *Republic* the connection between eros and tyranny (573b,c,d). The *Republic* must thus be read in counterpoint to the *Symposium*. Whereas the *Symposium* emphasizes (and possibly exaggerates) the potential greatness of eros while remaining virtually silent on its dangers, the *Republic*, conversely, emphasizes and even exaggerates the dangers, but virtually suppresses the potential value. In my view, we totally misunderstand Plato's intent here if we resolve this conflict by claiming that Plato 'changed his mind on eros' between the two dialogues.
13. Martha Nussbaum, *The Fragility of Goodness: Luck and Ethics in Greek Tragedy and Philosophy* (Cambridge: Cambridge University Press, 1986). See especially chapters 5–7. A similar point is made more moderately (and implicitly) by Mitchell Miller in his *Plato's Parmenides: The Conversion of the Soul* (Princeton: Princeton University Press, 1986). The full and 'non-imagistic' access to the Forms which Miller sees Plato as arguing for seriously would seem to make the project of wisdom completeable. Under these circumstances, it would be difficult to construe philosophy as 'tragic'. See especially pp. 18–25.
14. Hence the significance of the title of chapter 6 of *The Fragility of Goodness*: 'The Speech of Alcibiades: A Reading of the *Symposium*.' op. cit., pp. 165–234.
15. Vlastos, Gregory, *Platonic Studies*, 2nd edn. (Princeton: Princeton University Press, 1981), pp. 1–34.
16. Nussbaum, op. cit., pp. 167 ff. for the emphasis on individual love in Alcibiades' speech, pp. 173 for her recognition that Aristophanes' speech also exhibits this personal emphasis.
17. Ibid, p. 198. Nussbaum makes clear that she takes the teaching of Socrates' speech, consistent as it is with the 'otherworldliness' of the *Phaedo* and *Republic*, as Plato's own view. See for example pages 152 ff. and 192 ff. On page 195 she characterizes 'personal eros' as 'the plague' which Diotima cures!
18. If only this view were maintained consistently when considering dialogues such as the *Sophist*, *Statesman*, or *Timaeus*, where Socrates is virtually silent!
19. It is no less significant that she is a woman, though the importance of this is not directly germane to this paper.
20. Drew Hyland, 'Taking the Longer Road: The Irony of Plato's *Republic*', forthcoming in *Revue de Metaphysique et de Morale*, and

especially Hyland, Drew, 'Plato's Three Waves and the Question of Utopia', forthcoming.

21. For other ways in which the philosopher of the *Republic* is tragic, see Harman, John D., 'The Unhappy Philosopher: Plato's *Republic* as Tragedy', *Polity*, vol. XVIII, no. 4, Summer 1986, pp. 577–94.

8
Philosophy and Tragedy: The Flaw of Eros and the Triumph of Agape

CARL R. HAUSMAN

The *modus operandi* that drives philosophy by nature possesses a tragic flaw. Obviously, justification for this claim depends in part on what I mean by the ideas of tragedy and philosophy. In brief, I assume that the term 'tragic' applies properly to an agent who engages in a noble effort that inevitably fails and fails because of the nature of the agent. I shall elaborate on this conception later. The term 'philosophy', in the most straightforward sense, may be understood with the aid of the etymology of the word, namely, 'the love of wisdom'. However, this characterization of it in turn depends on what is meant by 'love' and 'wisdom'. Both terms will play a role in the discussion to follow, and the meaning I give them will, I trust, become evident in that context.

THE SCOPE OF PHILOSOPHY

Philosophy is essentially critical, systematic, and unrelenting in pursuing an ultimate goal. Being unrelenting and pursuing a goal are marks of the love that drives philosophical activity. And the goal of this activity may be referred to as 'wisdom', which is at least ideally final and which is understood as exhaustive and exclusive, including the legitimatizing of its own activity, so that it is reflexive – a point to be considered at a later stage of these remarks. As exhaustive, it is all-embracing, having as its scope all that can be known. As exclusive, it precludes all other possible claims to exhaustiveness, unless they are assimilated to it. The goal of philosophy, then, is something to be understood as categorical, apodictic (necessary), and unrestrictedly universal, having reference to all possible and actual classes of thoughts and objects of thoughts.

My characterization of philosophy obviously may be challenged. One possible objection is that it does not apply to all activities that have been regarded as philosophical. In response, I should first acknowledge that my main concern is to suggest how much of pre-twentieth and some twentieth century traditional, systematic philosophy possesses a tragic flaw. Thus, I am interested in philosophy in the 'grand tradition' – a tradition, let it be noted, that includes anti-metaphysical forays as well as materialisms, idealisms, holisms, etc., that may be aligned with metaphysics. Yet there are reasons for going further and proposing that the conception of philosophy that I have briefly outlined applies to some, if not all, the recent views of philosophy that might be thought to elude the tragic flaw because of their repudiation of philosophical aspirations to understand the fundamental source of all that is and all that can be said. It is appropriate at the outset, then, to try to show, at least briefly, that even philosophical views that eschew claims to extend their knowledge to the whole of things are tied to the kind of goal just described.

We may begin with a remark about one of the earliest advocates of the view that philosophy is restricted and not only cannot, and in principle ought not, to attempt the goal of finality: Protagoras. The principle attributed to him directly expresses a skeptical restriction on the aims of philosophy that Protagoras found in the Pre-Socratics, who attempted to identify the fundamental reality underlying all process. Protagoras proclaimed, 'Of all things the measure is man: of existing things, that they exist; of nonexistent things, that they do not exist.'[1] Thus, he proposes that Pre-Socratic metaphysics be replaced by a limited hope. According to Robinson's consideration of Plato's interpretation of Protagoras' words, the man who is the judge referred to is each individual rather than mankind. Thus, each living human being ought only to hope to determine the proper – conventional, efficient, and fruitful – way to live. However, Protagoras does not put forth his principle tentatively or in a limited way. He does not claim that his principle expresses one perspective among others. In affirming this maxim, Protagoras offers an apodictive, categorical, and all-embracing principle, a claim about the whole of things, because he asserts not only something about all things, but also something about the exclusive status of knowledge (the measure) that is proper for apprehending all things. He affirms something exhaustive about the whole of knowledge and its object.

If we now leap into the twentieth century and consider the so-called analytic tradition, including logical positivism, logical empiricism, and ordinary language philosophy, we see a similar if not identical goal of universality and all-inclusiveness. One assumption at the basis of these traditions is that philosophical language is not properly about objects; that is, it is not significant by virtue of referring to things available for inspection independently of the language that does the referring. Instead, it is logical in the sense that it is about relations among concepts about objects. In this sense, to be logical is to have a 'meta' status that is not confined to formal logic and that may include ordinary language analysis. In any case, this orientation itself may be regarded as either philosophical or meta-philosophical. If it is the latter, then either it is not relevant to the issue of whether there is a tragic flaw in philosophy or it is relevant because, as meta-philosophical, it may be assumed to have a philosophical status in the sense that it is offered as a philosophical claim about philosophy. I think the latter interpretation is correct. A meta-philosophical claim about philosophy does itself have philosophical status. It is a claim the significance of which is philosophical, even if its 'meta' relation to its object, philosophy, is supposed to be only logical. It is aimed at making a universal, all-embracing assertion about its subject-matter. It asserts something about all that is intelligible – in terms of science, philosophy, and common sense or ordinary languages that either are translatable into scientific language or into some ideal language amenable to philosophical logic. I shall briefly spell out this point with reference to several representative twentieth-century philosophers. However, let me first consider further the status of meta-philosophy.

I have said that even a meta-philosophical characterization of philosophy has philosophical significance. The chief reason for my claim has to do with the character of philosophy and the relation of assertions to their objects. A perceptual judgment such as 'The grass is green' purportedly refers to an object, an object that is at least phenomenally present and standing as a referent of the judgment. Further, the judgment is of a different order of reality or being than its object. Whether one construes the judgment as a mental act or as a proposition that either is a meaning independent of thought or a general rule for experiencing consequences that follow from acting on the judgment, what is referred to is distinct from and, as an object, is independent of the judgment in that it is not in itself a judgment. On the other hand, a second order judgment, a judgment about judgment, or about the significance of the relationships that judgments and their objects exhibit, shares something in common with its object. Its object at least in part is of the same logical or ontological genus as the judgment. In this sense, such judgments are reflexive. This, I suggest, is the kind of reflexivity that meta-philosophical claims about philosophy have. Philosophical inquiry infects the meta-philosophical inquiry in the sense that like philosophy, meta-philosophy is reflexive. With this brief answer to the proposal that meta-philosophy may escape the characterization I am proposing for philosophy in mind, I should like to return to that characterization, mentioning some examples.

Willard Quine prefaces *Word and Object* with a statement that is made categorically and presumably with reference to language as a whole: 'Language is a social art'.[2] And the book as a whole makes assertions about language, including the relation of language to truth. Consider also his discussion of Dewey's naturalistic view of language. He points out that observable behavior is the only evidence for deciding on meaning, as exemplified, in particular, in translating from one language to another. One might suggest that this point might be understood within restrictions imposed by a science of linguistics or a psychology, with no intended philosophical significance. Quine's discussion and Dewey's conception of meaning, however, are more than matters confined to linguistics or to psychology. They are offered as bases for telling us something about what is exhaustively true of mind and its relation to nature. Further, Quine is discussing theories in general and to that extent is engaged in a reflective activity that gives it universal scope with respect to making things intelligible.[3]

It might be objected that even if the analytic rejection of the traditional aim of philosophy commits the analyst to universal claims about all that is intelligible, nevertheless, what is said about philosophy exempts it from aiming at a vision of the whole of things. The analyst's view claims that the legitimate, underlying philosophical aim is not at bottom all-comprehensive, but instead is or ought to be, when explicit about its intent, limited in being committed only to the clarification or the exhibition of speech or thought patterns. But this objection assumes the meta-philosophical view, exempting the philosopher's speech about the aim of philosophy from the philosophy being considered. Thus, although the claim is that philosophy has misunderstood its own aim of being categorical and unrestrictedly universal, the meta-status of the analytic view, as already pointed out, is itself assertive and comprehensive in scope, even if methodological or logical in form.

The central point I want to emphasize is that the anti-metaphysical tradition in philosophy shares with what may be called the 'metaphysical tradition' – which explicitly makes metaphysical claims that are universal and all-embracing – the distinctive characteristic of philosophy as a field that aims at exhaustive affirmation and, as already suggested, that is reflexive. This tradition is well illustrated by Brand Blanshard in his early *The Nature of Thought*, and in later volumes devoted to various issues including ethics and religion.[4] The tradition is also illustrated by idealism in England and Germany and, of course, in rationalisms such as those of Descartes, Spinoza, and Leibniz, and in empiricism such as that of Hume, who points out that one cannot attack metaphysics without engaging in metaphysics.

In pursuing its aims as philosophy, the assertions or proposals of philosophers take themselves into account. Philosophy is essentially reflexive, because its aim is to be all-embracing, so that it cannot avoid taking account of its own status. Thus, even if a philosopher disclaims making statements about what is, the philosopher says something about what must be substituted as the proper domain of philosophical statements. And this, at least by implication, is to be concerned with the concerns of traditional metaphysics, which inquires about what is in the most general way.

If my point about philosophy holds for the analytic orientation, does it also hold for deconstructionist views in the continental tradition, and in recent developments in the United States characterizable as feeding on the linguistic turn, according to which all assertions about a reality are exhaustively dependent on linguistic fashions? It seems to me that writers committed to these views are also intent on reconstituting philosophy, offering therapeutic advice for misguided foundationalists and ideal language theorists. Even if it is urged – how, for them, could it be argued? – that language is not about the world except insofar as the world is what language games construe it to be; even if it is urged that it is futile to search for or be committed to a reality that is said to be independent, and accessible somehow in the (perhaps infinite) future, such an urging is nevertheless a glorification of something, a futility, entertained as exclusively universal. The contingency of all things and all vocabularies displaces the possibility of an ideal, universal vocabulary commensurate with decisive, fundamental principles of reason and feeling. If anything functions as a commitment to an exhaustive condition to be recommended for future philosophy, and for all other attempts to deal with human relations in society – and in the context of what natural sciences inquire about – surely this new form of relativism is as categorical and unrestrictedly universal as the relativism of Protagoras and other repudiators of philosophical fundamentalism. In any case, my suggestion is that anyone who purports to pursue or reject an aim from the vantage point of philosophy is committed in a way that exhibits a tragic flaw. Let me turn to a characterization of this flaw.

THE TRAGIC FLAW

My brief characterization of the conception of what is tragic at the outset identified as its key, nobility that necessitates failure. In order to develop this idea, I should like to begin with several points found in a characterization of tragedy that I offered elsewhere.[5] In this discussion, my focus was on an insight that I believe is evident in Sophocles' treatment of inevitability and choice in his dramas, *Oedipus Rex* and *Antigone*. Although many of the points in the discussion are relevant specifically to literary aspects of the presence of a tragic flaw in human action, the features that distinguish the condition identified as a tragic flaw can be singled out and applied to our topic.[6] In connection with tragedy and inevitable failure, four themes were considered: *conflict, fate, evil,* and *freedom* and *guilt*. These are applicable to the situations and personalities of the heroes. However, it is possible to specify some of the features of these themes when applied to the philosophical enterprise. With respect to the last idea, freedom and guilt, the latter component will be set aside, because it is a function of a psychological state or awareness, which is not for my purposes relevant to my claim about philosophy.

The first theme, conflict, is important because its expression in the context of tragic drama is the outcome of a determinate way in which the poles of the conflict assert themselves. Each antagonist –

'[e]ach force, each value, is asserted exclusively, as if it were supreme'.[7] The effort that is or becomes tragic is exerted as if it were unqualifiedly justified. The force that drives the antagonist is expressed as if it were infallible. The assertion of a tragic force is not sheer bigotry or blind intolerance, although a certain intolerance must accompany what is asserted exclusively. The assertion of a tragic force is directed toward what functions as a noble end for the agency that exerts that force. In the context of literature, such an agency is heroic – committed, courageous in self-sacrificing determination with respect to seeking the noble end.

The theme of fate in literary expression is associated with preordination and doom. When abstracted from this context, fate may be regarded as necessity, as unavoidable development, not necessarily in every detail, but necessarily in a determinate direction and toward an end. The main characteristic of this condition that is applicable to our topic is inevitability. What is inevitable is the unrelenting pursuit of the end that gives direction to the pursuit.

What is called 'doom' in the literary context is directly linked to the third theme, evil. In the life of a tragic hero, there is suffering and misfortune, eventually destruction that is either utter or partial. This is evil when considered in terms of tragic drama. Abstracted for application to what is tragic in philosophy, the idea of evil becomes the idea of failure, which is a state that is shared with the destructive component of fated evil. The inexorable drive toward a noble end that inevitably meets with doom is a drive that fails. Failure may not be complete, and it may be accompanied by partial success. Nevertheless, insofar as the essential function of the noble effort is thwarted, there is tragic failure.

The theme of freedom indicates that what is tragic is not an activity or drive that is blindly undertaken, as if the agent who expresses a heroic effort in aiming at a noble end were doing so mechanically, or according to antecedent causes that serve as the basis for completely predictable results. The agent chooses to act in accord with the inexorably driven activity that fulfills the development that must fail. There is a teleological character to the action of that which is tragic. And this teleological character does not qualify blind effort. In this sense, tragedy involves freedom. The hero assumes responsibility for the choice and drive toward an end. At the conscious level at least, the course of events that become tragic is freely entered. Thus, there must be room for departures from the

exact regularities of the activity in which tragic effort is expended.
These departures are not effective enough to break the necessity of
reaching failure. Yet they do permit certain developments that
could not have been predicted or deduced by informal or formal
logic. Variations are possible that are not predestined, while the
general failure with respect to the achievement of the end is
predestined. This mixture of necessity and spontaneity will be seen
to be crucial to the application of this characterization of tragic
action to philosophy. We must now turn to this application.

TRAGEDY IN PHILOSOPHICAL THOUGHT

The application of what has been said about the character of
tragedy as abstracted from its presence in literature may lead in
two directions. The first already has been indicated in what was
said in the beginning about the character of philosophy, namely,
that it is driven by a love of wisdom. The second has to do with the
condition of experience, or more generally, the cosmos, that
grounds the tragic flaw of philosophy. Consideration of this
application will move our discussion into the domain of
philosophy, and this raises the question whether my own view is
not subject to the tragic flaw that I find in philosophy in general.
This issue will be addressed later. Let us first turn to the direct
application of the conditions related to the themes of tragedy in
literature.

The four features that have been abstracted from the conditions
of tragedy in literature can be correlated with the two conditions of
philosophy, love and wisdom. The first feature, claiming or
asserting a demand exclusively, correlates with the condition of
wisdom. The other three features of tragedy are correlated with
love. I would like to take these conditions and features in order,
thus reversing the two dimensions of philosophy.

Wisdom, it will be recalled, is a state of knowledge that concerns
the whole of things. Its correlation with the first condition of
tragedy, then, is straightforward. In seeking wisdom, philosophy
would reach a state in which the expression of its knowledge is
categorical and unrestrictively universal. The force that drives it is
admirable, marking the drive of human intelligence to achieve
perfection. In the way of a tragic hero, the lover of wisdom strives
for and often presumes to have found a way to provide, at least in

principle, a complete account of things, a principle or basis for a vision of the whole of things. This is not to lay claim to a set of statements that leave nothing unsaid, but rather to say what is necessary so that all possible statements could be inferred from the insight of wisdom. And in this sense, the philosopher assumes, as philosopher, that what is appropriate to say is said exhaustively and exclusively. Like the tragic hero in literature that I have assumed in describing the features of tragedy, the wisdom-seeking philosopher may be regarded as having (or at least as aiming at) a kind of blindness. That is, an opposite point of view must be denied by the wisdom-seeking philosopher for the sake of the ideal heroically affirmed. It cannot stand on equal footing with the ideal. The philosopher's eyes must be closed to whatever does not fit the account that exhibits wisdom. Even if opposition is given a place in the whole that is envisaged in the account that has achieved wisdom, the opposition has less status than the whole to which it belongs. If it is not absolutely rejected, it is absolutely limited – restricted to a place of subordination or outright exclusion. For instance, for Hume, necessary connection understood as a relation in matters of fact such that its denial would be a self-contradiction is excluded from the proposed wisdom of his empiricism. More generally, *a priority* is excluded from knowledge of matters of fact. For Charles Peirce, intuitions are not excluded, but are subordinated. Intuition is permitted as long as it is not proposed as having cognitive status. It plays a supportive role for cognition, although cognition cannot be understood as deducible from it.

The love that is directed toward wisdom is driven. And if it could reach its beloved, wisdom, it would terminate, being merged with its goal. There is a gripping power in philosophical effort, a compulsiveness to become clearer and to reach finality. This effort can be understood in the light of tragic fate in the sense that it follows its course in accord with a necessity, a preordained pursuit in its unrelenting demand for critical attention to whatever it finds and reflective concern for probing beyond any given moment of thought. If it pauses, it does so within a larger process that is necessitated by its aims. This unrelenting pursuit of its goal is the mark of the kind of love that is called eros. This way of understanding the love of wisdom was, of course, made explicit in the work of Plato. It is Socrates' eros that drives him in his pursuit of his mission. The characteristics of eros are described in Plato's *Symposium*. Eros flows from a lack that is to be filled. Eros seeks the perfection of the ideal that lures it. It is driven toward a union with its beloved, its goal of complete intelligibility. The conception of the love of wisdom in terms of eros is important for a qualification that I shall introduce later. At the moment, our purpose is to see how this love is structurally like the assertiveness of the tragic drive. Like eros, what is tragic is driven. Like eros, it seeks exclusively. And its demand is for an ideal that it envisages.

Let me pause here to raise an issue that suggests a qualification and a paradox in what I have been claiming. One might ask whether Plato and philosophers in general may be aware that the pursuit of wisdom must end in failure. There is evidence that Plato thought as much, particularly in his refusal to offer a conceptual, rational account of the Good and his introduction of the paradox of the realization of a perfect state. And the very radical skepticism that I have said is asserted exclusively and categorically, may be an acknowledgement of the failure of the pursuit of wisdom. However, there is a peculiarity in such an acknowledgement. If awareness of failure were internal to the philosophical view that the philosopher wants to develop, then the development itself would be futile. That is, in accord with philosophical inquiry that is driven by eros, if failure were held explicitly before attention, the assertion of the view, for instance, of the Platonic doctrine of human aspiration and the end of thinking through understanding the doctrine of Forms and gaining insight through the myths that surpass dialectical discourse, would be to assert its failure from the outset. The move to myth in the case of Plato might be taken as the exhibition of this acknowledgement. Yet it seems to me that the myths are offered as ways to an insight that must be seen as related to the dialectical development of a view that is completed by the myth. The very presence of the myth reveals that eros is still alive and that wisdom is a goal. Thus, the awareness of failure is expected to give way to success.

If the awareness of the futility of seeking wisdom is external, then it takes on a meta-philosophical status; that is, it is meta with respect to the whole of the particular pursuit of wisdom under-taken by the philosopher who is aware of the tragedy of philosophy. This alternative is addressed in the attention I shall give later to the question of whether the claim I am making exemplifies itself.

The third feature of the tragic, evil, is present in philosophy as its flaw. As suggested earlier, the flaw is a function of failure, and in the case of tragic failure, it is inevitable. As just suggested, Plato acknowledges this inevitability of failure, as he recognized the eros of philosophy. The physical and empirical condition of the human soul limits the fulfilment of the goal of philosophy. A vision of the Ideas or Forms is what lures philosophical thought, but insight into them, such as is expected of the rulers of the ideal state, depends on knowledge of The Good, and this knowledge can only be referred to by analogy – by the symbol of the sun, by the journey through the cave to vision under and into the sun, and by diagram. Only the ideal wise person can transcend limitation to this kind of speech. Eros can never reach its beloved. It must fail.

The last feature of tragedy to be correlated with philosophical love is freedom. As already indicated, one might conclude that there is no room for freedom in the scheme outlined for tragedy according to which both the drive and failure in achieving its goal are conditioned by necessity. However, as also indicated, there is room for departures from a strict logic of events within the web of necessity. Thus, eros is not bound in every detail to the development of its effort in its pursuit of its goal. If this were not so, there would have been only one philosophical position in our heritage. The necessity of the tragic venture is internal to the choices made in the argument, clarification and probing that characterize each philosophical endeavor. This is to say that there is freedom internal to the necessity that governs the unrelenting force of philosophical eros. The development of a philosophical view occurs in a context of inevitability. Yet the larger context does not require that each detail be predetermined. Only the comprehensiveness of the end sought for is necessitated – not in minute detail, but in the overall shape of wholeness. The individual stages are not necessitated. In correspondence with the tragic as it is drawn from literature, this freedom is integral to and constitutive of the necessary happenings that push and pull thought onward toward the envisaged complete account of things. Analogously, Oedipus' decision to kill the person who, unknown to Oedipus, was his father, was a decision that could have been different. In that sense, he decided freely and was responsible for his choice. It was not this free decision itself that necessitated failure. It was the general laws of human nature and the cosmos that necessitated the general condition of his failure. So too when Hume decided to regard empirical knowledge as founded in impressions, he decided freely to adopt a fundamental assumption inherited from his tradition. However, it was not this decision itself that ensured failure, any more than was Descartes' decision to adopt an apriorist foundation. Instead, it was the conclusion each affirmed about the whole of things that yielded failure because the very determination of the affirmation implied wholeness that was not wholeness – a wholeness that as determinate is not after all exhaustive and comprehensive. What is important at the moment is that each move on the way to the conclusion is free insofar as that move could have been otherwise.

However, I want to suggest that there may be a more radical kind of freedom. The account of what I mean is integral to what I shall say about the issue mentioned earlier, namely, that the discussion of our topic is itself a philosophical effort; thus it may fall prey to its own claims and must be doomed to failure. What kind of failure would this be? And what consequences follow for one possible direction in which philosophy may be pursued in the future?

THE FUTURE OF PHILOSOPHY AS TRAGIC

The proposals I have made about the tragic dimension of philosophy have not been offered as the ingredients of a philosophical position. They have been made from a perspective that relates philosophy to certain ideas in literature, and they have been intended as reflections on the significance of philosophy for one who is committed to arriving at a position. This purpose may be thought of as meta-philosophical. Yet, as pointed out in connection with some of the contemporary critiques of traditional philosophy, having a meta status does not relieve the meta-philosophical of the philosophical aims which it is about. Reflecting on philosophy requires a consideration of the whole to which philosophy is said to be committed. And reflection on philosophy in a sense illustrates the very point made about philosophy, that it is unrelenting, driven, erotic, for this reflection is itself a continuation of the philosophical drive. It is an extension of the search for wisdom. Consequently, the discussion in this paper must be subject to the flaw common to philosophical pursuits. Does this mean that the claim that philosophy is tragic, that it cannot escape failure, is itself flawed, so that the statement that there is a flaw is necessarily flawed? In making a claim about philosophy as such, it seems that I must propose a determinate view, a bit of alleged 'wisdom'.

I think that the possibility of being wrong is essential. Thus, if I am right about the tragedy and thus the flaw and inevitable failure of philosophy in the achievement of its ideal, then I must acknowledge that flaw in what I have said, insofar as what I have said is philosophical. However, granted the inevitable fallibility of what I have proposed, there are two qualifications that should be highlighted. First, the failure need not be located in the thesis that philosophy is tragic, but in the overall stance that my view must take – that is, in the position that is implied or presupposed. And this, or that part of which I am aware, will be suggested in a moment. Second, even if the flaw lies in the claim that there is an inevitable flaw in every philosophical enterprise, this possibility does not preclude what I think is the associated possibility that the undermining of my claim by what it claims is itself subject to being undermined as long as philosophical thought continues. For as long as philosophical activity occurs, it must be headed toward something not yet achieved, and this leaves it open to the limits that yield error. I shall leave this response as it stands. More important is the first suggestion that the flaw in what I have proposed lies in the larger position that is presupposed.

The philosophical outlook at the basis of the claim that philosophy is tragic is a form of fallibilism, and this fallibilism, I think, is closest to that of Charles S. Peirce. I say this not simply because he declared himself as a fallibilist in affirming his version of pragmatism, called 'pragmaticism'. There is an additional reason that centers on a relatively overlooked part of Peirce's philosophy that is found in a series of papers he wrote for *The Monist* in the 1890s. In that series, he introduced an idea of evolutionary love, agape, that clearly contrasts with the love identified as eros. He does so in the context of discussing his view of cosmic evolution, as well as the history of thought. Although agape is mentioned by name very few times in his writings, the idea threads its way through them and is particularly evident in the last stages of his career. My purpose, however, is not to discuss Peirce's doctrine of agapasticism, but to make use of the idea of agape as he thought of it in order to merge the points made about philosophical love with the point about my presupposed position as subject to the philosophical tragic flaw described in this discussion.

If the conception of philosophical love is broadened so that it is not interpreted exclusively as Platonic eros, but is interpreted so that it includes agape, the presence of the flaw and inevitable failure of philosophy can be given a proper place, a place that suggests that inevitable failure implies a flaw that is a virtue – a suggestion that might be appropriate for interpreting the flaw of the tragic hero in literature. This does not lessen the failure, but it suggests that the failure is to be both admired and sought after, insofar as it is the expression of a condition of the inevitability and limitations of the agency that engages in philosophical activity.

Agapistic love is not, like eros, a love that is driven to overcome a lack. It is a love that flows from the possession of something that is conferred on what is lacking. It is a giving. However, it is a giving that does not require predetermined acceptance or a specific kind of response, if it is accepted by a receiver. The receiver may oppose the source of the gift – may be 'hateful' to the source; yet the source permits it to go its own way. What is important about this giving, then, is the openness to something other than the agency and the agapistic effort. Thus, agapistic love is permissive of flaws. It does not propose that what it gives to must do and be in just the way that agape is and acts. Agape is the love of creative development. It leaves open to what it loves the possibility of departure from its own determinations. Thus, if philosophy can be agapistic as well as erotic – and erotic only with respect to non-final goals – then it can accept its own flaw. It can support the freedom described earlier as integral to the necessity of the tragic drive.

Let me formulate my point in a somewhat less figurative way. Philosophical argumentation that is headed toward wisdom must be open – ready to accept – its inevitable failure to achieve the perfection of an exhaustive account that is universal, necessary, and comprehensive with regard to experience and nature. I am recommending that philosophers strive to reach wisdom even though they know that they cannot reach it. This striving is the expression of something that is more like Peirce's agape than Plato's eros.

The upshot of these reflections is not that the future of philosophy should lie in trying to overcome its tragic nature, but rather that philosophy live with and foster this nature by insisting on its own growth, which is possible by virtue of its own failures. This is not to recommend that we abandon philosophy to the contingencies of language. It is to recommend that we unrelentingly persist in transcending the constraints of determinate outlooks gained in the pursuit of a receding vision of the whole.

Perhaps this is a version of what Sophocles had as a vision in his own tragedies, and why *Oedipus Rex* was followed by *Oedipus at Colonus*. The tragic hero's flaw is the tragic hero's redemption. Philosophy's tragic nature is its redemption and superiority over itself.

Notes

1. I follow John Mansley Robinson in *An Introduction to Early Greek Philosophy: The Chief Fraqments and Ancient Testimony, with Connective Commentary* (Boston: Houghton Mifflin, 1968), p.245.
2. Willard Van Orman Quine, *Word and Object* (Cambridge, Mass: MIT Press, 1960), p.ix.
3. Willard Van Orman Quine, 'Ontological Relativity', in *Ontological Relativity and Other Essays* (New York: Columbia University Press, 1969, pp.26–68.
4. Brand Blanshard, *The Nature of Thought* (New York: Humanities Press, 1964).
5. Carl R. Hausman, 'Sophocles and the Metaphysical Question of Tragedy', *The Personalist*, vol. 47, no. 4, Autumn 1966, 509–19.
6. I use the word 'literary' and the conception of literature with reference to expression that functions aesthetically. To function aesthetically is to function so that attention is directed toward its object for its own sake, for its intrinsic value, as such value constitutes or enhances the content and form of the expression. In the present context, I must bypass the many issues connected with characterizing what is properly called 'literary' or 'literature' in this sense of aesthetic function.
7. Ibid., p.510.

9

Being at a Loss: Reflections on Philosophy and the Tragic

WILLIAM DESMOND

I

Howl, howl, howl, howl! . . .

A violently reiterated Howl is not the usual way to initiate a philosophical meditation. Neither Aristotle's list of categories nor Kant's table make mention of any Howl. Hegel's *Science of Logic* contains no concept corresponding to Howl. There is no Platonic *eidos* of Howl. Indeed the Howl seems to shout down, shout against all categories, drowning out the civilities of reason in its brute explosiveness. Perhaps we might think of the cynics, the dog-philosophers as not silencing the Howl. But Hegel saw nothing much in Diogenes', bastard offspring of Socrates. Nor did he take much notice of Diogenes' self-description: the watchdog of Zeus. And many philosophers are much more Hegelian than they realize, or care to know. We will shrug it off. With sweet reason on our side, we will say: Why have a bad conscience in turning from the Howl? Where can Howling find its place in the ideal speech situation? This Howl is no voice in the grand 'conversation of mankind'. The rest is philosophical silence.

Yet this Howl is different. A silence that merely shrugs it off betrays philosophy. For this Howl breaks forth as one of the great conceptless voices in the 'conversation of mankind'. Perhaps it would be better to say the Howl is a 'transconceptual voice'. Thereby we keep alive this ambiguity: is the Howl other than conceptual, being empty of concepts, or is it more than every concept, hence full of a challenge philosophy must strain to think? For this reiterated Howl is the agonized voice of Lear, coming on stage with the dead body of Cordelia in his arms.

154

> Howl, howl, howl, howl! O, you are men of stones:
> Had I your tongues and eyes, I'd use them so
> That heaven's vault should crack. She's gone for ever.
> I know when one is dead and when one lives;
> She's dead as earth.
>
> (*King Lear*, V, iii, 259–63)

The philosopher has no category of Howl. Who then are the men of stones? Is Spinoza a man of stones in describing his philosophical desire: not to laugh, not to weep, not to detest, but only to understand? Is this what philosophy will do? Give us eyes and tongues, but eyes and tongues that are stones? We cannot, we will not speak about this Howl. We will be silent about heaven. Will we, like Anaxagoras, turn the sun into a god of stone? How then will we look on life and death? As if philosophical reason had nothing to do with life or death? And where then are our categories for that simple phrase that assaults the disarrayed mind: 'For Ever'?

Lear's Howl is a transconceptual voice in the 'conversation of mankind' that not only ruptures all logical systems but threatens the very basis of that civilized conversation. It threatens, not because it will not hear the other, but rather from excess of hearing, from excess of exposure to an otherness that destroys every human self-sufficiency. Can philosophy listen to this Howl and not risk the ruin of thinking? For when one hears that Howl a crushing night descends wherein the mind is threatened with blacking out or going blank. The mind shudders, as if a dark abyss had opened and swallowed all sense. Rational mind undergoes a liquefaction in which all intelligibility seems to be reclaimed by a malign formlessness. There is anguish before this Howl.

The Howl is an outcry. It reminds us of the great outcry of Dostoevski, in the howl of Ivan Karamazov, against the suffering of innocent children. What is the source of this outcry? Why listen to it? Thinking too much on it – will it not make us mad? Like Lear's Howl it issues forth from a depth of our exposed being that seems to elude conceptual encapsulation. The Psalm says it: *De profundis ad te Domine clamavi*. But what are those depths, what cries out from those depths? The Howl as an outcry is a cry from the heart. But what is a cry from the heart? What otherness has stirred the heart to this outcry? Must philosophy default here? Can there be a systematic science of such cries? Would not a systematic

pretense be nonsense, a folly of logic? Such a cry, such an outcry, is
elemental. If logic would that it were not heard, if it tried to stifle
the outcry, would not logic prove itself to be metaphysical
madness? Does the outcry need tragic saying? Can tragic art alone
make us hear this Howl?

But our listening to the agony of Lear's outcry is not over. Have
the men of stones the tongues and eyes for this savage saying:

> And my poor fool is hanged: no, no, no, life?
> Why should a dog, a horse, a rat, have life,
> And thou no breath at all? Thou'lt come no more,
> Never, never, never, never, never.
>
> (*Lear*, V, iii, 307–10).

This Never is an absolutely crushing word.[1] Perhaps never has the
word Never been uttered as crushingly as by Lear. Can
philosophical dialectics take us into this Never, beyond this Never?
Can the universal of logic or Hegel's world-history ever unharden
the irrevocability of Lear's savage, reiterated Never? What can
philosophy ever tell Lear, what alleviation give him in his
elemental grief? What consolation could the Platonic eidos, or
Husserl's *strenge Wissenschaft* ever offer? What, to reverse hearer
and listener, does the conceptless voice of tragedy tell philosophy?
What can we philosophers hear in this Howl, in this For Ever, in
this Never? In their metaphysical horror is there incitement to think
about essential and unavoidable enigmas – tragic enigmas forcing
philosophy to its own extremes where its concepts begin to break
down? Can philosophical mind break through to a deeper
metaphysical thinking even in this breakdown?

II

I step back from the edge to approach these questions. First I will
speak of philosophy and the tragic, most especially in relation to
Plato, considered by many, Nietzsche not least, to be the arch
enemy of tragedy. I will say that this is too simplistic: philosophy
has a complex, plurivocal identity, not reducible to scientific
cognition, though not exclusive of rational cognition. Philosophy
can be especially attentive to certain fundamental tensions between
determinate knowing and significant indeterminacies of being

beyond encapsulation in specific concepts. In a subsequent section I will reflect on such tensions in relation to Lear's Never and the related notions it calls forth.

I am not primarily interested in tragedy as a problem in aesthetics. Modern aesthetics tends to be too much in the grip of an aestheticism that compartmentalizes art: in its excessive insistence that art is art, that art is for art's sake, that art is resistant to any intrusion from what is other to art, post-Kantian aesthetics ends up divorcing art from its origin in the fundamental creative and tragic powers of human existence. In elevating art into a false self-sufficiency, it ends up diminishing art's metaphysical power. This power interests me. I ask: What is it about *being* that is revealed by the tragic? More specifically, what does it mean to be in the guise of *being at a loss*? Tragedy reveals one of the ultimate forms of being at a loss. In a tragic situation we were faced with boundaries from which there is no escape. We are backed against a wall, as it were. We are pushed without easy recourse into a dead end of being. How we are and what we do in this *cul de sac* is revealing of what it is to be.

If my interest is metaphysical, I immediately add that metaphysics here escapes the stock Heideggerian charge of 'metaphysics of presence'. As is well known, Heideggerians accuse all of metaphysics, from Plato to Nietzsche, of being some form of the 'metaphysics of presence'. I say: If metaphysics can meditate on the tragic in the guise of being at a loss, then it is ridiculous to see all this as 'metaphysics of presence'. Being at a loss shows tragic experience as already deconstructing the 'metaphysics of presence'. True, there is a philosophical tendency that would immediately want to convert being at a loss into some totally rational picture, see the loss as a mere prelude to a positive founding, a being refound, a new foundation, and so on.

I believe metaphysical reflection is capable of a more complex response. Being at a loss it not a mere absence, relative to which a dialectical interplay can be quickly initiated. Here an absence does not dialectically provoke its contrary presence, such that tragedy would be the play of absence and presence, with the presence more clearly grasped by the philosopher than by the tragic artist or the person undergoing the tragic. This again is too simple. Certain exposures to being at a loss seem to be unsurpassable in the direction of a positive finding that we can articulate on this side of going under into death. Or: a certain suffering knowing of being at a loss may itself be what is affirmative in tragic undergoing. Metaphysical meditation on that suffering knowing is solicited.

We begin to see the emergence of the crucial tension between philosophy and the tragic. Traditionally philosophy has presented itself as the quest for a rational account, indeed a rational account of being in the most comprehensive sense: a *logos* of the whole. The implicit presupposition of this entire quest is that being as a whole is ultimately intelligible. Should we think radically enough, should we take our logos, logic, to the ultimate boundary, then being as a whole will reveal itself as available for intelligence, for reason. *To gar auto noein esti te kai einai*: to be and to think are one and the same. This utterance of Parmenides (frag. 3) seems to be the complete antipodes of Lear's Howl. Parmenides' saying is susceptible of a number of interpretations, but these are not the point here. The point is that philosophy seems driven by the conviction, should we say faith, that being is not ultimately tragic. True reason will never be at a loss; true reason will be the intelligent *finding* of the deep logical intelligibility that is inherent in the nature of things.

Philosophy does not deny that enigmatic and recalcitrant events do strike us, or that, to all appearances, we do experience being at a loss. But these are often seen as the ambiguous, perhaps duplicitous appearances that a more penetrating mindfulness will surpass. Parmenides says (frag. 6): the many wander like hordes that are double-headed, *dikranoi*: two-headed, in two minds, at a loss what to think one way or the other. The many do not find being but are beings at a loss for logos – they cannot say what being means. Appearances appear tragic but being in itself is not tragic. In being, in itself, there is no loss. Hence Parmenides' description of being (frag. 8) – a well-rounded sphere, neither more here nor less there, but homogeneous throughout, without gaps or ruptures. The description of beauty in itself in Plato's *Symposium* reiterates the apotheosis of such being without loss, beyond all lack. Time is the sphere of loss, for time is a perpetual perishing, time is decay, decrease, decease. Death is the ultimate loss of being, and the ultimate before which we experience being at a loss. Parmenidean pure being is deathless.

When philosophy sees itself as a complete rational finding, beyond being at a loss, it predominantly thinks of itself as a science. To be scientific is to be capable of giving a determinate account of things, a logos of a *tode ti*. Systematic science would be the apotheosis of never being at a loss. To every perplexity, every enigma, there would be a determinate response to be made. If philosophy were exclusively systematic science, it would ultimately be a systematic exclusion of the tragic. For in principle one should never be at a loss in systematic science. If one were radically at a loss, the suspicion would surface that the scientific claims for complete determinate intelligibility were questionable.

Suppose, by contrast, we think now of some great tragic heroes in relation to their *knowing*. Consider Oedipus' will to know: he refuses not to know the truth, but the truth is too much; in an excess of dark knowing, he must blind himself to continue. He may be personally guiltless but his knowledge, self-knowledge, brings measureless suffering, not *eudaimonia*, as Socrates suggests knowing will bring. Consider Hamlet: he too is marked by a thirst for knowing that goes to the boundary of man's metaphysical predicaments; he knows and does not know that his father was murdered; he alone bears the burden of knowing/notknowing; he has to put on an antic disposition, use the mask of madness to deal with his wrenching situation; his knowing is not that the real is the rational *sub specie aeternitatis*; his is the cursed knowledge that 'the time is out of joint'. Where is the consolation in this knowing? His knowing essentially puts him at a loss what to believe as genuine, who to trust, what to do. All his knowledge brings is suffering. Yet both knowing and suffering are unavoidable.

Consider Lear again: the cushioned King has to become unsheltered to the extremities, stripped to his elemental humanity before the powerful elements, endure his passage through a madness more knowing than his regal sanity; and at the end there is the Howl and the Never that assault the calm of our philosophic faith in the basic intelligibility, indeed value, of being. Lear's tragic knowing brings him to the condition of being utterly at a loss. The Howl says it all – namely, that Lear does not know what to say: the public communicability of discourse retracts before the horror and all intelligible saying seems to founder. Tragedy brings a knowing that shatters every naive faith in the intelligibility and worth of being or saying. Is philosophical mind then at a loss? What can it think about such extremities of being at a loss?

No doubt about it, philosophy has a strong *eros* to overcome loss, to not be at a loss, to place reason where tragedy faces rupture. What then do we do with the devastation of losing, of radically being at a loss? What, for instance, does the philosopher do with the erosion of being that time inexorably works? I say the philosopher because I want to underscore the particularity of the philosopher as a living thinker. A propensity of philosophers has been to displace reason's attention from the particularity of the philosopher to the putative universality of philosophy as such. The consolation of the logical universal usurps the idiocy of the particular as particular. I use the term idiocy here in the Greek sense of *idios*: an intimacy of being at the edge of, if not outside, the system of public reality, an intimacy not indifferently available to anyone and everyone. (This idiocy will be important below in discussing the Never.) What of this idiocy of the particular philosopher as particular? The philosopher as a particular human being is washed away by the erosions of time. To be is to be bound to a process of genesis that not only brings into being but always brings about the demise of being. The erosion of the being of the particular, the loss of being for the particular is ontologically constitutive for every particular being. This cannot be denied.

Indeed I claim that we are marked as metaphysical beings, as well as tragic beings, only because this ontology of loss is intimately known by us. If we did not intimately know being at a loss, it is not clear we could fully raise the question of being in any other sense. Nor could we be characterized as beings who undergo or behold the tragic, or who bespeak the tragic in works of art and religion. Obviously the sense of the tragic is only possible in a human world; but it is not possible in a merely humanistic world where what is radically other to the human is not given its proper due. Tragedy arises because the human being becomes metaphysically aware that there are rupturing others that inescapably disrupt, destroy any sense of ontological self-sufficiency that human beings might feel or claim on behalf of their own being. We are metaphysical beings in the measure that the tragic breaks through, in the measure that we know our being to be one that loses itself, that loses its way. We know that our way of being is unavoidably a way of loss. Being at a loss is a more deeply constitutive dimension to being human than might initially be suspected.

Nevertheless, wherever possible we try to stand our ground before being at a loss. Philosophy can be a mindfulness that tries to find its way in loss, that is, it can be a finding of being in the losing of being, a mindfulness that thoughtfully tries to be at home with being in being at a loss. Here the identity of philosophy that emerges is other to its identity as systematic science. Losing, failure, breakdown, the eruption of the indeterminate are acknowledged as absolutely essential here. Logic offers no final answer with being at a loss. Nevertheless I am trying, philosophically, to speak of loss as essential, without reducing loss to the logical consolation of a conceptual essence.

So it would be very wrong to think that philosophy must always simplistically displace metaphysical concern from the rupture of being at a loss towards the neutral logical universal. The complicated situation has never been one of simple opposition or 'either/or'. In my remarks now to follow, with respect to the view that philosophy has no simple univocal identity, I will speak of Socrates and Plato, to a lesser extent Nietzsche and Hegel. Philosophy has a more complex plural identity which includes but is not exhausted by the will to systematic science. What is more than systematic science in philosophical mindfulness is related to the metaphysical meaning of being at a loss, and hence also to the tragic.

Thus, one way to read Plato is as a strongly Parmenidean thinker: the doubleheaded nature of the doxic many is not to be taken seriously, especially by one who has seen the circular self-sufficient plenitude of being in itself, absolute being without loss. Yet the doubleheadedness reappears in Platonic philosophy. Philosophy reduplicates a plurality that the Parmenidean ideal ostensibly leaves behind. On the one hand, related to this ideal we find the logicist concern with contradiction: contradiction is the doubleheadedness in thought that the philosopher tries to shun. Hence the concern with equivocal language, double language that is potentially duplicitious – logos will try to disarm or expose the duplicity of equivocity by formulating all questions of being in sheerly univocal terms: there is one meaning and one meaning only.

But then, on the other hand, we must grant in Plato the articulation of *positive plurality* as constitutive of a genuine philosophical dialogue. Nor is such a dialogue just a smooth, seamless exchange between a philosopher and others. It is born out of perplexity: someone is at a loss what to think and asks another for his views or response. The experience of being at a loss drives a philosophical dialogue, and needs the plurality of its constituent voices. Many voices, many heads are necessary to respond to the condition of being at a loss. Hence the plurality of voices in difference or contradiction is not necessarily a merely negative thing. In response to being at a loss, plurivocity constitutively energizes the very dynamism of philosophical interplay and exchange.

But you will say: this is the negative dialectic that inevitably will subvert itself; the being at a loss drives beyond itself through the inherent momentum of logos as dialectically unfolding; the negativity of loss will negate itself and produce a positive finding. Thus the faith in logos is preserved and we always end up with a rational account beyond all loss. But if so, why do so many dialogues end in an impasse, an *aporia*: they end up at a loss. This is glaringly at odds with all those cliches of Plato as the 'metaphysician of presence' *par excellence*. The dialogue drives logos to a new height of articulation, but also to a deeper acknowledgment of being at a loss. Logos in aporia, logos at an impasse: these are constitutive for the Platonic sense of philosophical thinking. It is as if the wonder that is said to be the originating pathos of the philosopher *reappears* after he has done his best job in giving a determinate logos. The indeterminate perplexity reappears, wonder resurrects itself, in a different sense of being at a loss, now at the limit of logos itself.

I find it peculiar that Aristotle is often honored as the philosopher of tragedy in the ancient world. But his *philosophical practise* is very antithetical to Plato's here. In a far more insistent way, Aristotle wants a determinate logos of a determinate somewhat, a *tode ti*. This is why he rejects the philosophical appeal to myth. This is why, when he reiterates Plato on wonder, one suspects that wonder has been dimmed into intellectual curiosity, the telos of which is not a deepening of metaphysical astonishment, but the dispelling of curiosity in a determinate answer to a determinate question. Aristotle significantly invokes *geometry* when claiming that the acquisition of knowledge issues in a *reversal* of wonder (see *Meta.*, I, 983a15–25). (I will remark below on 'geometry' and tragedy. I note that it is significant that Husserl links philosophy and geometry, not only in *Ideas*, but even in the *Crisis*.) If Platonic wonder can be deepened but not dispelled, this is because being at a loss can be bespoken but never eradicated. Why? Because man as metaphysical is an *indeterminate question* to which no determinate answer will ever reply or correspond. If there is to be an answer, it must somehow include the truth of indeterminacy itself.

The greatness of being at a loss, of running into an aporia is precisely its reminder that just this indeterminate openness is ontologically constitutive of the human being. A totally determinate science, in claiming to give a complete explanation, would actually be a falsification of this ontological truth of the being of the human. Its very success would be its most radical failure. All we have to do is become self-conscious of this and the force of being at a loss reinserts itself into philosophical discourse again. This is always happening in philosophy. No sooner does it make some claim to knowing, but there begins the process of deconstructing the completeness or adequacy of this claim. In finding its way, philosophy immediately initiates a way of losing that thenceforth subverts its own provisional peace. Philosophical mind's true and enduring condition is one of metaphysical insomnia.

The anti-philosophical philosophy of deconstruction does some of its main business in bringing philosophy to aporia: making philosophy acknowledge that it too, in the end, is brought to loss; that thought is being at a loss which sometimes hides its own loss in dialectical rationalizations. Of course there is some truth in this. But I say: philosophy has *already* always been at this point: always at a loss. This is the very perplexity that generates thought, that in turn is always deconstructing itself. This too reflects the skeptical principle in all genuine thinking. Those least infected by the skeptical principle are the minnows of the philosophical tradition. Hence deconstruction fishes best with the small fry of thinking, not the sharks. To reduce Plato's sense of logos and aporia to the metaphysics of presence is to draw in a net empty of Plato the philosophical shark. As a developed philosophical strategy, skepticism is nothing but mind's alertness to its own being at a loss before perplexities it finds intractible. Philosophical mind comes to know itself in its own breakdown. It can also break through into thought beyond breakdown. Skepticism, like deconstruction, tends to give us breakdown without breakthrough.

When logos runs up against an aporia different responses are possible. One might deny that the aporia is really an aporia, and redefine it as a merely temporary block on reason; reason will eventually find a way beyond and in the end there will be no beyond, there will be no other to reason. This is one typical philosophical strategy: there will be no others to philosophy, since all reason has to do is continue and the other will no longer be other, because it will be conceptualized, will be thought. The other of thought, in being thought, will be thought once again, and so it will not be the other of thought. We end up back with Parmenides. And so philosophy will meet itself again at the end of the road. The god of this philosophy cannot be tragic, because the ultimate picture will be thought simply thinking itself; there will be no loss, no self-loss; all will be embraced in the circle of self-thinking thought.

Another response is silence. The rest is silence, it says at the end of Hamlet. Philosophers have known the power of silence. I name but two: the younger Wittgenstein in the *Tractatus*: logic falls silent in the face of the mystical; Aquinas at the end of his life when he refused to continue to write and said of his work 'It seems to me as so much straw'. Being philosophically at a loss and silence are intertwined. But silence, like being, like being at a loss, can be 'said' in many ways. There is the empty silence of meaninglessness. There is the silence of an acknowledging, full of reverent respect before the other. There is a silence of despair. There is a silence of peace beyond measure. There is a tragic silence: this is a transconceptual silence that rends the silence, all silences, the conceptless silence of Lear's Howl.

It seems to me that the great systems of philosophy are encircled by a silence that they do not, perhaps cannot name. The silence that circles the system, the philosopher, turns his speech of clear concepts into the chiaroscuro of the tragic. But the philosopher as idiot can be haunted by this silence; this can make him more than systematic scientist. The unsaid haunts all saying; but some saying carries the silence of the unsaid in itself. This is most evident when the philosopher is also a poet. Plato and Nietzsche are the two great examples. Their thought is plurivocal; thinking is not the monologue of *noesis noeseos* or Hegel's self-thinking Idea. Tragedy raises the question of philosophical silence in philosophy's very lucid speech itself. We probe the philosopher when we ask about his silence: What does his speech avoid, what does his speech respect, what does his speech ignore, what does his speech dread to say? All such questions call for an awareness of the different modalities of philosophical silence. Consider Spinoza's motto *Caute!*, his one word of command, or perhaps warning. Who is he commanding or warning? What is he afraid of? What then does the motto mean? Many possible things, all beyond univocal logos. The tragic itself is always beyond univocal logic.

One thing we do not want at the limit of tragedy is the chatter of conceptual analysis that thinks it has the measure of an enigma when it makes a verbal distinction. At the opposite extreme to this analytical evasion, there is the possibility I develop in *Philosophy and its Others*: not only thought trying to think its other; but thought trying to sing its other. To say how the Howl turns into song is too large a theme here, though I will offer a few hints at the end.[2]

I return to Plato as a philosopher who thought in the shadow of the tragic. I do not simply mean the shadow of Greek tragedy, though this is true. He was concerned especially with tragedy as a religious drama in which appears the inscrutable will of the gods, even in the mask of their resistance to reason. The wrath of the god that mocks the pretensions of human reason was something deeply disturbing to the implicit faith of philosophy, namely that being, at its deepest and most ultimate, is intelligible. God is not envious is the refrain in the *Timaeus*, a refrain reiterated by Aristotle, by Aquinas and significantly by Hegel himself. Hegel says it because he holds God to be self-disclosive: there will be no enigma in the ultimate which resists the approach of reason; God is simply reason and the nature of reason is to manifest itself, reveal itself, make itself available to the philosophical mind. Likewise Plato was concerned to purify the gods of the masks of irrationality they seemed to wear in tragedy.

For the suffering in ancient tragedy has a sacred modulation; what is at stake is sacred suffering, and the tragic hero is not out of the ambit of the sacrificial victim of the gods. If one's basic faith in that being is transparently intelligible to mind, this sacred violence of the holy provokes shudders. Where is the *episteme* of this sacred violence? If the gods are infected with such an otherness to reason, an otherness violating to reason, we seem to peer into an ultimate arbitrariness in the nature of things. At bottom being does not appear completely intelligible to the tragic vision.

Moreover, there was the proximate tragedy of Socrates. The man who seems most rational meets a death that seems least reasonable, with respect to both justice and truth. Platonic philosophizing sought to penetrate Socrates' tragedy to the intelligibility, the life of reason at work in this philosophical life, in the loss of this life in a senseless death. If the life of reason cannot be found to be at work in this life here and now, then for Plato the loss is also the loss of the here and now. The work of reason will be said to transcend this life. And as the work of reason transcends this life, so in fact must it transcend this death. Again we see the desire to save philosophy's faith in intelligibility. The problem is that, if we anticipate ultimate reason and justice beyond this life and death, we then return, in some form, to the question of the ultimate light or darkness of the gods. Plato knew this too; else he would not have Socrates tell the myth of Er.

Plato wants to see the light. Nietzsche did not see *this* light. At the bottom of things he saw darkness. At its deepest the nature of things is such as to give rise to horror; in itself being is not intelligible. Still reflecting Schopenhauer, the bottom of things is a dark origin, in Nietzsche's case, a Dionysian origin that erupts and is given shape in the tragic drama, but which in itself exceeds all form, for it is the forming power which in itself is formless.[3] That is, the ground of being for Nietzsche, what he calls *Das Ureine* in the *Birth of Tragedy*, is not intelligible in itself. Intelligibility is a consoling construction of concepts that we and philosophers like Socrates create as a shield from too violent an encounter with the Dionysian will to power behind it all.

A major point here is: Schopenhauer says the Will is on *the other side* of the principle of sufficient reason; so in a sense there is no sufficient reason for the ultimate Will. Nietzsche runs swiftly with this insight in relation to philosophy and the tragic: the ultimate origin is beyond the principle of sufficient reason, and hence to the extent that philosophy is contained by this principle, it cannot properly think the tragic. There is a suffering that comes through in the tragic that exceeds the ministration of the principle of sufficient reason. In face of this suffering we need art more fundamentally than we need philosophy.

Who, for Nietzsche, embodies the principle of sufficient reason? Socrates, of course. Socrates wants to disarm the a-rationality of the tragic, neutralize in universals the sacred suffering that springs from the dark Dionysian origin and that the tragic drama makes present, that tragic drama celebrates. Philosophy fakes its own being at a loss, disguising its conceptual consolations as 'truth'. Tragedy looks into this fearful darkness, yet it bespeaks this darkness with a certain celebrating joy. This joy is our brief salvation from despair and meaningless suffering. It is our encounter with death and our unreserved yes to being, despite the destruction and the terrible. Deep down life is inexpressibly joyful: this is what the tragic says to Nietzsche. Philosophy is treasonous to this suffering and this joy; it turns away from both towards the abstraction and the concept; Socrates offers his therapy for the darkness of life in dialectics. For Nietzsche this is the epitome of philosophy's impotence, its powerlessness before the tragic.

This is not Nietzsche's last word about philosophy and the tragic. If this is Nietzsche's judgment on traditional philosophy, it is not his judgment on the promise of philosophy. He himself clearly wanted to be the first Dionysian philosopher, the first philosopher of the tragic, the first tragic philosopher. Philosophy in the tragic age of the Greeks was already marked by this promise, only to be aborted, nipped in the bud by Socrates and Plato. But even Socrates was a masked Dionysian: he too suffered from life; he too wanted a saying of being that would enable the transfiguration of being, in a manner analogous to the transfiguration of life and death that the sacred suffering of the tragedy enacts. The antithesis of tragedy and philosophy is not an ultimate antithesis, though clearly the way to transcend this antithesis cannot lead us back to Socrates and Plato and their heirs – so Nietzsche thinks.

Once again the relation of philosophy and the tragic raises the question about the very identity of philosophy, and indeed, after Nietzsche, its future identity. Can philosophy honestly name the otherness of the tragic without disarming its horror or neutralizing its challenge by means of its conceptualizing appropriation? If philosophy can try to think the tragic, must it redefine its modes of thinking, such that it opens itself to what may resist its categories, perhaps even cause their breakdown? Would not this also demand a rethinking of the relation of the poet and philosopher, and in a form that finds the Platonic view unsatisfactory? Or must we also be cautious with Plato here too? Is not Plato's philosophizing also a mask of the tragic poet?

Nietzsche's views force us to make a more general remark in line with earlier points about systematic science, namely: if the scientific view were completely applicable to the whole of being, there would be no room for the tragic. Scientific mind treats being as valueless in itself. The question of the worth of what is, the very worthiness of being, does not directly arise for it. This question points to a convergence of metaphysics (as asking about the meaning and truth of being) and ethics (as asking about the goodness of being). (In Nietzsche's case, metaphysics and ethics are subsumed into aesthetics.) The tragic exposes mind to a radical experience of being at a loss. Ingredient in this loss is the possible loss of the worth of being: the horrifying possibility is brought before us, not only that being lacks an ultimate intelligibility, but that at bottom it is worthless, it is valueless.

Tragic experience seems to suffer being as drained of any value. Being is, but is as nothing. Better not to be at all, perhaps: a saying Nietzsche repeated after Schopenhauer, who himself repeated the Greek Silenus, companion of Dionysus, and the figure to whom the drunken Alcibiades compares the enigmatic Socrates. Metaphysics tries to be mindful of such issues, science does not. Science is itself a mode of mind that devalues being, drains being of value: the being there of the world is taken for granted as a given fact; the being there of what is arouses no ontological astonishment, or metaphysical nausea, or aesthetic jubilation, or religious celebration. Scientism – in claiming that science will answer for the whole – is thus identical with nihilism: the assertion of the valuelessness of being. Nietzsche himself understood this, and blamed philosophy for being the remote source of ths nihilistic scientism, which paradoxically is driven by hatred of the tragic, that is, epistemological dread of its suffering knowing. The paradox is that the scientistic impulse presents itself as beyond love and hate. In fact its 'love of truth' hides a hatred of the tragic for its recalcitrance to conceptual encapsulation.

The silence of science returns philosophy to the saying of art. The metaphysical question does arise in art, and painfully in tragic art: a great hero comes to nothing, his being is shown to come to nothing. In this loss of being what then is the worth of being? What is worthy being when all being, even the greatest, seems inexorably to come to nothing? Science has nothing to say about such questions. There can never be a science of the tragic, and were the scientific mentality to try to impose its norms on the totality, the result would have to be a blindness to, a denial of, perhaps a repression of tragic experience. The irony, contradiction, here is that this repression embodies a metaphysical violence that has its own implicitly tragic dimension. We normally do not couple Spinoza and metaphysical violence, the noble Spinoza who in austere purity of mind philosophises *sub specie aeternitatis*. Yet there is such violence in Spinoza's claim to treat human beings and their emotions like he would treat solids, planes and circles. This sounds high-minded, since the philosopher seems willing to sacrifice the pettiness of his restricted ego purely for disinterested truth. But such a putative will to truth is potentially a violent repression of the truth of the tragic. There is no geometry of the tragic. When philosophy thinks it is the geometry of the tragic, this is tragic for philosophy.

I think Plato knew this. Over the entrance to his Academy is said to have hung the saying: Let no one enter who has not studied geometry! Yes, but this does not say, *only* geometry; nor that once having entered, all modes of mindfulness will be reduced to geometry. Again I reiterate that the philosopher's self-identity can be forged in a deep awareness of being at a loss. This is relevant here. A crucial place where the limits of logos come up in Plato's dialogues is the *Phaedo*. Socrates is in prison on the eve of death. He accepts that there is no escape, no way out for him. Is this death tragic? Is the philosopher at a loss in the face of it? Will geometry help one through the portal of dying? Where is the geometry of death?

I am within traditional respectability in raising the issue of philosophy and the tragic here. Certainly Hegel, even pan-logist Hegel, thought of Socrates' death in tragic terms. Dialectical reason is at work even in tragic death. For Hegel there is a clash of two justified principles or powers. Socrates embodies the new principle of subjectivity: inward thought makes claim to absoluteness over against the social substance. Against this is the social substance itself, whose unreflective ethical *Sittlichkeit* was the fundamental ethical embodiment of the people's *Geist* at its most ultimate, religiously, morally, aesthetically. Both those powers have their justification, but the emergence of the first from the second produces an inevitable clash between the two and the downfall of both. The unreflective ethical *Sittlichkeit* was at a loss what to do with Socrates as embodying the radical freedom of thought; Socrates himself was at a loss in asking ethical questions in a form which traditional *Sittlichkeit* could not answer. This double being at a loss necessitates for Hegel the loss of both as distinct opposites and their falling to the ground. Socrates was guilty, for Hegel; but Athens itself was infected with the spirit it condemned in Socrates and so in this sense was condemning itself. It was already unknowingly in the spiral of dissolution that the Socratic spirit represented – the dissolving powers of thought before which nothing seems to stand. Thinking brings us a loss of unreflective tradition, shows what is hitherto accepted and lived as coming to nothing.

Hegel's view is very illuminating in its dialectical sense of the togetherness of opposites. But I am not interested in displacing the tragic issue onto a neutral universal, not interested in displacing the issue from the particular philosopher to the stage of world-history or to philosophy as systematic science. Ultimately, for Hegel, the particularity of Socrates and his death is *world-historically redeemed* as preparing a more thoroughgoing victory for reason in history. Hegel displays the philosopher's faith in the final ascendency of rational intelligibility. Universal spirit as world-historical is the victor. But what of the tragedy of Socrates as *this* philosopher? What redeems the death of this particular self as idiot?

Plato is deeper here and more revealing for our purposes. He presents Socrates as a particular human thinker. Socrates explicitly says in the *Apology* (32a) that to survive as a philosopher it was necessary for him to live as an idiot (*idioteuein*). He would have been dead earlier if he had not lived as an idiot. Thus he outlived 'the sects and packs of great ones that ebb and flow by the moon', as Lear – about to be imprisoned and become 'God's spy' – calls the factions of feverish politics, the world-historical mighty. Plato's Socrates does not give us systematic science or a world-historical account in exoneration of his philosophy, his life. We are given an apology for an *individual life*. Though that life involved the search for the universal, the life itself was the mindful existing of a *this*. Only a *this* can apologise; a universal does not apologise, nor does it live the inviolable inwardness of an ethical life. This latter is part of Socrates' tragedy. There is no way to make sense of the enigma of Socrates if we think that his life was exhausted by a logicist obsession with the ideality of universal definition. One does not live or die for such a definition. The ideal sought must be different from a definition encapsulated in any logical category.

Socrates' death makes us reconsider the enigma of his life as philosophical. We begin to sense that there was something ineradicably *Once* about this life. Death revealed to us, to Plato, the Once of this life, in confronting us with its Never: once Socrates was but now never more. Why was Plato too sick to attend the dying Socrates? What was this sickness before death? Is there any 'geometry' to heal it? Can we imagine Plato howling: Why should a rat, a horse, a dog have life, and Socrates no life at all? Will Socrates ever come again? The answer is: Never, never, never! Hegel will say to this: No, no, no! Socrates will always come again. But he will not come as *this* Socrates, but as universal thought. But Plato knew: *that* is not Socrates. It is Socrates as a this that concerns us; it is Socrates as a this that apologises for philosophy; it is not the universal using Socrates as an instrument that apologises; it is not the Socratic spirit. Socrates says: I, I, I and the I is ineradicably particular, irreplaceable. There was only one Socrates, one and one only, even though this unique particular claimed to speak on behalf of the universal.

It is for this I, not for philosophy as such, that we cry at the end of the *Phaedo*. At the end, we weep for an *other*; it is the death of the *other*, Socrates, the beloved other that had his friends and Plato at a loss. (Below we will see that it is the death of the beloved other,

Cordelia, that pushes Lear to the most extreme loss.) The tragic issue is not just concern with *my* death à la Heidegger, but with the death of the other – Marcel and Levinas would agree. But perhaps the deepest moment in the *Phaedo* is when Socrates covers his face after taking the poison, and his body began to mortify, petrify with the advancing poison, as if becoming stone. The universal has no face; the universal Socratic spirit has no eyes wherein terror or fear or exhaltation or consent might appear. But Socrates as idiot, as an irreplaceable this, has a face, has eyes.

Why must those eyes be veiled? What was in those eyes of the dying Socrates? Composure? Terror? Did Socrates crack in the face of the Never, all his previous arguments about immortality notwithstanding? Did the impersonal universal lose its power in this final moment? Or do the eyes have to be covered up because the eyes reveal the absolute singularity of the person, the absolute particularity of the philosopher? The death of the singular philosopher, the veiling of the eyes in the final moment, is completely enigmatic to philosophy as systematic science. There are no concepts within any system that can tell us about those eyes looking on death, looking out of death, on life.

The I as idiotic is in the eye in a manner that is evident nowhere else. The idiocy of the I is its ontological intimacy, and this intimacy of being appears in the eye. In the face of death, the eye is the place where the face may manifest the person's yes or no to being, to death, to the Never, to the Once – if indeed this yes or no come to manifestation at all. Socrates' eyes are covered because there is no public universal that can encapsulate what might have appeared in them. You might say: terror appeared, and then imply that terror is public; we all share terror; terror before death is universal. True. But this is beside the point in relation to the intimacy of the eyes, their idiocy from the point of view of the universal, its stony eyes.

Consider how, regardless entirely of death, we find it extremely difficult to hold a person's eyes; there is a dangerous ambiguity about eye to eye contact. How much more powerful is the dangerous ambiguity when the living survivor is making contact with the eye of the dying one. What passes from eye to eye, what metaphysical terror is there in this communication, what metaphysical consent? What passes between the eyes is an intimacy of being which no impersonal universal can ever bespeak. This is why Plato, the poet-philosopher, gives us an *image* here, not an impersonal universal. The manner in which Plato covers the eyes is a stroke of philosophical genius. There is nothing to compare to it in all philosophical literature. Plato says nothing; but the writing of this silent gesture before death witnesses what cannot be said.

I note here how visitors to Nietzsche after his breakdown frequently commented on his *eyes*. The visitors seemed to see in Nietzsche's eyes a *knowing beyond sanity*, that invariably shook them in a brief disruptive revelation. The terrible eyes struck them in every sense, as if the dead eyes, the mad eyes were the eyes of tragic wisdom; and then just as quickly the veil would be redrawn and the vacant face of idiocy would look out at them.[4] I note too the prominence of the theme of eyes in *Lear*: sight and blindness, "reason in madness." We recoil at the horror of Gloucester's plucked eyes, empty sockets like Oedipus' gouged eyes – gouged with the malignant cry 'out vile jelly where is the lustre now?' Is this all that the eyes and the ontological intimacy of the I are: vile jelly? Were Socrates' eyes, Nietzsche's eyes just vile jelly – where is their lustre now? Lear advises Gloucester: 'Get thee glass eyes'. Gloucester already knows: 'I have no way and therefore want no eyes;/I stumbled when I saw' (IV, i, 18–19). Death opens the eyes of weeping. Weeping eyes cannot be understood in terms of Sartre's Look; the actuality of weeping is totally inexplicable in Sartre's reduction of the promise of the eye to the Look. The Look is the apotheosis of the eyes of stones, the Gorgon's eyes that turn to stone. But stones do not weep. Nor does 'geometry'. Only flesh weeps. Only flesh knows the tragic.

By contrast with Hegel's *Aufhebung* of Socrates' particularity into the world-historical universal, Plato offers us the particularity of an apology, even though the life apologized for may include the search for a universal more than personal. The philosopher is often between these extremes, tempted to sacrifice the first to the second. The artist is also between these extremes, but his temptation is perhaps the reverse, the sacrifice of the promise of the universal for the particular. Both need each other to allow the epiphany of universality in particularity, as well as a non-reductive acknowledgment of the particular as particular: to name the particular without reduction, and to grant the universal without desiccation. In trying to find the middle, the lure of the extremes will be differently modulated by the artist and the philosopher.

If Plato does not offer a Hegelian *Aufhebung*, this does not mean we lose all faith in logos. Death is the place/noplace where the philosopher's extreme being at a loss is manifest. In the thought of death we try to think what cannot be thought, for to think the thought of one's death is to think oneself as being.

Logically, we are caught in an aporia. Existentially, we are faced with the temptation to give up on logos. Hence it is here that we find Socrates' warning in the *Phaedo* against misology. This is extremely significant. I see it as Plato/Socrates' gesture that philosophical logos must not simply give up before the ultimate experience of loss. Being at a loss before the loss of being – this is impending death. The philosopher's response cannot be a question of conceptual chatter continuing. What does one do at this point, if anything? What can one say?

Socrates' gesture of philosophical *faith* is to continue talking. But I stress that the talking is not logically univocal but irreducibly plurivocal. Here philosophical speaking has more than one mode, more than the argumentative statement of thesis and evidence. Apart from the significant fact the Platonic dialogue itself is more than a logicist monologue, within this dialogue Socrates raises the possible need of philosophical song or music. He himself blends with the swan of death, the songbird of Apollo. This again evidences a view of philosophy very different to systematic science. Song and system cannot collapse into one totality. It is true that Socrates offers different 'logical' arguments with regard to immortality. But these are logically easy to trouble, as Socrates himself grants. On being logically troubled, and in the face of the consternation of his interlocutors, Socrates goes so far as to compare his philosophical speech to incantations and charms. Finally Socrates offers a myth.

Songs, charms, arguments, myths – different voices of a plurivocal philosopher. There is no one voice in the face of death, in the face of being. Why this plurality of different voices? Because Plato is a plurivocal philosopher, responding to the living/dying philosopher as a plurivocal this. Socrates was like a father to his friends who, bereft of him, would be as orphans the rest of their life (*Phaedo*, 116a). Nor can we forget the weeping of Xantippe. And then the silence – 'best to die in silence', Socrates suggests (*Phaedo*, 117e) – and the masterful gesture of covering the eyes, as death creeps over the body. The *covered* eyes: Are they the eyes of death? Are they the extra eyes of posthumous mind (see below), mind looking on being from beyond the ultimate loss? Are they the eyes of a Never that crushes all hope of a beyond? Socrates is dead, dead as earth. Then the eyes *uncovered*: staring, fixed, immobilized, stones; their once vibrant presence extinguished, never to come, never; dead as earth.

This is not logic; this is not system; this is not the abstract universal. All of this is an image, a philosophical icon. At one level the image says: Philosophy must go on. But at another level it cautions: It can only go on if it is honest about loss, if it keeps before its thinking the image of death, the memory of the dead.

III

I said before that there is no geometry of the tragic. Nor is there a geometry of death or of the memory of the dead. I have also denied that philosophy can be reduced to the determinate cognition of the determinate. 'Geometry' would be a figure for totally determinate or determinable knowing that seeks utterly determinate intelligibility. That there is more to philosophy as plurivocal, I now want to illustrate in terms of a non-geometrical meditation on Lear's Never. In trying to think through this Never, there opens up both a sense of metaphysical horror and of ontological astonishment. We again face the issue of the value of being, questioned in an extremity of being at a loss.

Metaphysics, I think, is always shadowed by the Never. In turn, the Never is unthinkable without a sense of what I will call the '*Once*' and the '*That it is*' of a being. Need philosophy flee this shadow into universal cognition? Does tragedy stay closer to the truth of the Once, the Never, the 'That it is'? Beyond all determination, all self-determination, tragic loss is not recuperable at a finite level. There is a loss of being that transcends finiteness, an aporia that allows no surpassing at the level of finite determinacy. How are we to think of this loss beyond finitude, since it take shape in finitude? It is beyond because is entails *being at a loss before finitude itself*. Is this being at a loss before finitude a loss beyond finitude, pointing to the other of finitude? Is the Never ever softened in an everafter that allows some recuperation of meaning?

We must relate the Once and the Never to the 'That it is'. A being is, and is but once, and then is no more – ever. Only we know this, only we. This is why the human being is the metaphysical being. Tragic and metaphysical knowing of being at a loss are only possible for a human being, not for a rat, a dog, a horse. It is not simply that we are capable of rising intellectually to the impersonal

universal. This is true. But there is a more intimate kind of
knowing where metaphysics and the tragic overlap. This takes
shape in response to the Once and the Never: the gratuity of mortal
being, the necessity that it pass out of being, lose its being in time,
the chance we are offered to say thanks in the interval of the Once,
before the night of the never more, thanks for the gift of time itself.

When Lear says Never, we hear him beseeching why a certain
being should have being at all. Why should a rat, a dog, a horse
have life and thou no life at all? He is addressing a particular thou.
We recall Hamlet's fateful question: to be or not to be. But the
metaphysical question assumes a more violent form after Lear's
Howl. When we try to think about his savage Never, thinking
becomes faint, becomes lightheaded, as if it were about to swoon,
to undergo a blackout. For the Never names the irrevocable and
the irrecoverable. It names them irrevocably. We are here at an
extreme extreme. It is like the cliff that Gloucester is induced by
Edgar to see in his mind's eye: 'How fearful/And dizzy 'tis to cast
one's eyes so low! ... I'll look no more,/Lest my brain turn, and
the deficient sight/Topple down headlong. '(IV, vi, 11–12, 22–24)
Gloucester's cliff, like the metaphysical enigma of being, is a cliff of
the mind. At the edge of the Never, one is overcome by a kind of
metaphysical vertigo, as though one were about to throw oneself
off the mind's own cliff or ridge. It is as if one were to undergo a
death by the thinking of this sheer abyss. One has to be blinded,
like Gloucester, to surrender oneself to it.

That Lear addresses a thou indicates that the Never presupposes
a certain attunement to the singularity of the singular. The Never
invokes the sheer 'That it is' of a singular being, the being of
Cordelia – not the being of an indifferent thing, not being as an
anonymous universal. It is this being as particular, the idiotic
being, the intimate being of Cordelia as the singularly loved child
of Lear. Again I use 'idiotic' in a sense related to the Greek *idios*: an
intimacy of being not indifferently available to anyone and
everyone, a neutral public.

The thought is this: Cordelia came into being, offspring of the
father, marvel of a child, loved beyond measure by the father,
though the father was also foolish and cruel. The singularity of her
'That she is' is not replaceable by the being of anyone else or
anything else. The being of the 'That she is' is not substitutable for
any other 'That it is'. The 'That it is' of any this or that is a singular
metaphysical marvel. This is the sheer being there of a thing, or a

self, or a human being. This sheer being there is enigmatic. It floats on the void, in that the shadow of its possible not-being haunts its sheer being there. The 'That it is' is shadowed by its own possibility of never being again. Together the Never and the 'That it is' point to a certain absolute singularity of a Once. That Cordelia is in being, that this 'That she is' is unrepeatable, irreplaceable, that this sheer being there will in time not be there ever more, all of these point to the time of the particular being as an absolutely singular Once.

The difficulty for the logicist mind is that it thinks in terms of concepts or genera or classes or universals or sets which are precisely tailored to the repeatable, the non-unique, what is not singular but what the singular shares with all other instances of the same genus or universal or class or set. The logicist mind shuns the idiocy of being there. So the sense of being that is carried by the 'That it is', by the Once of the 'That it is', by the irrevocability of the Never that is the destiny of the mortal singular being – all of this is deeply recalcitrant to logical conceptualization. The very act of conceptualization, by its very nature, displaces us from the singular as singular: something remains about this that is idiotic to the logical universal.

I stand on the shore and see the flow of wave after wave; they form, crest and crash on the sand. I struggle to identify a particular wave as particular. The sun glints for a moment on a singular form, but in the same moment, the form is deforming, reforming, endlessly ushered elsewhere, endlessly othered by the undying energy of the sea. I cannot fix the This that is Once, and then is Never again. It briefly rises to the surface of the sea, and flowing into another, it subsides into the maternal waters again. I say: the wave. And I see many waves; they all are waves; all are instances of a common genus; big and small, angry and smooth. But the glint of particularity is no sooner received than it vanishes. There is joy in the glint, but terror in the vanishing. The glint of particularity is the singularity of that wave, the self of a this. Try to fix it, mind cannot. Mind is at a loss, it passes by the mind, and yet it is known as passing by. It is noted in the passing of its thisness. The human being, child of time, is the glint that mindfully arises and vanishes on the maternal sea of being. Nor need the passing be smooth transition; it may be abrupt violence.

Can we be mindful of the Once as the sheer now of being now? The Once reveals a particular that, in being, is in a process of perishing, but that as determinate spills over our every effort at fixed determination. I do not think of this 'spilling over' in a merely negative light: it is not an indefinite vagueness that should be philosophically replaced by a determinate concept. The particular resists conceptual determination because of its ontological richness. It 'spills over' because it is the concretion of 'more' than determinate being.

This means rejecting Hegel's view of the matter. Hegel's discussion of sense-certainty in the *Phenomenology* seems to reduplicate and answer the difficulty I have here. Hegel repeatedly claims to show that the immediate is mediated, that to name the particular is always to invoke a discourse of universals: the this becomes a universal this; the now becomes a universal now, time; the here becomes a universal here, space, and so on. Hegel essentially subjugates the sheer being there of a being to a set of universals which are then said to both articulate and give us the truth of the original immediate this. Sheer ontological astonishment, always terror-tinged, before the sheer being there of a being is immediately covered up with a net of concepts. The rest of the *Phenomenology* will continue the cover-up and claim that this cover-up is simply the process of completing philosophy as a science of systematic determinate knowing. A similar point will apply to Hegel's *Logic* where being is the emptiest of universals and hardly distinguishable from nothing into which it dialectically must dissolve.

The sense I am struggling to say of Once and Never and the sheer 'There it is' of a this, is at a tangent to Hegel's. It grows from a conception of philosophy different to the Hegelian one of scientific system, with its stress upon the determinate knowing of the determinate. Unlike Hegel's consciousness and sense-certainty, Lear, the father, loves the child as a sheer this. The love of the parent reveals an ontology of particularity that is unremittingly attentive to the this as this. The this is not simply an instance of a universal; in this love the metaphysical fragility of the this is known. The metaphysical frailty is the sense that this being has a singular being that was never before and never will be again as this sheer onceness, sheer unrepeatability. No being or universal can substitute for this being, ever, never.

This metaphysical frailty concretizes the sense that the Once is shadowed by the never more. Never more is ontological necessary to the definition of the 'more' of the 'Once' as non-repeatable. My sense of the particular as idios demands we see it as its own world unto itself, but it is not a bare or indigent particular. Quite to the contrary: it is more, not less, than any abstract universal. Nor is this sense of the nothing that comes with the Never the same as Hegelian negation. For Hegel's 'nothing' is caught up in the dynamism of determinate negation, hence every negation will yield a positive result. If there is an outcome with the Never, it is not that Hegelian one.

My point is not to deny mind's need of universal structures; this is part of all philosophy. The point is not to falsify certain particulars by something like Hegel's dialectic of sense-certainty. It will not do to say that all immediacy is mediated and, *mirabile dictu*, the dialectical dynamism presses relentlessly forward again. Some particulars take root in one's being and cannot be uprooted without violence. There are particulars that, as it were, hook into one's throat and, struggle as one may, one cannot pull them out. The Never hooks into the throat of thought and rasps the smoothness of its conceptual voice. It cuts into philosophy, making a wound that may never be entirely healed. Particulars which are idiotic, intimates of being, have a certain inward otherness, invisible to any form of objective thinking. This intimacy of being resists objectifiable identification, is other, idiotic to objective thinking. It resists total saying in determinate concepts, resists being brought out completely into the public domain of conceptual discursivity.

The Once, the Never and the 'That it is' means that there is and will be no repetition. Being as the 'That it is', floating once on the nothingness whence it came and whither to our eyes it is once again returned – all of this is idiotic. The Never thus says a No to Nietzsche's eternal recurrence and its once more. The Once is a No to this eternal recurrence too, I think. Every unique particular, that is, everything, will never be repeated. There is only once, and once only. If there is an eternity it must be radically other. It cannot be a repetition, for even repetition would be other than what it repeated, and the once would renew itself as other than what it once was. This is what is implied by a metaphysics of agapeic creation.[5]

We might here think of the irreplaceability of the This in terms of Job's second children. Surely we miss something absolutely fundamental if we think that a second set of children can replace or substitute for the first children that are dead? We miss the irrepeatability of the Once. Perhaps there is here something that is ever escaping from us. We are in the process of loss always and we don't even know it. Even as we think we master this or that, this other or that other is slipping from us and mostly we do not even know it. Tragedy brings home the permeability of all being by loss: to be is to be at a loss.

This may not apply thus in the world of means and ends, of pragmatic utility. But that world is one of the replaceable: one thing can substitute for another, one thing might be as useful as another and for an end outside itself. Such a world lacks in intrinsic values, lacks the irreplaceable, the unrepeatable. The tragic shows that the instrumentalized world feeds off a flattened ontology. The world of utility is a narrowing and a falsification of being. Tragedy involves the destruction of the instrumental illusion. Every quotidian value comes under stress if not destruction. Even the highest instrumental values of regal politics are seen as less than ultimate. Lear will be stripped to his humanity, and will have nothing left. And there will be more insight through this 'nothing' than through all the regal power of the instrumental world.

In that sense, world-history can be a lie from the standpoint of tragic knowing. This is why there is a kind of Hegelianism for which the intimacy of the tragic is a closed world, for it sees things too much in terms of the public arena of world-history. It cannot comprehend the idiot wisdom of a Lear.[6] It cannot attain the extremity and radicality of what is seen and said there. Perhaps there is no 'place' for this in human existence. Perhaps we can only die after beginning to see what is revealed here; die or be utterly transformed. But this transformation would be death also to the intrumentalized self. It would be a blank, horrifying emptiness; the instrumentalized self would see nothing, nothing there. The judgment coming from there would say: Never, never, never – and you have lived this lie, and now must break, break absolutely, or you die a different death. Thus we might liken tragic insight to a process of being drowned: the air of everyday instrumentalities is withdrawn, we cannot breathe, we are being asphyxiated by a knowing that we cannot process, cannot digest. We are being brought under, going under, undergoing, in shock from a lightning-bolt out of the Once and the Never. Yeats once said: 'blackout – heaven burning into the head'. This black knowledge is a blindness, a madness, a death, a howl, as when a knife pierces one.

The Never then is at the antipodes of Hegel's *Aufhebung*. The

Hegelian negation as determinate negativity is always prelude to the *Aufhebung*. As I before said: Never is a crushing word; Never is *the* crushing word. But what does it mean to be crushed? Is there a dialectical account of being crushed? Being crushed is like a retraction of the energy of being into an inarticulate void, not a determinate negation. It is like a stunning blow to the head: one may never recover from the metaphysical concussion received; once hit, one will always be concussed by this Never; one will always, evermore find it difficult to keep one's balance: one's being has lost its equilibrium, is always in danger of tilting over and itself falling into the abyss. The mind staggers like a drunken man. This is madness from the point of view of philosophy's official image. But was there not a secret metaphysical staggering in the great philosophers, Hegel included?

Lear was once a kind of Hegelian himself in thinking of being in terms of the public stage of the kingdom, the Hegelian universal of world-history. Exiled from this stage, passing through madness, Lear discovered the intimacy of being, the wisdom of its idiocy. In effect Lear rejects Hegelian dialectic in saying to Cordelia, still alive, that they would take upon themselves 'the mystery of things,/ As if we were God's spies; and we'll wear our,/ In a walled prison, packs and sects of great ones/ That ebb and flow by th' moon'. (V,iii, 17–20). There are no final mysteries for Hegel's dialectical concept. Can we call Hegel 'God's spy' when he compared his *Science of Logic* to God's thoughts before the creation of nature and finite spirit? No. The *Logic* is silent about what Lear sees. Hegel's God, as the world spirit of world-history, dialectically ebbs and flows by the moon, borne in devouring time by the packs and sects of great ones, Hegel's world-historical nations and individuals. Hegel's dialectical theodicy fails for all Lears, mute before the elemental grief of father and mothers, mute before murdered children, the Golgotha of the intimacy of particularity. The rational comfort of dialectics does not comfort.

The idiocy of the Never as lived from within brings home the intimacy of horror. This intimacy is at the limit of sense, and our response to it is itself at the limit of sense. We experience here a metaphysical helplessness which we ought not to euphemize or fake with the bustle of pseudo-explanatory discourse. No rationalization will ever do away with this being at a loss. Here is a destructuring indeterminacy, a negative otherness that resists total recuperation in the logic of dialectical concepts, a collapse of the energy of being, a metaphysical oppression, that resists being reduced to any mediated account.

When one comes to the edge of the Never, one looks over into nothing. It is an edge of being that is no edge, for the other of being here is not a simple negation of being. It is the irrevocable revocation of being: the nothingness of being as beyond being and yet as the destiny of mortal being. But paradoxically the 'nothing' of the Never is 'too much', a dark excess of irrevocable revocation of being. This dark excess is beyond the dialectical economy of Hegel's system of determinate negation. It is an indeterminate negation which is yet quite determinate – for it is this self that will die or is dead – but indeterminate because the very determinacy of the Once is itself the intractable enigma or mystery. The *tode ti* is here an idiotic particular because it cannot be subsumed into a universal without betrayal of its thisness. Precisely as a determinate *tode ti* it is recalcitrant to conceptual determination either in its thisness or in its possible universality. A different thought of the This is required than either an Aristotelian or a Hegelian one.

Here we might compare Lear and Abraham. This is entirely relevant, for the invocation of Abraham served Kierkegaard well to charge the Hegelian system with its betrayal of the This. Unlike Lear, Abraham was *asked* to kill his child, sacrifice his son. Bear in mind: Abraham has a child in old age. Presuming that his eyes were not already stones, one imagines the aged father, the father preparing for death, looking upon Isaac with a sense of the sheer Once of his being there. Isaac was a gift out of nothing. Abraham must have intimately known the metaphysical density of the Once, the irreplaceable This, indeed the idiocy of its gift given the extemity of his own age – the madness of an old father, but a madness gifted by God for whom all things are possible. Again we cannot make sense of the Never without a sense of this absolute Once. Here a metaphysics of creation is deeper than a dialectical logic of the self-generating Idea. The latter does not allow for sufficiently radical otherness, and hence for sufficient newness, onceness, as does the former.

When God asks Abraham to kill his son, the violence in this request is unparalleled: the irreplaceable is to be destroyed, to be treated as if it were nothing. But ontologically this is impossible. There is a sense in which even God cannot undo His work, once given the otherness of its being created. Though the This was a gift out of nothing, once in being, the This is absolutely irreplaceable –

all the more evident too, given the extremity of Abraham's age. God cannot undo this, even though He order the death of the This. Yet Abraham consents to God's attempted revocation of the irrevocable. Abraham now stood at the edge of the Never. In some sense, he faced into the Never as the result of his own willingness, his own choice, and so must have consented to its crushing burden. He is willing to give up the Once of Isaac. I cannot conceive of his willingness except as invaded by metaphysical nausea and horror. Sickness of heart inundates him but it must be kept down, smothered in silence before God. This silence horrified and obsessed Kierkegaard. He wanted to admire the silence but secretly had to stifle his own nausea before the horror.

Lear cannot smother his rage in silence, though he prays for patience. He prays for patience because he is being crushed. He cries out in his intolerable loss. Perhaps he cries out because the regal I of Lear was not yet dead in him. Yet this regal I is part of the glory of human particularity, humble or hubristic, its glint of free selfhood. Lear does not willingly go up to be crushed by the Never. It visits him, even though his own foolish acts offered the welcome to it in the form in which it did come upon him. Abraham is willing to be crushed and yet has faith that beyond the Once and the Never is God and His promise. This sense of the beyond is not thus evident in Lear. Nor is Lear given back his Cordelia as Abraham is given back his Isaac.[7]

Can we discover any alleviation at all in this contemplation of the Never. As one possible approach, I suggest we consider Dostoevski's experience of, as it were, outliving his own death. The younger Dostoevski was condemned to death for subversive politics. As a condemned criminal I think of him as living with the thought of the Never. On the morning of his death, he faced the Never: never again the sun rising, never again the fragrance of the air, never to hear birdsong at dawn, never again the face of a familiar loved one: never, never, never. On the morning of his execution, Dostoevski was already half over the edge of death, already thinking, trying to think what cannot be thought. We know the rest of the story: absolute reversal from death to life – the absolute surprise of reprieve, the shock of the impossible. Dostoevski experienced being pulled back again into life, but not without the taste of the unthinkable. I think of this as like the violent shock of being brought back to life, like a resurrection from the dead. Instead of never being again, he was given back the Once again: once again to be, to live.

The metaphysical consolation, such as it is, is this: The sheer 'once there is' of being at all strikes home. Dostoevski sensed the sweetness of the morning air, as if for the first time, as if never before, as if the sheer moment of resurrection to life resurrected all life to its virginal freshness. It is like the fairy tale that begins: Once upon a time. This Once recalls the mythic time of such an aboriginal freshness of being, the time of the origin beyond all time, the time out of time of creation from nothing as pure gift. The resurrected Dostoevski must have rubbed his eyes: I am here. I am. It is. It is inexpressibly good to be, simply to be.

This 'I am' is not the 'I am' of Descartes' *cogito ergo sum*, I think therefore I am. This resurrected 'I am' is one that the power of thought, purely on its own, cannot bring into life, back into life. This 'I am' comes as a gift from an unnamed other. This 'I am' testifies to a gift of being from the other that no thought thinking itself could ever conceive as *being*. Not *cogito ergo sum*; but I was as dead, as nothing; but now I am, in a reversal from death to life, from never to once again; a reversal that pure self-thinking thought cannot effect or indeed conceive. This 'I am' is a release from the prison-house of immanent subjectivity, a release towards the otherness of being because of the gift of being from the other. Encounter with, or being brushed by the Never resurrects the Once in its splendor. The value of tragic insight offers itself in the precipitation of this ontological joy. One must sing 'I am'. I must sing the 'to be' of being as gift.

There begins Dostoevski's initiation into what in *Philosophy and its Others* I call posthumous mind[8]: a thinking of being as if from beyond death, being in the worthiness of its present joy. Tragic insight crosses over from life to death, and looks back on life, crosses back and lives life otherwise: life in death, the Once resurrected. Dying, and yet to look on being there with the extra eye of death: this is what I call posthumous mind. The eye of death has been added to the mortal living one; henceforth one is split between the here and the beyond, the once and the never more, and the more that may be beyond the never, beyond life and death. The theme of being at a loss returns. It seems one must lose everything to be able to see anything properly. One must be brought to a complete loss to be able to see things once, and once again. To see the simple `there it is' of what is: to see the marvel; to sing the marvel of being. `Thy life's a miracle', the son Edgar tells the father Gloucester, after the blinded father has fallen into the abyss of mind. The beloved father too is for the exiled son an irreplaceable This.

And yet Lear's Howl comes back again and again and the word 'marvel' sticks in the throat. Where is the song then? Lear's Never seems to give us, not horror and pity à la Aristotle, but horror without the pity, pitiless horror.[9] At the end of *King Lear*, there is no resurrection of the Once. Nevertheless, looking on Lear, we are made to ponder the possible resurrection of the Once. The horror of *King Lear* is that this resurrection seems to have *already* occurred when Lear and Cordelia are taken to prison and Lear speaks of being 'God's spies'. Lear is actually as if dead by this time. He speaks as if from a condition of posthumous mind. On waking to Cordelia's presence, Lear actually says: 'You do me wrong to take me out o' th' grave:/ Thou art a soul in bliss ... Where have I been? Where am I? Fair daylight?' IV, vii, 45–6, 52). Fair daylight – the words recall the restoration of elemental being for Dostoevski. But then all of this is snatched from us in the Howl, Howl, Howl. We thought we had crossed over to death and returned. Kent says (V, iii, 319): 'He but usurped his life'. But Lear has to actually cross over into death itself. We cannot really outlive time in time itself. The ontological enigma of death has to be endured. 'Men must endure/ Their going hence, even as their coming hither;/ Ripeness is all.' (V, ii, 9–11) The irreplaceable cannot be replaced.

Through the tragic suffering of being at a loss, the question rises again to torment the philosopher: If one has ever been brushed by metaphysical astonishment before the Once or metaphysical horror before the Never, why should we confine the irreplaceable only to the loved particular? Why should not a rat, a dog, a horse evoke the same sense of ontological enigma? Why not explode Hegel's dialectics of sense-certainty with the mystery of a rat's being – or for that matter Krug's pen. This is perhaps a variation on Parmenides' question to young Socrates about dirt and the *eide*. Hegel runs away from the dirt of Krug's pen. Plato is better again in making Parminides tell Socrates that philosophy too must think the hair, mud and dirt, the repugnancies of being from which at first reason recoils (*Parmenides*, 130c–e).

Thus in a deep sense, and with the blessings of untragic Parmenides, there is no reason at all why philosophy should despise the being of a rat. True: the beloved This is for us the place where most often the enigma of being breaks through. The metaphysician can ask: Why should a rat, a dog, a horse have being at all? They too exhibit their sheer 'That it is'. Though we might eat them as meat, in themselves they live the intimacy of being in their own way, every entity a gift out of nothing by agapeic being. But when I turn thus from the beloved This to the despised This, from the child to the rat, the point is not at all for philosophy's eyes to become as rational stones. It is for philosophy to be the metaphysical thinking of agapeic mind.

Notes

1. Shakespeare scholars argue about the difference between the Folio (1623) and the Quarto (1608) editions. In the Folio there are 5 nevers, in the Quarto 3 nevers. As the reader will come to realize, for purposes of the metaphysical reflection undertaken here, the difference between 3 and 5 is not of ultimate significance. One Never can be enough, Once is enough. I thank Robert Miola for bringing to my attention the point about the different editions.

2. See *Philosophy and its Others: Ways of Being and Mind* (Albany: SUNY, 1990), ch. 6 on thought singing its other. Nietzsche speaks of the birth of tragedy from the spirit of music. It is not entirely clear how, in Nietzsche himself, something like Lear's Howl might turn into Nietzschean music. How do we get from the howl to the music? On what I call 'aesthetic theodicy and the transfiguration of the ugly' in Nietzsche and also Hegel, see my *Art and the Absolute* (Albany: SUNY, 1986), 150–9.

3. See my 'Schopenhauer, Art and the Dark Origin', in *Schopenhauer*, Eric von der Luft, ed. (Lewistown: Mellen Press 1988), 101–22.

4. On the eyes of the mad Nietzsche as seen by some visitors, see *Conversations with Nietzsche: A Life in the Words of His Contemporaries*, ed. and introd. Sander L. Gilman, trans. David J. Parent (New York: Oxford University Press, 1987), e.g. 242, 246, 247.

5. Is there any sense in which the idea of *sub specie aeternitatis* has some applicability here? Even Spinoza says: we feel and experience ourselves to be eternal. Do we need a sense of time's other, traditionally called eternity, to make sense of the Once and Never of our time? Here eternity could not mean the impersonal universal, the eternity of the dead ideas. It would have to be something like the living conversation of mind that outlives time, as in Socrates' dream of the other world: this other world is not simply the world of ideas, but of *thises – particular* heroic humans to whom Socrates wants to talk. *Philosophy and its Others*, chapter 6 reflects on time and time's other. On agapeic creation, see my *Desire, Dialectic and Otherness: An Essay on Origins* (New Haven: Yale University Press, 1987), especially chapter 8. On the critique of 'static eternity', see *ibid*, chapter 4.

6. On idiot wisdom, see *Philosophy and its Others*, chapter 6.

7. The theme of patience is very important, both for *Lear* and our reflection here. But it would require another meditation.

8. On 'posthumous mind', see *Philosophy and its Others*, especially 278ff., 300, 304, 368n20.

9. Hence the difficulty sometimes felt in staging the final death scene. Shakespeare's sources have a restoration and happy ending. In the eighteenth century the ending sometimes was changed. Dr. Johnson said that the death of Cordelia was so shocking that we would want to avoid it if we could.

10
Myth, Tragedy and Dialogue: The Language of Philosophy

JOHN M. ANDERSON

PHILOSOPHIZING

To philosophize is to strive to articulate and develop the nature of human being. It is to say I am living in circumstances which surround me. I am aware of wonders which call for my free response. Who am I, and why am I here? Who can I become? What does this mean? I try to discern myself, and of course am at once aware that I would not be myself unless I wanted to be more than I am or could be, and know more than I can know.

ODE TO HUMAN BEING

There is much that is strange, but nothing
that surpasses humans in strangeness.
They set sail into empty space amid the smoke and
blasts of their engines, tacking in the light of sun and
the softer light of the moon.
They weary the ground beneath their feet, the Earth,
even that which is home.
Harsh and untiring,
casting over her from year to year, the
flesh of furrows, reaping away, back and forth, collecting
the food she yields them, this way and that, with knives
and machines.

And humans, pondering and plotting,
penetrate the asteroids like light-gliding birds and pan
the surface of the moon for gold and diamonds. Seeking in

the depths of the oceans the native creatures.
With guile they overpower the shark that roams the
waves by night as by day.
On land they yoke the hirsute neck of the stallion and the
undaunted boar.

And we have found our way
to the call of the word,
and to wind-swift all-understanding,
and to the mores which rule over cities.
We have considered also how to flee
weather and frost to the light and warmth within sky
probing walls.

Everywhere journeying, naive and yearning, we come to
nothingness.
Through no flight can we resist
the one assault of death,
even if we have succeeded in cleverly evading
painful sickness.

Clever indeed, mastering the ways of skill beyond all
hope
we often accomplish evil,
sometimes help others.
We wend our way between the bounty of the earth
and the promise of the sky,
carelessly rising high above our place.

Those who for the sake of power use up the endowment of
origin lose their place in the end.

May such persons never frequent my hearth.
May my mind never share the presumption
of a person who does this.

Sophocles rewritten

PART I

INTRODUCTION

Tragedy, its concept and meaning, has a long tradition. The word, in English, no longer carries the symbolic meaning and conotation that it once had and still deserves to express. Now the word is used to name a very sad event, a disaster. If it refers to a play it names a serious work dealing with a central character and leading to an unhappy or disastrous ending by accident or the result of a flawed character. In a modern work the flaw is usually moral weakness, social pressure, or an abnormal psyche.

Despite this I say that tragedy should be returned to its original position as a fundamental aspect of human life and living. As human we are limited. We are aware of that, not merely as evidenced in particular ways, that is we can run only so fast, can write only so many volumes, expect to live only so many years, and so on. We are aware of limitation as a horizon. That we cannot specify. That we cannot say. None the less that is a fundamental part of our lives. It is this horizon tragedy plumbs and has plumbed since its origin and growth from the myths of prehistory. It is this we lose by focus on our daily needs and in the distorting pride engendered by literal power. It is this depth we must search, for searching is our nature.

There is growth and becoming and often meaning in the folds of human living. Humans become as their growth unfolds and enfolds. Not already patterned, not fixed to any pattern, but growing and changing, and as free they may open themselves to the dark fullness of the earth and to the ever-arching sky light, to become a strange but meaningful incarnation as of the Whole which is more than dark and light, or any parts, and yet neither totality nor merely an object constructed of one element nor any or many parts.

Plato says this: '...our eyes give us the sight of the stars, the sun and the firmament...it is these wonders which compel us to consider the universe and to accept the greatest gift of the gods, the capacity for philosophizing'. Here he assumes wonder to be compelling confusing presence calling us to philosophize. Later Aristotle says much the same thing. 'It is owing to wonder that men now and at first began to philosophize: they wondered originally at small difficulties and later about greater ones such as the moon, the sun, the stars and then about the genesis of the universe. Here Plato and then Aristotle distinguish between knowledge of facts and philosophical truth, emphasizing a distinction even then made long ago, and passing it on to others.

SOCIETY

This inwrought depth of quality, our involvement in wonder, wonder which is also each of us, bespeaks our being as free becoming. Responding to wonders, wondering, we may qualify and have more character. We often try to attain this, and strange as we are, we try to possess the necessities of living at the same time. The satisfaction of both, we remember, has happened in early life in a family. But at best the family offered temporary solace. And now we have relations to each other in societies of various kinds in which both can hardly be found.

The societal relation itself has ensured little more than cooperation for the attainment of power necessary for the satisfaction of needs. Yet the results of our cooperative efforts are ingenious: tools, buildings, roads, ships, machines, plants and animals, common sense and technological knowledge, and much more, including wars with both beginnings and ends; but they include few instances where the achievement has been enduring response to the call of wonder.

Yet we yearn for the ideal society which will do this. We have often tried to put together such a polity by introducing qualities and patterns from the family, from religions, from art. Thus polities built with more than the bricks of their walls and roads have been proposed. Apropriately these have been named Utopias, for they are not to be found anywhere in the space their buildings occupy. Even modest ideals when embodied introduce oppositions and commitments which tear polities apart, as in the Holy Roman Empire, the Shaker communities, the Athenian democracy, the Communist experiments. Usually the break is either a result of inability to produce the necessary goods for the satisfaction of basic needs, that is the inability to organize for power when Wonder is the focus of attention, or it is a result of the dedication of the citizens to their own special, and apparently different wonders, which interferes and even makes impossible their relations to each other as themselves wonders.

MYTHS

But society as cooperation limited to the satisfaction of needs embodies only an aspect of our living. We can cooperate for power, but we can also limit our needs and our need for power. We can seek to articulate our effort to express our freedom by responses to wonder engendering myths, and ignore power. Myths develop from our free response to the dark background of clear perceptions. Our perceptions are here and now. They are present and objective. Myths are not only present in consciousness to some extent, but have presence. They are examples of free attainment of presence and constitute evidence that the clarity can be achieved without objectification, without the here and now. Myths, however often retold, are remembered. They are always 'Once upon a time', and never brought into the present. We find the presence of myths elaborately developed by art early in our history, for myths and art seem coeval.

Such enhanced myths are more complex responses to circumstances than the clarifying objectification by consciousness which is perception. They are most often developed when perceptions are touched by the confusion of wonder. They are responses which preserve wonder. Myths are efforts clarifying content but resisting full objectification of their content. That they preserve by thought and imagination mirrors the confusion as well as the clarity of human nature. Myths are deliberately ambiguous and at the same time as content of consciousness, clear. In this way myths as clarifying, but not clear, bring to consciousness evidence of both our participation in circumstance and the horizon of our freedom from it, that is our existence in presence.

Art in Myth

We have long sought and still seek to bring the meaning of our free becoming to presence by developing perception as myth. And in the myths of the past as well as those of the present we find art used to aid us in the clarification of the call of Wonders to our creativity. It is with the help of art that we answer this call and express our freedom in bringing to consciousness the creative drive in myth-making as the creativity of our living. We look to the helpful muses and to gracious luck for the key to the half concealed secret of our freedom.

Let us consider an old myth told and retold on this theme:

THE WATERS OF NON-EXISTENCE

The symbolism of Maya is developed further in a magnificent myth describing the irrational adventure of a mighty sage, Markandeya, during the interval of non-manifestation between the dissolution and re-creation of the universe. Markandeya, by a miraculous and curious accident, beholds Vishnu in a series of archetypal transformations: first, under the elemental guise of the cosmic ocean; then as a giant reclining on the waters; again, as a divine child, alone at play beneath the cosmic tree; and finally as a majestic wild gander, the sound of whose breathing is the magic melody of the creation and dissolution of the world.

The myth begins with a review of the deterioration of the cosmic order, during the slow but irreversible passage of the four yugas. Holy Dharma vanishes, quarter by quarter from the life of the world, until chaos supervenes. Men are filled at last, with only lust and evil. There is no one, anymore, in whom enlightening goodness prevails, no real wise man, no saint, no one uttering truth and standing by his sacred word. The seemingly holy Brahmin is no better than the fool. Old people, destitute of the true wisdom of old age, try to behave like the young and the young lack the candor of youth. The social classes have lost their distinguishing virtues; teachers, princes, tradespeople, and servants sprawl alike in a general vulgarity. The will to rise to supreme heights has failed; the bonds of sympathy and love have dissolved; narrow egotism rules. Indistinguishable ninnies conglomerate to form a kind of sticky unpalatable dough. When this calamity has befallen the once harmoniously ordered City of Man, the substance of the world organism has deteriorated beyond salvage, and the universe is ripe for dissolution.

This most degenerate age is devoured by the fire and the dust of the holocaust. This is laid by a torrential rain which gradually collects to form the ocean of non-being, the night of Brahma. In this night of non-being the great god Vishnu sleeps; all has become and remains implicit. And yet the ocean of non-being is filled with the waters of life, so that even as Vishnu floats sleeping upon the ocean he dreams. And in the dream of the god, the sage Markandeya lives a life of perfect holiness. Yet while living this dreamed life, the sage inadvertently slips from the mouth of Vishnu and falls into the waters of non-being. In consequence he finds himself swimming desperately in the dark waters and finds his situation unbelievable; indeed, he supposes that this might be a dream, for the strangeness of the situation is totally beyond his human powers of comprehension. But before the sage can adjust to this situation in any way, Vishnu stirs in his sleep and, scooping him up out of the water, returns him to the dream. This one excursion into absolute strangeness is followed, in the tale, by two more. In the next Markandeya again slips from the dream of the god into the waters of non-existence, but sees floating upon them the great figure of the sleeping god. He is again scooped out of the water by Vishnu and returned to the dream. And finally, when he slips into the waters for the third time, he sees upon them an island where the great and venerable god Vishnu is seated and playing as a child. In the myth Markandeya is pictured as being returned, at last, to the dream of perfect existence, never having grasped the wonderful significance of his adventure.

(Matsya Purana, clxlvlii 13–25)

Myth-making gives birth to figures, persons and complex events interpreting us and our situation and, to safeguard their implicit wonders, places these in consciousness, a theater that is *theasthai*, a seeing place. In the theater of the mind wonder can be introduced, clarified, and protected from those powers of collective action which produce goods to be possessed and used up. On this fertile stage, with scenery and scenes prepared by art, figures larger than life are born and live their lives freely and more significantly than we do in our restricted collective action. Art's telling and retelling of myths on this stage enlightens the wonder of their lives and shows them to be the richer lives we could and should live, makes the events of heros' lives take place on the path leading into radical possibility, the path we too, as free, should be on, and along which we, too, should find ourselves as human, moving beyond into presence.

In the presence attained in art we look for and come closer to the untold ground of our living. But although the enlightenment art offers is good, we are well aware that the insight is multiple and ambiguous. That, as always, we shall remember only the shadows of meaning, that we shall be still at a loss for words or signs to explain the presence in which we have participated and almost found ourselves and our fate.

When we respond to wonder in the rhythm, sounds, music of dance, and above all in its intoxicating performance, we develop, retell, restate and refine myth. When we paint scenes on cave walls and carve reliefs and statues, as of the earth mother and her progeny, including ourselves, we do so to hold wonder, to penetrate by regeneration the veil concealing its secret. Wonder, interwoven in myth and brought to presence by art bespeaks the call exciting our yearning to participate in, to find ourselves of, that beyond us.

In the theater, a seeing place, we set the wonder of Wonder at a distance on the stage and so seem to bring it to consciousness and clarity by objectification. As *performance*, as dance, as story, however, we re-experience both the ambiguity of wonder and of free human becoming. In performance we re-peat, re-discover, re-examine and re-live wonder in the quality of our behavior, and so discern as the thread of freedom, its ambiguity. By doing this in the art of tragedy we discover we can intend to bring our deepest drive to focus and so be led to stand upon the threshold of the *aporon*, the wasteland, the greatest wonder, the openness, which discloses our fate as still its secret. Thus even in the art of tragedy its deepest meaning is its emphasis on the ambiguity of wonder, its emphatic confusion, and its re-statements of this, and of ourselves.

RELIGION

That we have insight beyond that available in our ordinary societal lives is attested by wonders, and its significance has often been expressed in myth clarified by art. That this clarification can be developed to a startling degree by the generation of presence which is art, suggests that it might be possible to attain even more than the ambiguous vision of tragedy.

Artists intoxicated by their involvement often suggest art is revelation. If this were so the clarity attained would be disclosure of another world, that is a world not only beyond that of our collective actions, but beyond what any myth helped by art can tell us about ourselves and our place. For such radical disclosure to be possible we need more than the small infinities of the many wonders which confront us and call for our myth-making and artistic efforts at disclosure. We need a wonder surpassing any artistic achievement, an incredible wonder which is in itself the illumination, the clarification which is the truth of all wonders.

In the West and in the East the short period of our history (600 BC–AD 200) is studded with a series of exceptional illuminations. These unbelievable wonders inspired more than development as myth, and, even, more than development by art. While any response to them was evidently inadequate it was evident in some cases that this impossibility should be expressed both in elaborately written and highly developed graphic forms. It is not surprising that this was understood to justify elaborately developing the extraordinary places for human existence already sketched in myth to inconceivable lengths. During these years and subsequently, such accounts have been stated and restated to show, however indirectly, humanity's ultimate nature and place as an entirely new life and world.

This was done in different ways in the accounts of the Judaeic, Christian, Hindu, Islamic and Buddhist religions, for example. Because of the revelational clarity of their insight these religions often conflicted in sharper ways than do the variety of such expressions formulated in myth and in tragic drama. While there are patterns in Euripides' tragedies which conflict with those of Sophocles, the essential ambiguity of their presentation as myth and presence can be attributed to artistic expression and would also be expected as essential for reflecting the transcendent significance of wonders which, as transcendent, cannot be fully accessible to human understanding. The art developing myths, even when this reaches the heights of presence in tragic drama does not claim the clarity of response to wonder that has often been claimed by revealed religions. Nor does it incite the human violence resulting from the disagreement of the different religious 'certainties' which produced the great slaughter of the many religious wars in the course of the last 2500 years, and is still a continuing threat to human dignity and survival.

GREEK SCIENCE

At about the same time, although somewhat earlier than the development of revealed religions, the prideful human desire for clarity was supported in terms which, since the western Renaissance, have come to be understood as the key to the development of science. About 585 BC it occurred to Thales of Miletus that he could both respond to the Wonder of the Sun and also focus his attention on its finite aspects, the objects and facts consciousness discloses clearly, and so predict that there would be an eclipse of the sun within a year. And for another example that he could respond to the infinity, the wonder, of the Ocean and also measure the distance of ships at sea and the height of very tall objects on the shore. That is he attained the supreme clarity of scientific knowledge, useful knowledge which could be checked by reference to facts already known; that is knowledge which is true from any point of view, that is universal knowledge. To preserve Wonder while apparently turning away from it to details, he introduced a very significant assumption. He assumed that in some sense all finite things are themselves distinguishable but not separable parts of The Whole, and also themselves wholes of distinguishable but not separable parts. To justify this assumption he added that The Whole is Water and that its parts are also water.

By considering all things to be simply distinguishable quantities of water, the call of the One as Wonder can still be heard. We need only note that the distinctness of things is easily washed away, that is as blobs of water the many flow together into The One; and add that, acknowledged as whole, The One is easily dispersed as in 'rain drops'; and so may be acknowledged as many. According to Thales either understanding includes the other. Thus Thales could claim to devote his energies to attaining a great deal of knowledge about the many without losing the intuition of The One.

His view, although placing much more emphasis on the many, is similar to the more refined eastern intuition of No Thing, as in Tao and Buddhism. That is, as human we are ourselves ambiguous and in consequence can be and are sometimes involved in The One (No Thing) as many things and at other times we intuit the Many Things as No Thing (One). Human being, thus, is at once One and Many.

A restatement of Thales' assumption which also emphasizes the many and the consequences of this emphasis, can be found in Euclidean geometry which was developing at that time. It is assumed in Euclidean geometry that space is made up of points and that all points are interchangeable, that any individual point can be replaced by any other. These are the many.

Since a point has no width, breadth, or length, or indeed any qualities except location – which is assigned as relative to an arbitrary choice of a reference point – since a point has no qualities as such, its contribution to the whole of Space is the same no matter where it is thought to be or what other points are thought to be present. This uniform contribution establishes the *homogeneity* of Euclidean Space as a Whole and makes all translations of figures and objects possible without changing them. It does not matter where figures or objects are. Thus the figures and objects as constituted by points do not break up empty space, The One. They are as much empty space as they are individual circles, squares, etc. And The One, empty space, contains as homogenous points, Many Things.

The Greeks were not immune to the temptation of clarity, however, which led them to emphasize the many in their art, and in the pantheon of their religion, as well as in their science. Still they were careful to include The One. In art they produced statues, temples (as the Pergamon Altar), paintings, literature, where individuality shines, but is carefully justified by dedication to The One, as re-presented by the gods. Such dedication was done by artistic involvement understood as contributing to the art the power of presence in which The One is unveiled.

However even if rites do protect The One from veiling by the many, the Greeks were very much aware that, even with rites, it is difficult to avoid imposing limiting conditions on The One which objectify that. For example, Leucippus' and Democritus' theory of *The One as constituted by very small atoms differing in shape and size*, which serve as unperceived building blocks for construction of objects and patterns with differences based only on quantity (size) and location (shape) does impose size and shape on The One which, then, as objectified cannot be a Whole of parts which dissolve into that. Even Thales' claim that The One is water, although persuasive, is hardly acceptable, for it suggests The One is an endless Ocean. And, of course, the distinct properties deducible from the axioms of Euclidean geometry are attributed to Euclidean space, and objectify it as such, thus depriving it of a claim to be The One as such.

At this time the Greeks struggled with the philosophical problem of understanding the Wonder of The One in terms which would include the many without loss of Wonder, and the Many in terms which would constitute The One as Wonder. They sensed in this issue a call for philosophical consideration. In fact they formulated an alternative to the various theories of the homogeneity of the many which tainted The One by objectifying it as quantity, a totality of separable parts.

The nature of an alternative to the assumption of homogeneity of the many and a totality of finite parts was stated at this time by the Eleatics and restated by the Qualitative Pluralists. Thus the most interesting of these, Anaxagoras, denies homogeneity of the many when he insists 'Among the small there is no smallest'. His assumption denies the existence of ultimate identical parts without qualities, and he says 'things are not sliced off from one another with an axe', as separable existing points or atoms would be. He also insists that qualities are not separable but of infinite gradation. This denies the possibility of distinguishing such items as ice, water, steam, air or whatever, by specifying quality as such. Without a unit of measurement and separability of the units the many cannot be homogeneous and serve as separable building blocks of *The One*. And without specifically different qualities, that is, with the infinite shading of qualities, Anaxagoras assumes The One cannot resolve into The Many. Anaxagoras' assumptions imply that there is an initial wonder which as a Whole calls the appearances of the many to their ground.

There is in his thought the suggestion that The Wonder of The One is Mind which orders and arranges as the level of the Whole without parts. Human mind cannot be conscious of this for such a Whole is not an object. None the less it can intuit this. This intuition, Anaxagoras says, can be expressed as the realization that the world of the Many of which we are conscious is only an instance of an infinity of such worlds in which thinking has produced and will introduce the many. Thus Mind as Whole without parts introduces Totalities with parts. We can think this as occurring, but we cannot comprehend this Wonder.

Human thinking has no direct access to this infinity of worlds. Human thinking is based on finite parts, but we do have an intuition of The One as a Whole in which parts dissolve. The possibility of an infinity of worlds, each a totality, suggests that Mind thinking can think both The One and the Many, but that human thought cannot. We must think one or the other, and then realize that our intuition of Wonder, of the Whole, requires our commitment to move beyond the idea of totality even though we cannot claim to reach The One. Knowledge we have, but Wisdom lies beyond.... This is the approach to the *aporon*, the threshold of the intuition of No Thing.

As Thales, Anaxagoras and Lao Tze might have said, a Whole dissolves separable parts and is The One, quality. Our effort to disclose the ground of quality makes the presence of the many an infinity of worlds, and deepens the presence of ourselves as reflecting not only that which is more than we are, but an infinity of thats which reflect us. In the infinity of worlds our own presence as quality reflects, more evidently, more than we ever are.

WISDOM AND/OR TRUTH?

In classical Greece the evidence that scientific truth, analysis and logic, based on the assumption of homogeneity, could provide universally acceptable knowledge and guarantee practical results was understood. But it was not understood to justify introducing a separate discipline and a new highway to knowledge for these purposes and at the expense of wonder. Although the Greeks were exceptional mathematicians and scientists they were also exceptional philosophers. They believed that while quantitative knowledge based on homogeneous parts was significant it did not, as did qualitative intuition, lead to wisdom. And, most of the scientists of the time were committed to the love of wisdom, even as they sought specific knowledge as well. Even as late as the western Renaissance many scientists tried to avoid any split with religion or philosophy, and many philosophers tried to avoid a split with religion and science, as had the Greeks.

In the development of myth by telling and retelling, and its further development by art into drama and especially tragedy and comedy, the Greeks had showed time and again that a deepening awareness of human nature in its freedom was possible along the older path. Tragedy does not offer a definition of human being. Tragedy presents no specific and final knowledge of human being, but it does show us that the pursuit and attainment of objective knowledge produces, if it attenuates the presence attained by tragedy, a truncated expression of human being. In the West the development of artistic tragedy still leads to significant discussion and thought in art which discloses the depth of our being.

The Modern separation of science from religion and philosophy did not develop fully until the time of Descartes, who argued that, since the universal wisdom pursued by philosophy could never be attained by humans, as the Greeks and later thinkers had clearly shown by their failure, it would be best to accept the truths which could be attained by focusing attention on facts and forms. That is, on the clarity of relations and patterns referring to the facts and objects which are the intended content of conscious experience. Before this time there were so many humans fascinated by wonders that most could not turn from them to the details of empirical data and concern themselves with precision of scientific truths. It had taken centuries for enough humans to realize that by defining truth to be absolute clarity, it would be possible and seem desirable to live a life of seeking and wielding power over the environment.

PART II

THE LANGUAGE OF USE

We are already engaged in a discussion of human being, its place in the circumstance that seems to surround us and the merits of various modes for its expression and development. (1) We have spoken of societal expressions as aimed at filling human needs, and of the development of this response by science to enable us to express ourselves more fully, and so reveal more about us. It is evident that this development into technology has revealed startling aspects of us and our ways. (2) We have also spoken of myth and of art's development of myth in order to say more than myth alone can say about us. In fact we have noted that the development of myth by art into the tragic drama has produced major insight into a second aspect of our being. (3) The historical settings of these developments and the understanding of the thought of those involved suggests that human being is dual and that such duality is sharp and fundamental. And that this duality which appears early in human history and has been well expressed in tragedy now appears in a much sharper and more threatening way than ever before. That now the need for comprehension appears even more necessary if major distortion of civilization is to be avoided.

In our discussion, it has been necessary to use, so far more or less subliminally, a rather different language than that of myth, art or science. The articulation of the most penetrating art, the tragedy, is found in the acting, the speaking, the text, the scenes. These cannot be used here although they may be referred to and repeated in our thinking, and in our evaluations and discussions. The language of science is constructed for the occasion, and consists of signs referring to facts and objects. This cannot be used here since we are involved participants in the circumstances of which we talk. Our involvement, however is not that of the language of art.

The language we use thus has a peculiar status. It is selected at any one time for various reasons, but it cannot be formalized or described since it must be open to modification in order to accomplish its task. Thus we must note that we may understand its nature, but only to a degree. What we can say about it here and now is that there is just one such language serving on any such occasion, namely the one we are in fact using, all others mentioned are spoken about in the language we use. This language of use should contain whatever linguistic patterns and devices we think are necessary for our purposes. Of course we may be initially wrong about our choice, and forced to change the language we use by additions and modifications as we proceed. We make such changes when the language used has led to error and failure.

In using a language to enquire about the meaning achieved in and by dramatic articulation, we must note that we do so because the language or languages of the drama are not entirely successful in telling us who we are and who we ought to be. If the drama could tell us this no discussion would be necessary, except to correct errors. But the articulation of drama, even though it has been developed over thousands of years (in the case of western thought beginning with the Greeks, since 800 BC) it has not been able to resolve or even present certain problems of human nature. One such problem is the understanding of the heroic nature of the hero, another is the meaning of tragedy and/or comedy itself. It is these problems we need to discuss in another language: the language of use.

It is in the language we use (as in the one I am using), that is, a philosophical branch of the tree of life, that is articulation like other modes that human beings have modified for use to communicate with each other and evaluate the dramatic re-enactment of human living. Certainly, if it is to be used, a philosophical language must be able to formulate the norms developed in drama, or able to accept modifications necessary to do this. For this purpose philosophizing will be close to tragedy. However, neither I (nor anyone else) am in a position to guarantee the language of use can do this adequately.

COMEDY OR TRAGEDY?

There can be in comedy a developing focus on the limits of an individual's action and his evident ruin by that of which he is not conscious much like the focusing and symbolic development in *Oedipus Tyrannus*, or other tragedies.

In a scenario, something like one of Charlie Chaplin's short comedies, he returns home, tired after a long day at work. Hoping to relax and recuperate he opens the in-a-door bed, pulls it down only to see it fold back behind the door. He tries again, but again and again the bed acts in accord with its technical nature to frustrate Charlie's wrenching human efforts to retire and dream. Charlie cannot achieve his goal, and at last, standing alone facing the unsolvable problem as impasse, he accepts this evidence of his finitude, accepts his ruin, but reaffirms his freedom by spreading his coat on the floor, gratefully lying down and falling asleep to allow his blissful dreams to develop without restraint. The flowering of the scenario in the wasteland as a dream, is at once the ruin of the fool and the impossible solution of the unsolvable problem as brought to presence by comedy.

The contents of the dream satisfy him fully, for as freely emerging they are wonderful. However, as he awakens he is no longer merely in the dream, but the artist as well. Awake, he is conscious at once of the success of the dream as his own artistic fabrication, and of his own failure to create art powerful enough to change his nature, and so avoid ruin. Still he accepts his limitation to fabricator of dreamed illusion and his failure by walking off hopefully into the setting sun and through darkness toward... (a new day?). In this act he addresses his audience, asking for their help in supporting his art and himself in moving beyond the objectified world, and offering them the talisman of art, the presence of wonder which they need to confront the problem of their finitude. But we too are finite and are limited in our interpretation and support of the play. How can we guarantee that our interpretation is more than our illusion, our support more than transient? Still at this point we do stand with the author free and aware of the wonder and the threshold his and our finite efforts symbolize, and so moved to see each other as grounded in the mystery, as offering response to develop dialogue which can change us and, if spreading and continued, be passed on as the radiance of each to all, that is to create the symbol of meaning mankind could be.

We all know, on the basis of my example and Socrates' authority, that tragedy and comedy, while not identical, are the same; that is, the author of one could, in principle, be the author of the other. In *Oedipus Tyrannus* we can discern the mirror image of a comedy: Oedipus faces the unsolvable human problem of how to act with pride and still avoid ruin. Can we develop this image and sketch *Oedipus Tyrannus* as *Oedipus Komodia?* Certainly the play could be rewritten without patricide, Oedipus' marriage to his mother and her suicide, and without sentencing his children to a fruitless life, and himself to Colonus. The incidents replacing these could be hilarious and salacious parodies of patricide, suicide, incest (including the use of such names as *mowify, dauister, husson*), seducing the audience by flirting with the reality and making the play laughably lewd. Then Oedipus would discover, shrewd detective that he is, that he has been most successful in not perpetrating these never-committed crimes. Then he could be safely proud of *nothing*, and he and we, his audience, could understand his colossal negative success as the impossible solution to an unsolvable problem, that is as the illusion of a solution requiring that the artist's creative efforts convince the audience when Oedipus cannot.

This makes the play a festival of song, *Komos aeidein*, and Oedipus the fool who at great length solves no problem at all, but by adding to and deepening the issue makes the impossible solution of the unsolvable problem a symbol and passes it on to the artist and the artist to the audience to deepen in their own way, that is to pass the radiance on to emerging human beings, to make this radiant becoming more than a symbol.

And comedy can be rewritten as tragedy. If Chaplin's film opened with scenes in a factory producing in-a-door beds, showing him working as foreman and presenting the devastating effect of the repetitive patterns and dangerous working conditions imposed on the laborers (as he did in *Modern Times*). And if Chaplin's returning home to fight with the bed had re-presented these, as in fact the killing of his father, the suicide of his mother and the despair of his children, leaving him hopeless and broken, the movie could have been a tragedy.

This could be done by developing the fight with the bed as the rupture of his marriage, destroying symbolic keepsakes and pictures of happy picnics and holidays, leaving their home in shambles and driving his children terrified and sobbing under the bed. Then Chaplin's great technique in staging the fight with the bed in that way would bring to him and us awareness of the illusion he has lived, the belief that technological society brings the good life to all. At that point he, as protagonist, would be ruined but free to transcend his illusions, to refuse to return to work, to quit his job, to reach out to his children to try to recover and develop the human bond which technology so easily destroys. He could then, as author, understand his negative success as symbolizing the impossible solution to the unsolvable problem of being human, and so requiring that he deepen involvement still further by assuming as author the task of transcending his efforts as protagonist. But at this point, in either comedy or tragedy, the author, even if Chaplin, cannot extend the scenario and restore the family. At this point symbolizing falters and leaves the author alone to face and accept his inadequacy and, if he can, bring the audience to awareness that the scenario must go beyond this. At this impasse, the author, failing to say in the play what must be said, must confess he cannot say this, and offer the gift of whatever radiance he has attained to his audiences, and they to all human beings, thus providing them with the light for further, deeper disclosure, the gift of symbolizing. But let us consider just how the drama does this

OEDIPUS TYRANNUS

One of the earlier and greatest tragedies in the Athenian and Western Tradition is *Oedipus Tyrannus*. While still a youth, Oedipus learns from a drunken guest at a festival that the gods have foretold his fate: he will kill his father and marry his mother. He acts immediately and continuously to avoid this taboo. He is ingenious and his quick responses to changing situations seem to avoid any possibility of the realization of these threats. It is evident that he is a man who is in control, and yet in the very circumstances which demonstrate his ability to succeed he unwittingly kills his father and marries his mother. It is evident that being in control is inadequate.

Yet what should he have done to be truly human? What, if not success, could make him heroic? It is true that he is called a great man at the beginning of the play by the priest who asks him, in the name of the people whose king he is, to save Thebes from the present plague. The people ask this of him because it was his solution of the riddle of the Sphinx, a puzzle of little difficulty at most, that had saved them and their city once before. At that time, in thanks, they offered him their widowed queen in marriage and made him their king. Now they assume that another such achievement, this one perhaps more difficult, exorcising this plague and exhibiting his competence again, would increase his fame and make it more enduring than bronze. This happens. But today his fame often seems to contemporary audiences to be based on the competence and objectivity he evidences in his determined efforts to avoid the fate the gods presage. Modern audiences often think of him as a hero because he strives so hard and accomplishes so much. Yet his achievements warrant only the admiration, sympathy, and the sense of injustice that many now feel for him.

Oedipus is a hero neither because he does his best, nor because doing his best leaves him ruined, nor because his world disintegrates around him, nor because he suffers. He becomes a hero only as his presumption changes to awareness that all his efforts to control have been irrelevant, that to live as truly human he must turn from a world understood as a scene for success, a world of practical action, to look for an impasse, an *aporon*, a trackless wasteland to which he has been blinded by intricate detail, the objective distance, and the objective view required for practical action.

Oedipus is a hero because as ruined, as facing chaos, he is now on the threshold of the wasteland and free. He becomes great as he turns from the determined path his finitude defines, blinds himself to all that he had accepted as true, and so as free to accept radical change, to become he knows not what, yet committed to move beyond.

Oedipus: There was no other way but my free act blinding
myself
My vile self now shows its vile birth...
I can still weep for you my children,
though I can't see you...
Do not take them from me.

Kreon: Let go your power, too.
You won power, but it did not
stay with you all your life.

WHAT DOES TRAGEDY ENACT?

To begin evaluation of the drama as formulating the meaning of human living, that is, as telling us who we are, what we can know, what we should do, what we should believe, let us consider the striking emergence of the drama in the West in Greece. This would be about 800–700 BC. How much earlier is hard to say. Before that time, very probably, the drama began to take shape in more or less extemporary group activities and dancing re-enacting events in the life of the gods and by the time of classical Greek tragedy was focused in terms of the life of Dionysos.

To a modern audience the gods offer shadowy patterns drifting behind the myths which constitute the evident narrative of the play. To the classical Greek audience, however, these patterns of Dionysos' life were the rich background of human life, and so the source of the deepest human truth, truth which is more than objectification by consciousness.

Dionysos, the god who becomes human, even to being born and dying, that is having a beginning and an ending, and so a finite narrative, which is exemplified by the play as such, but which, as not the narrative performed in the play, deepens this to suggest to an audience its obverse as well: the inwrought yearning of humans unfolding and accepting that other which offers the possibility that they could somehow become radically more than they are.

From the rituals improvised and performed in the mountains or during early festivals, through the staged productions of classical Athens, the changes rung on this theme are many. But those clearly enhancing transcendent imaging include: (1) The introduction of actors, who are also celebrants donning masks to appear as living the lives of other humans and of gods other than Dionysos, but reflecting his masks to present no objectivity, and so to disclose the miracle of art, presence; (2) A playwright and director (who may be one) whose work before a performance, during it and after it takes time to move beyond time, that is attaining presence; (3) A chorus often speaking for the author from outside the play, reminding forgetful audiences of needed information, and suggesting to them possible responses to the incredible events presented, thus indicating that the place in the play of an audience is not accident, but one demanding responsibility to sustain presence both during the performance and after it.

There may well have been an uninvited audience at the early rites in the mountains of Greece which preceded classical drama, as Euripides' *The Bacchae* clearly takes for granted. There was an invited audience at the yearly commemoration of Dionysos by performances and festival at a temple and theater dedicated to him in Athens. Although the uninvited audience in the mountains may have been involved in much more spontaneous ways than the tiers of male citizens in the theater dedicated to Dionysos at Athens, the explicit recognition of the audience's contributions required to penetrate to and enact the image of human possibility the drama presents, was a major step in the development of drama as ritual. If the enhanced quality, the wondrous experience, caught in early enactments of Dionysos' life suggested commitment without reservation, to regeneration by excited but hesitant onlookers such as the young women mentioned by Euripides, who having left their newborn babies at home gave suck to wolf cubs to ease their aching breasts, the later drama also called for explicit audience change and contribution to sustain these wonders as presence.

The ritual, the symbols, which the playwright, director, actors and chorus have wrought to enable movement beyond time and to which they ask the audience to contribute by continuing, somehow, the performed ritual beyond the final curtain. To continue beyond the curtain-fall is to deny an ending to the play, and to make its ritual the movement beyond that. This characterizes human being as oriented toward that beyond. But let us remember that comedy can also express this movement, and also charge the audience to continue beyond.

THE DRAMA AS SYMBOL

In all drama, but especially in comedy and tragedy, the ordinary world can be re-presented as deceitful, that is presented as so explicit and detailed as to fully determine circumstances and so limit the possibilities of human response. Sophocles' drama portrays Oedipus' driven competence as reflecting his confidence that he knows exactly what to do in the well charted circumstances in which he finds himself. Oedipus acts with confidence for he sees clearly that there really is no reasonable alternative to his actions. Indeed his confidence hides from him the possibility that he is responding to the lures of a baited trap. His action never wavers and the gate of the trap snaps behind him: He has been caught. He kills his father and marries his mother.

How could he be free and escape this fate? To be free he must break his sharp focus on the clear objective data that consciousness commands. He must see beyond the objective world. However, the objective world exists and cannot be destroyed. If being were reduced to nothing or even muddled, this would annihilate human being as well as all else, for we are, at least in part, of that. The results of this meddling would be worse than Oedipus' sins.

What can be done is to regenerate the degenerate nature of Oedipus' seeing from objective sight to the insight of a seer, as by the blind Tiresias. Oedipus' degenerate vision does blind him to the emptiness of objectivity, that is he does not recognize what he sees as the trackless wasteland, the *aporon*, which is the obverse of objectivity. But after he pierces his eyes with his mother's brooch and is literally blind, he no longer sees only clear and distinct situations which must be dealt with by constructive external action rearranging parts, he now sees this as *nothing*, a wasteland, which commands his free and creative, his subjective, response to move beyond it. His vision has changed and, as he says in the play, he is free.

To show the hero or fool as prepared for this creative leap through the veil of clarity, the playwright, director and actors emphasize at the beginning of the play the finitude of the references and connotations of the text, and of the activity in the performance. Thus presented as all too finite, the hero and fool seem less than human and so importunate. But when they stumble and are ruined, they lose their preoccupation with objectivity and their inordinate pride in handling finite situations, and, in consequence, are able to hear and see through the misleading cacophony and confusion of finitude, the clear call from the high tower and the golden light illuminating the sign confirming trust in the unknown. Promised support they transcend their finitude as they die and/or in some other way also inexpressible in ordinary terms, commit themselves to be more. At this point, however, the drama itself fails, that is, it ends, and its ending is presence lost, and emptiness, that is, a finite gesture which has no content.

It is at curtain fall that the audience often misses its cue (the messenger), for too often it sees no sign, no light, no seers among its members. It sees itself, caught either with the hero and/or fool in the details objectified by consciousness or with the author in objectified illusion, that is the text and performance. At this point the audience errs if it rises in standing ovation only to leave the theater and return to the street and, perhaps, hope for a return engagement. The symbols of text and performance, the presence, like music after any performance, fades away from the audience, to leave them with even less than most art objects.

But to remain in the street ignores one's own sense of loss and the message of the artists', players', director's and stage hands' efforts to support the protagonists, and the performance as presence. The performance responds to the wonder which inspired the myth and develops as the wonder of art. The audience's efforts must be enlisted to carry this presence beyond the curtain fall.

The playwright, director and actors express this demand by example. When the performance is over they begin work on another performance, or on an earlier play, or they turn to work on a new play. Such efforts carry presence beyond the finitude of the play, beyond its illusion. But do they pull the audience out of the street toward that which is other than finite, into the creative action which makes acceptance of other content, and so symbolic response possible?

Certainly the details, the finitude of content emerging in and characterizing much human living, can and do as such exemplify human finitude as failure. And as surely the call of the other which is heard in the last scene of tragedy (or comedy) is not intelligible. Yet all tragedies, as the hero dies, make a gesture to engage the audience, to hand to them the radiant torch of presence, and ask of them help in passing this on to others. In this gift lies the assumption that the human being can carry this torch beyond.... But how?

Sophocles' play *Antigone* is a splendid example of a radical approach making this insight explicit and demanding the audience's acceptance of the task and their response to it. More evidently than other tragedies it states the problem, that is the problem of accepting the wasteland, nothing, that is, the problem of responding to nothing, the problem of producing something from nothing despite the old contention, *Ex Nihil Nihil.*

Antigone begins where tragedies are said to end, that is, accepting death. Antigone embraces death before she appears in the play, affirms it throughout the play, and her death ends the play, but not her presence. There is no gradual degeneration of human affairs and circumstances to force the regeneration of seers. The curtain opens on the wasteland, and the task is clear: but what is the message, what can be done, how can we act? *Antigone* thus exemplifies for any audience immediate involvement with the other as absolute other, as involvement which must create symbolic presence. The whole play becomes a symbol. It has no beginning and no ending, that is the presence attained never wanes, never waxes. It is just there. It cannot be modified in any way. No doubtful resolutions for the protagonists can be introduced.

The audience has only the choice of accepting or ignoring the other, participating in the other or not being involved in presence, the first step toward the other or not. The protagonists have no choice. They are brought before Antigone's commitment to death and must deal with it. The drama is the course of their dealing, and their death. But is it more?

Antigone's commitment before the start of the play, during the performance, and after the curtain, exemplifies for the audience unqualified transcendence; the acceptance of the other as part of her heritage and as necessary for her living, and expressed in her living as absolute presence. This participation symbolizes her performance. She is free from the moment of her acceptance of death, that is long since. There is in or about death nothing in particular to be said, nothing in particular to be done. The finitude of the text and its performance makes it at most an approach and ultimately of no concern. It is already a failure. And yet it begins in death and ends there, and yet it is offered by the artist as a gift to an audience.

But if a play as finite fails, how can it, as Nietzsche insists, be wonder which 'wants deep, profound eternity'? Does the play speak from a high tower bringing to an audience which already has a sense of its unrecognized involvement with the other, the message that enlightens them, and is the audience carried by the play beyond its finitude into living symbolic expression?

How could this happen? It could happen through the changes their involvement in art wrights in them as well as the playwright and cast, the changes like those occurring within the hero or fool, through which they stand free on the threshold of the wasteland. There each is free to turn away from what has been done, that completed, that said, and as free, to *hear* the ringing harmonics of their changes as qualifying them for awareness of the radical quality of indeterminate possibility, and the substance of hope.

The playwright bespeaks this change of the audience by his example, by his contribution to the quality of the play, and by accepting the call to change himself and so to qualify by involvement again in another play, that is in something more....

To stand on the threshold of the wasteland, Socrates' *aporon*, discloses not only the chaos of practical living, but the capacity of artistry, even of philosophy, to break its apparent bounds by the free action of those engaged, that is the protagonists, the artists, the audiences, in developing as quality. Their awareness of changing can be their becoming not only as nominal articulation, but also as the complex becoming of themselves as of a horizon, a Whole prior to any parts, rather than a totality. In our changing we are aware not only of trailing finitude, but of the horizon of disclosure, limning more than is ever understood or perceived, and of our need to accept and live that limen again and again.

Because Athens wished to take from Socrates this horizon, and because he would be less likely to attain it elsewhere, he accepted the role of martyr: he could not live as truly human without that. To live as truly human Socrates had to live with others who were aware of the same need, to question and be questioned without limitation. Just as Oedipus must be free to blind himself to the illusion of the ordinary world in order to live. And as Chaplin claims freedom by offering *impossible solutions for unsolvable problems*. And as Lear, in his *emerging greatness*, qualifies for freedom.

To act freely is hoping, for there is no implicit limitation in freedom. Hoping is celebration, commemoration of meaning's origin in wonder. It is awareness not of any specific possibility, but of wonder. As free I wonder as I wander. *The wasteland is not merely open, is not 'nothing'. It is the indeterminate possibility which is the result of freedom and the ground of hope. Without these true human life cannot be lived.* The wasteland is where we can meet each other as free and speak truth.

HOW DOES PHILOSOPHY SPEAK?

We have now been able to adumbrate a fundamental norm which myth, art, and religion approach by adopting the language of use which can be philosophical, for it is the language which is not only ours but as always there, that of being too. We can re-present this norm in a somewhat different and better way than myth, art, religion and science have done, a way that avoids objectification and makes more evident its horizonal symbolism. In using this language we have continually modified it to suggest this norm, that is, becoming more....

The philosophical language used here enables us to say that artistic articulation in the service of myth, art and religion, does not refer to its medium but is of it. That is the distance introduced in artistic language is not at all the same as the distance introduced by reference in ordinary and scientific language. These languages create signs and objectify referents. Artistic language involves in its articulation not only its media in a narrow sense, but also, for examples, the protagonists of a novel, the contents of a poem, the elements of music, tones and harmonics, and the shapes and qualities which are the constituents of architecture. The language of art treats these as quality, and the language of philosophy as used here also does this, but to a lesser extent. By contrast ordinary language and the language of science are, although not pure, usually the language of separation, of quantity.

Art bespeaks the paradox of human being, of us as finite and more than that. But can it bespeak the resolution of this paradox?

In the words of the Chorus, Sophocles says,

> A human comes to nothingness.
> Through no flight can one escape
> the one assault of death.

And yet Sophocles' heroine avoids that one assault, for Antigone assaults death. She moves beyond the objectified world to stand as free on the threshold of the wasteland. Freedom commands choice which does not enjoin a specific pattern or the development of one. In becoming who she is, the heroine, Antigone, must first and always and willingly seek to become that she is not. She cannot say what that means any more than Sophocles can say that, or you can say that, but she can, as free, create its quality. *She can live her freedom even though neither her life nor Sophocles' tragedy can specify its presence.*

Awareness of her and ourselves as the freedom we can be is neither easily come by nor easily continued. We say we are finite but something more, something we cannot yet say. Becoming the *more-we-can-be* is our task. That we are forced to be aware of this, that we strive to become that we are not, and so ourselves, is to be aware of the root of meaning as wonder. Our fate is not only what we do, but also that given to us, and our acceptance (or rejection) of this. Not to accept freedom is to be blind to that we are not, blind to possibility, to the radiance of absence. Still, as a seer, we can only be aware of the radiant absence death limns. This is the greatest wonder: to seek and accept this absence, as *Antigone* shows us, is to live truly, to be free.

Let us say, *that* we cannot say, once more and at length, for indirection needs repeating to resist seeking direction. Let us consider the nature of a play as it develops without saying it does so. Let us remember that a play is an image not merely of Dionysos, but a repetition of his living. Thus the play's content has no beginning, it is the closed circle of his rebirth, growth, death, and his cycle is of the 'big year' as much as the small one.... And this is our question, how can we accept this mystery, what does this Wonder mean, what is our fate? We cannot say in words, we can only qualify by living what words cannot say and whatever living may bring....

A play is a response to that we are not, to wonder, but it is not a literal response. It is not setting sail on the frothing waters, not just turning over furrows, not daringly yoking the bull. Clever indeed are the works which do this, but let neither drama nor philosophy share their presumption, their hubris.

The play can carry the playwright and acknowledging audience as well as the heroine away from specific circumstance and action into presence. It offers neither fact nor objectivity, but possibility; suggestions not views; not scenes, but hopes. Like Dionysos it is nothing in particular. It is growing, blooming, declining, silence, and emerging again. This is sometimes presence and more. In response one opens, not to this or that, but is, as the play is, in its reverberations, open to.... Thus the very richness of illusion sharpens the awareness of absence, an absence of meaning in presence which calls for response which can replace hubris with the shadow of The One, with the absence of.... (*the Wonder, the Whole which is prior to any parts?*)

In Sophocles' *Oedipus Tyrannus* this call for response is the rich moment when Oedipus embraces the creativity of the family, his sister-daughters. In *Antigone* it is the moment of the invocation of

Dionysos. In Williams' *Outcry*, the moment when the audience has left the play within the play, and yet the play continues. In Shakespeare's *Romeo and Juliet* it is each of those many inseparable moments after each societal pattern which could support the lovers attesting love as all, but fails to do so.

In Socrates' conversations it is any *aporon*, epitomized by *It would seem from what has been said that Wisdom can be attained only after death*. In Plato's dialogues, it is the introduction of myth to say more, and when he says that the Republic, the ideal state, is possible only if a true philosopher would agree to rule it. In Wittgenstein's deliberate confusion it is when he says *My propositions are elucidatory in this way: he who understands me, finally recognizes them as senseless... then he sees the world rightly. Whereof one cannot speak, thereof one must be silent....*

But we, the author and audience, must also qualify as more. We can become that only if the enactment of the protagonists, the existence of the play, brings our lives into presence and qualifies us as it does them. A comedy or tragedy that is an enactment of the transcendent quality of its protagonists' lives carries the acceptance and hope which lies in finite failure. Handed on to us through their presence, their failure is imbued with hope that, if we accept it, can bring our life line into presence.

The protagonist in either tragedy or comedy who fails may enact failure as the impossibility of determining the patterns occurring in a finite context which would lead to more.... In doing that the protagonist presents his life as spinning a veil blinding him to indeterminate possibility and freedom, and thus calls on himself and the author and audience to be aware of the wasteland not only as a threshold, but also as the scene of freedom. It is the recognition of freedom which the presence of the play offers to the author and audience as hope.

This moment of disclosure occurs in *Oedipus Tyrannus* when Oedipus' only free act in the play is his self-inflicted blinding, for it is this which sets aside the objectified scene and opens for him the empty world which is possibility.

In tragedy and comedy, the protagonists and all those contributing to the working of art – the artists-director-actors – act to stand together with the audience, in recognizing the presence of art as the threshold of possibility. They do not agree (or disagree) concerning the nature of possibility, but standing together before the mystery, themselves emerging and recognizing each other as other, and emerging, they are to be of the breath, the deep aspiration, which resounds as possibility.

The articulating which is the working of art becomes the path nearing possibility. And when art develops as tragedy, comedy or some other forms by no means always drama, it places those involved beyond objective worlds by articulating distance as penetration, as nearing rather than as reference, and as related in their speach, in dialogue. Socrates' discussions evade objectification by recognizing others as other, and as contributors to dialogue. He hopes to involve his audience as presence in mutual recognition.

Dialogue when true, even as *written* by Plato and read by anyone, is distinguishable as being, among other things, that of which it writes, and that is being dialogue. As wondering, as starting nowhere, as surviving moments of *aporia* in its course, and as returning to no ending, dialogue is penetrating and so the disclosing of that it cannot specify, is itself the presence it images, a free, a wandering, going beyond.

Dialogue as participating leaps the distance the world introduced by an objectifying language. It offers presence to each of the persons it frees to stand on the threshold of possibility. These persons, as more than they were, or are, or will be, as the mutual recognition of the mystery each other is, are the presence in their dialogue. Their response to one another accepts the wonder of each as the emerging of mystery. Their words are the caul of their origin. What is said as dialogue can never name the structure of a world, but it can become a symbol and horizon, as Plato's radical insight in the seventh letter says:

On these matters there is no book of mine and never will be. It cannot be put into words like other subjects. Knowledge of it can only be attained by long association and joint concentration; it springs up suddenly, like a light kindled from a leaping flame, in the spirit, and from then on feeds its own flame. (341c).

So long as dialogue, the living language, the language of use, is used, neither it nor its nature nor its meaning can be specified, for it is not a limited language devised for some purpose, even such as fixing the structure of a world.

The return of the living language, as in dialogue, can be a free response to origin by one on the threshold to another standing there. As free response it is not limited to any language already used, neither to Greek nor to any other, nor to any brogue or patois, vocabulary, grammar or structure. It attests the origin of any limited language, either any already used or in use or any still to be developed. However this return is repeated, it remains for humans access to and acceptance of whatever ground of communication there is, for it gathers free persons as of this ground in dialogue as a wonder. And it is this dialogue, this wonder, which continues the penetrating becoming, the generation of words as symbols by the participants' mutual recognition of one another extending by unending addition of others toward the more each can be. These symbols are the wandering articulation of the more of human existence, and as this, extending the presence, the more of each, toward whatever possibility lies beyond.... *We are not parts of a totality, but are of a Whole prior to any distinction, any part.*

Index

absence, 17, 158, 213
action
  art-, 104–19
  human, 71–3
  of tragedy, 2, 26, 59, 68
  theory of, 10
  see also tragic action
Aeschylus, 1, 10, 82, 87–98
aesthetic devices, 61, 89
aesthetic form, 16, 51
aesthetic references, 76
aesthetic theory, 10, 11, 59
aesthetics, 158, 167
  Aristotle's, 158, 167
  existentialist, 101
  modern, 28
agape, 14, 151–3
agapeic, 185
Anagaxoras, 155, 188, 189
Anouilh, 41
Antigone, 2, 10, 16, 144, 209–10, 213
aporia, 134, 162–3, 173, 215
aporon, 16, 18, 199, 205, 208, 211, 214
Aristophanes, 13, 124–30
Aristotle, 1, 2, 4–11, 52, 59–62, 65, 70,
  72–5, 86–9, 108, 154, 165
  and action, 104–7
  and knowledge, 190
  and Nietzsche, 19–36
  as the philosopher of tragedy, 162
  and wonder, 189
art, 12, 16, 17, 57, 60, 64, 89
  and its metaphysical power, 158
  and myth, 191–4
  and Nietzsche, 28, 49, 166–8
  philosophy of, 32
  its relation to life, 73
  and tragedy, 87
  tragedy as, 104, 112–17
artist, 30, 73, 77, 89, 172, 210
  birth of, 112
  and comedy, 202
artwork, 76–88
  tragedy as, 8, 21, 65–6, 87, 104–19
Augustine, 6, 34

The Bacchae, 207
Bartok, Bela, 113

being, 15, 16, 34, 157–78, 180–5
Bernays, Jacob, 4, 19
Blake, William, 113
Blanshard, Brand, 143
Burke, Kenneth, 108

catharsis, 2, 19–36, 43, 60, 64–8, 71, 76,
  79, 86, 87
Chaplin, Charlie, 202–4, 211
Cezanne, 65
comedy, 75, 207, 209, 215
  Plato and, 123
  and tragedy, 128, 199, 201
  or tragedy, 202–4, 214
conceptual and tragedy, the, 154–5,
  161, 166, 168, 173, 176, 177, 178, 180
conflict, 20, 46–9, 71, 81, 87, 94, 144
content, 8, 208
  philosophical, 10, 58–60
cultural objects, 72–85
culture, 88, 89
  tragedy's contribution to, 72–80
creative process and tragedy, 116–17
creativity
  and agape, 152
  and eros, 130
  of the family, 213
  and myth, 191
  and Nietzsche, 34

death of tragedy, 31–9
Deleuze, Gilles, 35n2
Democritus, 197
Descartes, René, 2, 117, 143, 150, 183
Dostoevski, Fyodor, 155, 182–4

Electra
  Euripides', 91–5
  Sophocles', 93–5
  Euripides' and Sophocles', 2, 10
Else, Gerald, 36n11
emergence in tragedy, 113–19, 215
emotions, 9, 42, 57, 60, 64, 66, 68, 70, 71,
  74, 78, 79, 117, 168
enlightenment, 6, 7, 28
  and Hegel and Nietzsche, 51–4
  and the tragic, 39–48
epistemology, 9, 83

217

eros
 and agape, 151–3
 and Aristophanes, 124–31
 and Plato, 124–31
 and philosophy, 147–53
 tragic portrayal of, 131–5
The Eumenides, 63, 90–1
Euripides, 1, 10, 62, 87, 88, 92, 95–8, 102, 195, 207
existentialism, 98

fate, 61–4
 men's, 105, 194–213
 and tragic situation, 12–13
 as tragic theme, 144–7
failure, 13–15, 201–2
 eros and, 146–51
 and philosophy, 146–53
 radical, 162
 human finitude as, 209
 of text, 210
 see also finitude
Fergusson, Francis, 108
finitude
 and loss, 174
 Oedipus', 205, 208–9
 of the text, 210
The Flies, 2, 10–11, 90, 98, 101
form and content, 10, 58
form and the *Poetics*, 104
form and tragedy, 105–7
free becoming, 191–4
freedom as a theme of tragedy, 144–8
freedom and failure, 150–3
freedom and tragedy, 190–9, 205, 211–16
Freud, Sigmund, 10, 58, 70
Friedrich, Casper David, 113–14

Gadamer, Hans-Georg, 106, 120n11, 121–2n30
Georgopoulos, N., 21, 35–6n4
Goethe, Johann Wolfgang, 1

Hamlet, 58, 75, 78–9
Hawthorne, Nathaniel, 112
Hegel, G.W.F., 2, 6, 7, 11, 19, 117, 154, 161, 164, 165, 169, 170, 172, 177, 180, 184
 and the Enlightenment, 45–54
 as using tragedy, 58
 and tragic action, 106–8
Heidegger, Martin, 118, 119, 121n17, 171

Heraklitus, 34
Hesiod, 130
Homer, 89, 130
human condition, 7, 13
human nature, 19, 20, 51, 109, 124, 191, 199, 201
human situation, 12, 13, 126–7, 130
Hume, David, 117, 143, 147, 149
Husserl, Edmund, 156, 162

Ibsen, Henrik, 1
imagination and Schiller, 88
imagination and tragedy, 8, 57, 67–8
infinite, the, 18
Ingarden, Roman, 119n
Iphigenia in Tauris, 63, 92

Kant, Immanuel, 8, 66, 68, 117, 118, 154
Kaufmann, Walter, 1, 2, 104–5
Kierkegaard, Soren, 58, 181–2
King Lear, 2, 65, 78, 172, 184
knowledge
 Oedipus', 159
 tragic, 82
 versus wisdom, 198

Langer, Susanne, 2, 11, 105, 106
language
 of philosophy, 211–16
 of use, 200–2
Lao Tze, 199
Leibniz, G.W., 143
Leucippus, 197
Lessing, G.E., 4
The Libation Bearers, 90, 91, 95
limit, 111–12, 118–19
 see also failure
limitation as a horizon, 16, 189
logic, 32, 57, 76, 141, 146
 and tragedy, 156, 161, 174, 180
logical categories, 170
logical systems, 155
logos, 15, 157, 161–4, 173

Mahler, Gustav, 113
McKeon, Richard, 21
meaning
 and Aristotle, 63–4
 of human being, 18
 characteristically human, 104–17
 latent, 82
 metaphysical, 15
Melville, Herman, 107, 109–13

Merleau-Ponty, Maurice, 101
metaphysical
  meanings of tragedy, 15, 117
  speculation, 50
  theses contained in a tragedy, 7, 10, 98
  utterances in tragedy, 58
metaphysics, 30, 63, 140, 143, 174
  Hegel's, 107
  Nietzsche and, 49, 54, 167
  of presence, 158
  and Sophocles, 94
  and tragedy, 60, 175
Michelangelo, 113
Moby-Dick, 2, 109–13, 115–19
modernity, 70, 71, 81
morality
  and Nietzsche, 30, 34
  Hegel's and Nietzsche's evaluation of Socrates', 50
mystery, 12, 16, 18, 88, 119, 203, 214, 215
myth, 5, 6, 16, 17, 20–5, 33, 41, 87, 89, 90, 92, 95, 98–101, 116, 148, 162, 173, 189–95, 200, 206, 211–12

Nietzsche, 2, 4–11, 40, 58, 70, 86–9, 102, 172, 210
  and Aristotle, 19–36
  and Hegel, 49–54
  and the Enlightenment, 49–54
  and Plato, 156–68
Noguchi, Isamu, 114, 115
nobility, 13, 14, 61, 62
  and tragic erotic striving, 128, 130
  and tragic failure, 139, 144–5
nothing, 167, 178, 181, 208, 209, 211
Nussbaum, Martha, 120n7, 123, 131–3, 136–7n13

Oedipus at Collonus, 15, 153
Oedipus the King, 2, 12, 16, 62, 65, 105, 108–9, 127, 144, 153, 202–6, 213, 214
openness
  as ontologically constitutive of human being, 162
  to the other, 113–17
  as the *aporon*, 194
The Oresteia, 10, 91, 99, 108, 109
Orestes, 96
Othello, 2, 42, 58, 82, 83
other, the, 12, 107, 113, 115–17, 170, 181, 183, 209, 215

otherness, 16, 17, 117, 165, 178, 180, 183

Papanoutsos, E.P., 35n2
paradox of tragedy, 5, 20, 24
Parmenides, 158, 184
Peirce, Charles, 14, 147–53
Phaedo, 15, 169–73
Phèdre, 42, 108–9
philosophy
  analytic, 70, 141–3
  of art, 31-2
  linguistic, 70, 141–3
  phenomenological, 99
  positivistic, 70, 141
  practice of, 70, 84, 85, 162
  in tragedy, 2
  of tragedy, 30–3
philosophic fantasy, 80
philosophic life, 74, 165
Plato, 1, 4, 10, 12–15, 57, 74, 84, 104, 161–74, 184, 189, 215
  and the ancient enmity between poetry and philosophy, 80
  and Aristotle and political theory, 31
  and the eros of philosophy, 124–31
  and philosophical practice, 85, 112
  as tragic philosopher, 125–38, 142–8
  and the shipwreck of philosophy, 117–18
poetry, 8, 57, 68, 80, 84
poiesis versus imitation, 60
Pollock, Jackson, 115
post-modern, 70, 71
presence, 18, 191–215
  metaphysics of, 158, 162
Protagoras, 34, 140–1, 144
psychoanalytic theory of art, 9, 71, 116
psychology, 142
psychological treatment of tragedy, 10, 97, 98, 105

Quine, Willard Van Orman, 142

Racine, 41, 45, 107
rational explanation of 'tragic lift', 88
rational intelligibility of tragedy, 117, 155
rational findings of philosophy as science, 157
reality, 2, 7, 30, 54, 58, 59, 62, 67, 68, 75, 76, 79
  and art, 64
  and the tragic hero, 64
renaissance, 17, 35n2, 196, 199

The Republic, 2, 23, 123–4, 131, 134–5
Ricoeur, Paul, 103n6

Sartre, Jean-Paul, 2, 10–11, 90, 94, 98, 101
science, 15, 17, 80, 141, 201, 212
    and Nietzsche, 28–32
    Greek, 195–200
    philosophy as systematic, 155, 173
Seven Against Thebes, 2, 9, 73–5, 82
Shakespeare, William, 41, 62
Shelling, F.W.J., 55, 122n31
Schiller, Friedrich von, 2, 10–11, 86–87
Schlegel, Friedrich, 58
Schopenhauer, Arthur, 19, 23, 24, 29, 77, 105, 122n31, 166, 167
silence, 154, 164, 213
society, 10, 17, 80, 87, 190
Socrates, 1, 2, 12, 13, 74, 118, 130, 132, 135, 154, 161, 184, 203
    and the *aporon,* 211, 214
    and Hegel, 47–48, 50, 169
    and the incompleteness of wisdom, 126–9
    and Nietzsche, 166, 167
    and the philosophic life, 74
Sophocles, 1, 10, 41, 45, 87–8, 94–5, 97–8, 153, 195, 207, 212
Spinoza, Baruch, 143, 155, 164, 168, 185n5
subjectivity, 114, 116, 169
suffering, 33, 52, 71, 75, 86–9, 94, 97, 105, 108, 116, 159, 165–6, 184, 205
Starry Night, 114–15
Stevens, Wallace, 115
Stravinsky, Igor, 113
symbol
    drama as, 207–11
    of meaning mankind could be, 203
    tragic form as, 105–7
Symposium, 2, 123–4, 128, 131–5, 147, 157

teleology, 49, 50, 145
Thales, 196–7
theoretical explanation of tragedy, 89
thought, 8, 9, 10, 66, 68, 104
    philosophic, 149, 151
    primary and secondary process of, 71, 81
    in tragedy, 58, 69
Tolstoy, Leo, 24
tragedy
    the function of, 5, 19–36, 59

the pleasure of, 8, 11, 19, 60–9
the richness of, 8
the telos of, 25, 40
in philosophy, 2
as poetry, 68
and possibility, 8, 9, 16, 17, 18, 57, 66–7, 211–16
tragic, the, 2, 3, 4, 5, 7, 10, 14–16, 19–36, 39–54, 62, 123, 135, 149–53, 156–85
tragic
    action, 2, 62, 71, 97, 104–19, 146
    circumstances, 12, 97, 107, 109
    dimension, 12
    effect, 10, 11, 19–35, 86–102
    emotions, 2–9, 19–36
    experience, 10, 19, 21–2, 87, 102
    flaw, 2, 4, 42, 61, 144–53
    form, 105–7
    insight, 16, 83
    lift, 10–11, 88
    nature of philosophy, 14, 145–53
    sense of life, 7, 105
    view of life, 7, 19–36, 57
    situation, 97, 127, 130
    wisdom, 24
tradition, 76–7
transcendence, 17, 100, 114, 119, 195, 210
transformation of the self in the experience of tragedy, 179
truth
    disinterested, 168
    mythical, 87
    philosophical, 190
    scientific, 199–200
    of tragedy, 76

Unamuno, Miguel de, 105
universal claims of philosophy, 141–4
universal versus the particular, the, 169–81

value(s), 11, 21, 34, 67, 86–88, 94, 100–2, 106, 110, 114–15, 117, 167, 168
Van Gogh, Vincent, 111–14
Vernant, Jean-Pierre, 120n15
Voltaire, 40–49

Wagner, Richard, 24
whole, the,
    and Greek science, 196–8
    philosophy as a vision of, 147–50
    prior to any parts, 211–16
Wittgenstein, Ludwig, 118, 164, 214

wisdom, 135, 139, 180, 198, 214
  dreadful, 65
  philosophy as, 139, 146–8, 150–2, 200
  versus knowledge, 198–199
wonder, 12, 16, 17, 18, 117–19, 162, 190–216

Wyeth, Andrew, 114

Yeats, W.B., 74, 179